I0800153

IMAGES
of America

LONGWOOD

IMAGES
of America

LONGWOOD

Central Florida Society for Historical Preservation

ARCADIA
PUBLISHING

ISBN 978-0-7385-1392-8

Published by Arcadia Publishing
Charleston, South Carolina

Printed in the United States of America

Library of Congress Catalog Card Number: 2001093677

For all general information contact Arcadia Publishing at:
Telephone 843-853-2070
Fax 843-853-0044
E-Mail sales@arcadiapublishing.com
For customer service and orders:
Toll-Free 1-888-313-2665

Visit us on the Internet at www.arcadiapublishing.com

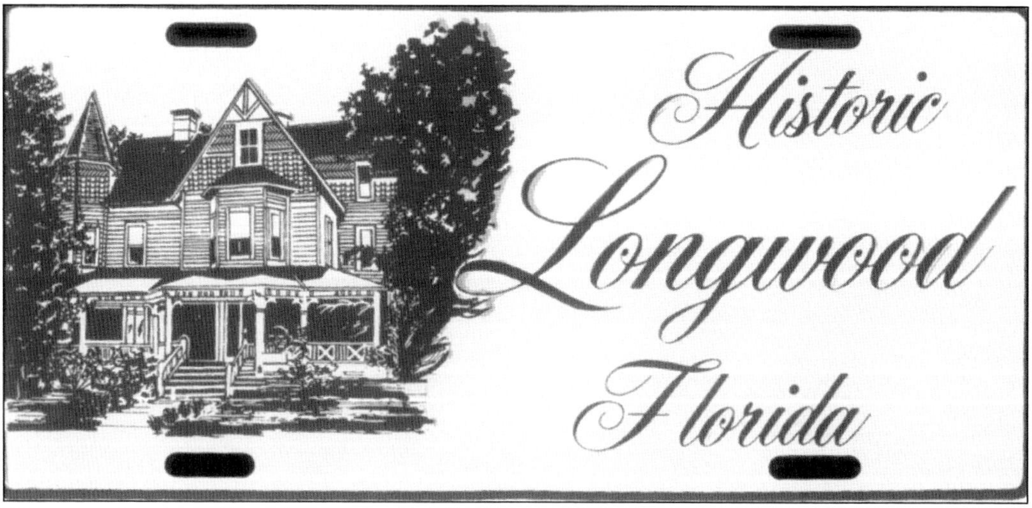

This city license plate shows the Bradlee-McIntyre House as part of efforts to promote Longwood as one of the few places remaining in Central Florida linking the past to the present. The Bradlee-McIntyre House, a Queen Anne–style winter home built in 1885 in Altamonte Springs, is now a museum in Longwood's downtown historic district at 130 West Warren Avenue.

Contents

ACKNOWLEDGMENTS

This book would not have been possible if not for the courage of the charter members of the Central Florida Society for Historical Preservation. Fred Bistline, Grace Bradford, Betty Jo McLeod, Dorothy R. Pearson, and Myra and Richard Venable invested their own money and rallied community support to move the Bradlee-McIntyre House and the Inside-Outside House to Longwood, which helped establish the historic district. The society's 2000–2001 Board of Directors—John Bistline, president; Lynette Dennis, vice president; Barbara Odom, secretary; and Debbie Dix, treasurer—provided much appreciated assistance and council during this project. The authors would also like to thank the many contributors of photographs, family stories, time and talent, including Areva and Forrest Barnes, Harry Beckham, Fred and Carolyn Bistline, John and Mary Bistline, Margie Blankenship, Gene and Lib Bothell, the City of Longwood and Mayor Paul Lovestrand, Ann Cooper, Lynette Dennis, Stella Fleece, James Russel Hammond, William O. McWorkman, Richard Miller, Barbara Odom, Martha Payne, Joe Pedro, Sarah and Alain Piloian-Girard, Fran Sanders, Charlie Searcy Jr., Richard Taylor, Fern and Spencer Whitehead, and Chalmers Yeilding. The society also extends a special thanks to Karen Jacobs of the Museum of Seminole County History. The authors would also like to thank Robyn Robison for layout assistance. Finally, Jim Robison would like to thank Lee Taylor, Lynette Dennis, and Barbara Odom for helping him create, edit, and compile this book.

Introduction

Longwood's historic district and its gift shops attract collectibles shoppers as well as those interested in some of the best preserved buildings from Florida's first tourism boom of the late 1800s and early 1900s. The downtown historic district's main landmarks, the Longwood Village Inn, the Bradlee-McIntyre House, and the Inside-Outside House, as well as the district's Christ Episcopal Church and shops in old houses, were built when Longwood and Altamonte Springs were winter retreats for wealthy Northerners. The Longwood historic district, earning recognition on the National Register of Historic Places in October 1990, includes more than 30 buildings dating from 1873 to 1926.

Longwood, as well as most of Seminole County, shares its frontier beginnings with the early settlement of Orange, Lake, Brevard, Volusia, and Osceola Counties that make up the metro Orlando area. The first settlers at what would become Longwood arrived during the lull between the end of the Seminole Wars in the 1850s and the beginning of the Civil War. The man credited with naming Longwood, E.W. Henck, found the Hartley family homesteading at Fairy Lake, which is now the Columbus Harbor neighborhood. Longwood and Seminole County's agricultural and winter tourism economy of the late 1800s and early 1900s disappeared by the mid-1900s as families converted much of the former farm and grove lands into new bedroom communities of Orange County and its major city of Orlando.

Tourism drives all of Central Florida. Of late, Seminole County has become popular for eco-tourism because of its many lakes, rivers, parks, bike trails, and nature preserves. Seminole County, bordered by the St. Johns and the Wekiva Rivers on the north, west, and east, is roughly equal distance from the Atlantic beaches of Volusia (Daytona Beach, Daytona International Speedway) and Brevard (NASA and the space coast beaches) Counties and Walt Disney World and the other world-known theme parks of Orange and Osceola Counties. The growth of Sanford's airport for international travelers and the only Florida terminal for the Auto Train again has made Seminole County a gateway for many tourists to Central Florida, much as it was in the 1800s. While many residents still make their living in the Orlando area and return to homes in Seminole County, Longwood has established its own historic-preservation identity while providing its residents with employment in the Interstate 4-corridor's growing high-tech market.

Jim Robison, July 2001

One

The Early Settlement of Longwood

Longwood has been a destination point for Florida travelers since coastal tribes used The Senator, an ancient bald cypress, to find their way over land from the St. Johns River to trading grounds at Spring Hammock. This was the wilderness sanctuary early tribes found when they escaped inland from the Spanish. Later, when Creeks and others from the tribes of the Southeast United States fled into Spanish Florida and settled new villages among escaped African slaves, they became the Seminoles. The word "Seminole" is adopted from Spanish and Creek terms for people who live away from others. The Senator, at more than 3,000 years old, is easily Central Florida's oldest tourist attraction and can still be seen today at Big Tree Park near Longwood.

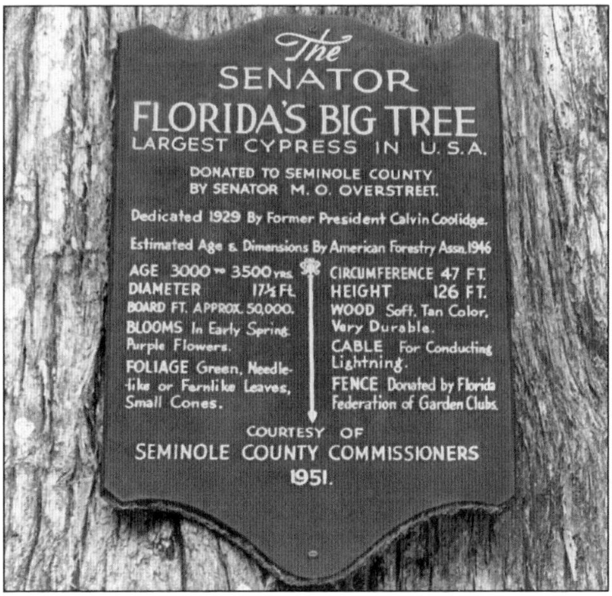

The Senator, easily Central Florida's oldest "tourist attraction," is at least 3,000 years old. This bald cypress is located in Big Tree Park in Seminole County's Spring Hammock Preserve.

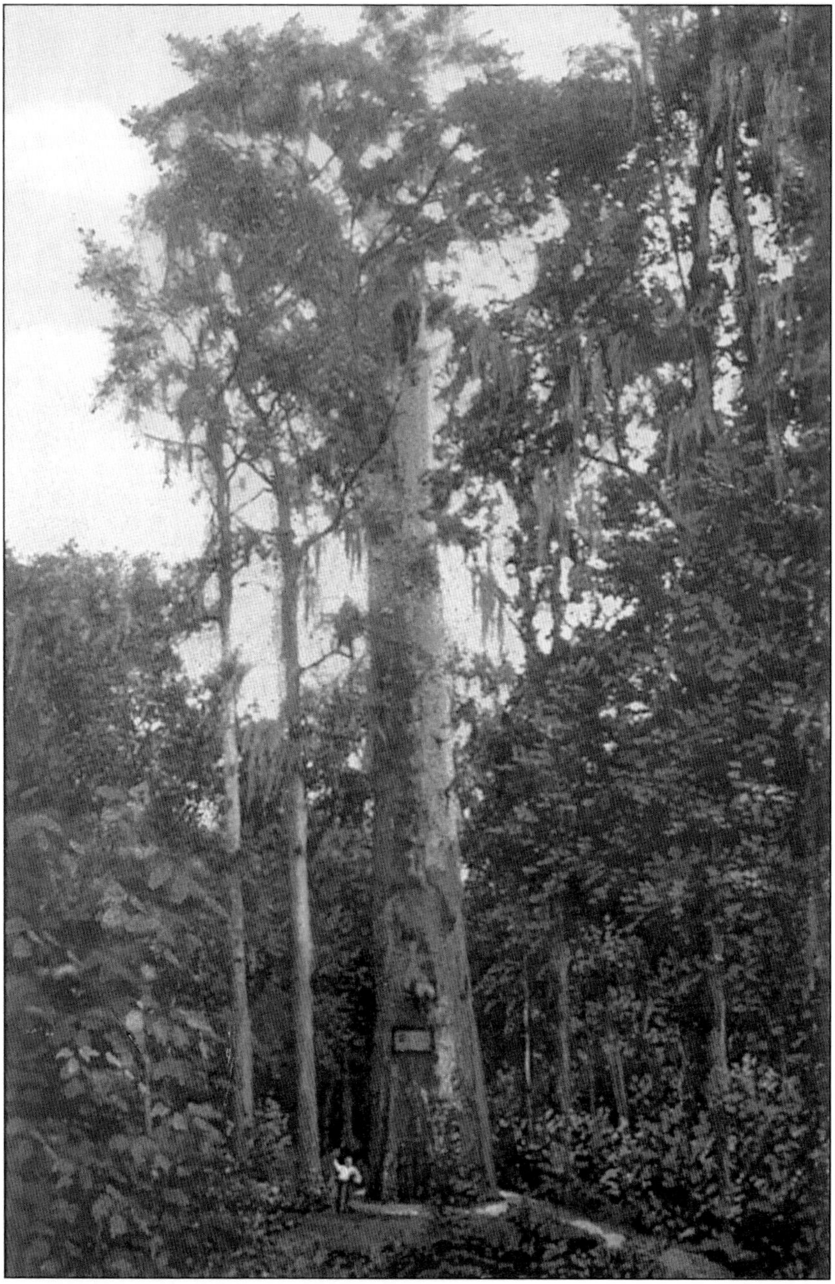

The area was once thick with bay, sweet gum, live oaks, longleaf yellow pines, and cypress hammocks scattered within low swampland. The land had changed little since coastal tribes followed the meandering St. Johns River inland thousands of years ago, using the towering bald cypress, shown here, to find their way to trading grounds. The ancient tree, now shorn of its top probably by a long ago storm, was visible from the river eight miles away. The first settlers also built mounds, or middens, piling sand, shells, and debris to create higher ground. U.S. Army soldiers from nearby forts at lakes Monroe, Harney, and Maitland searched for Seminoles throughout the region during the four decades of the Seminole wars, but much of the territory remained a remote wilderness until after the Civil War.

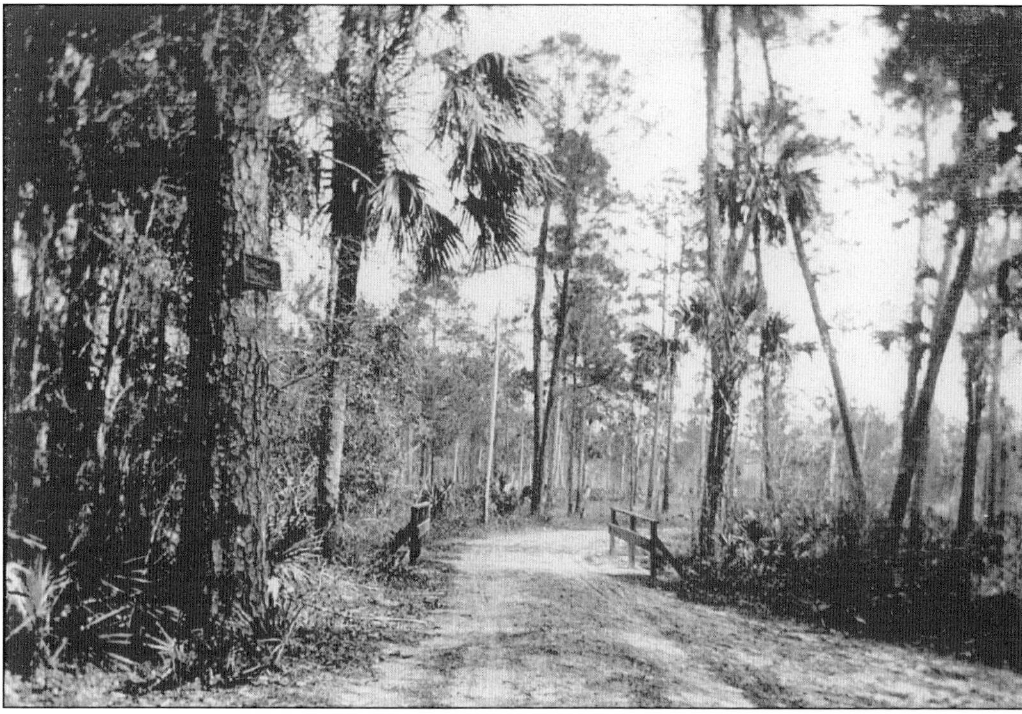

This is the old road to The Senator pictured above. Hardly anyone lived between Sanford and Orlando until after the Civil War. In late December 1871, surveyor J.O. Fries rode a lumber wagon pulled by a horse and a mule between Sanford and Orlando. He noted a lone house along the entire road and one small store in Maitland.

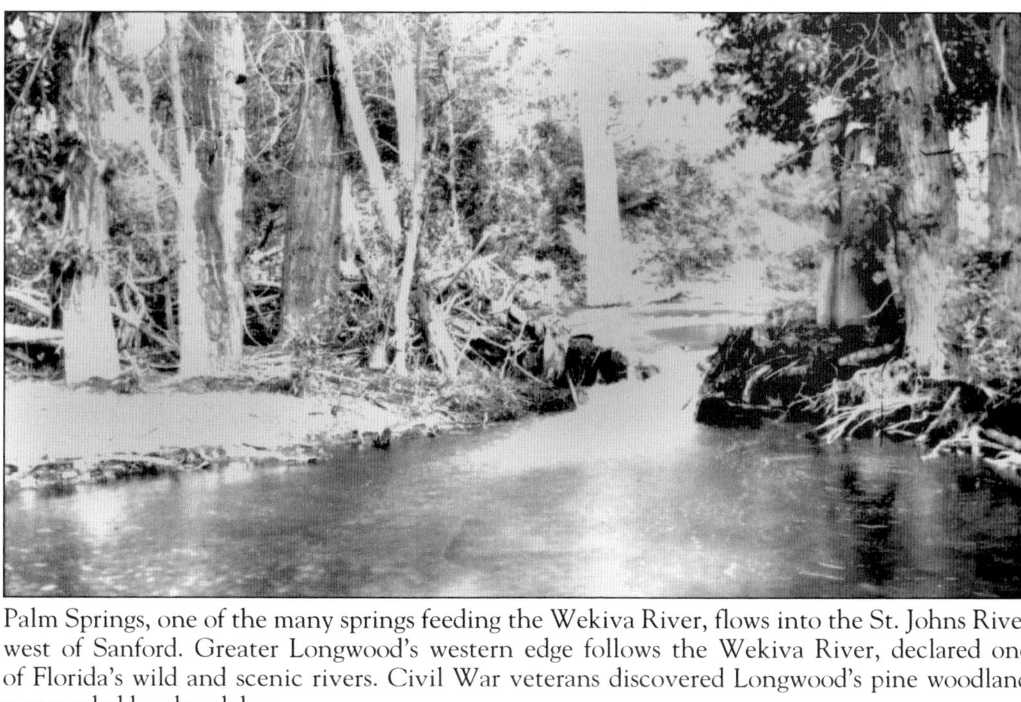

Palm Springs, one of the many springs feeding the Wekiva River, flows into the St. Johns River west of Sanford. Greater Longwood's western edge follows the Wekiva River, declared one of Florida's wild and scenic rivers. Civil War veterans discovered Longwood's pine woodland surrounded by clear lakes.

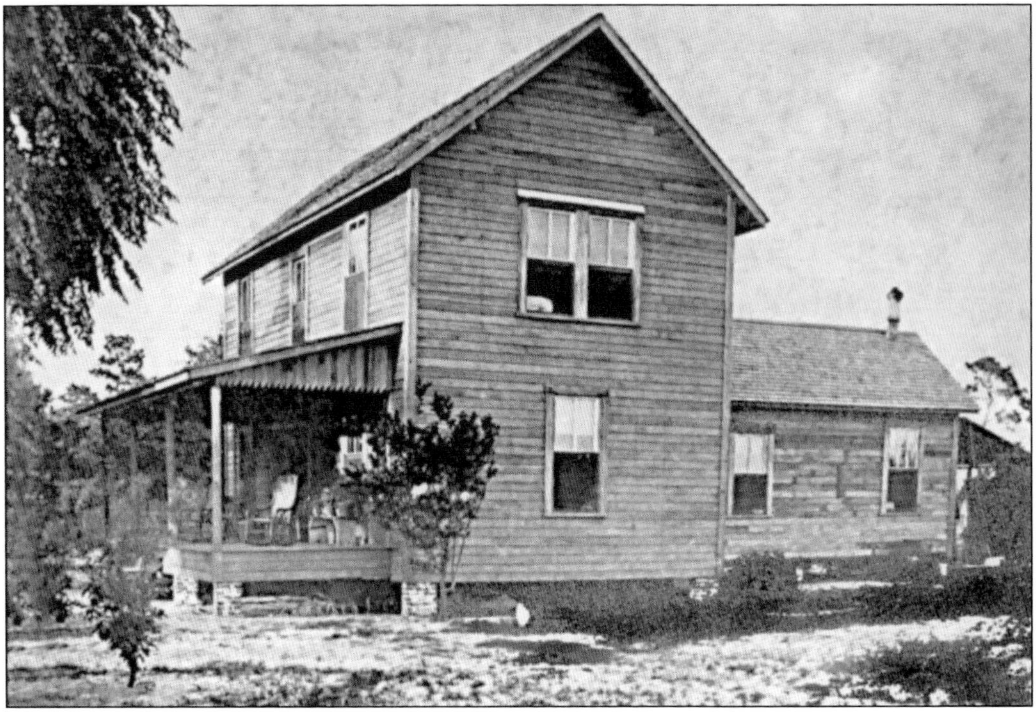

The homestead certificate for the Hartley House (above) is shown below. The house was built on Fairy Lake. At least six years after he settled at Fairy Lake, Lee J. Hartley registered his 160-acre homestead claim at the federal government's General Land Office in Gainesville. The document was signed Nov. 13, 1878, during Rutherford B. Hayes's administration.

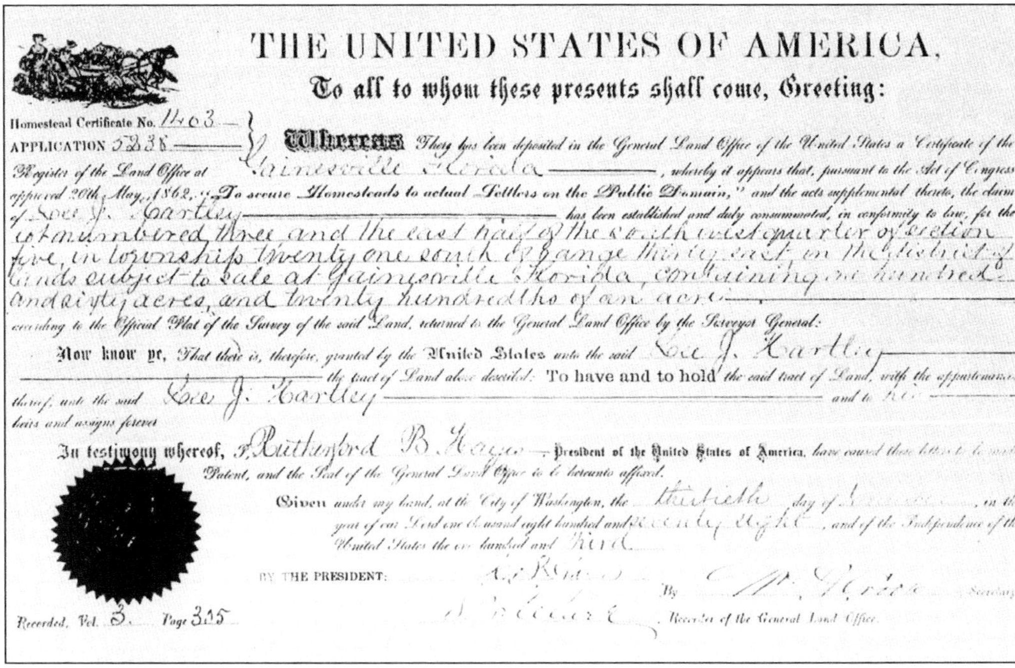

THE UNITED STATES OF AMERICA,

To all to whom these presents shall come, Greeting:

Homestead Certificate No. 1403
APPLICATION 5238

Whereas There has been deposited in the General Land Office of the United States a Certificate of the Register of the Land Office at Gainesville Florida, whereby it appears that, pursuant to the Act of Congress approved 20th May, 1862, "To secure Homesteads to actual Settlers on the Public Domain," and the acts supplemental thereto, the claim of Lee J. Hartley has been established and duly consummated, in conformity to law, for the lot numbered three and the east half of the south west quarter of section five, in township twenty one south of range thirty east, in the district of lands subject to sale at Gainesville Florida, containing one hundred and sixty acres, and twenty hundredths of an acre according to the Official Plat of the Survey of the said Land, returned to the General Land Office by the Surveyor General:

Now know ye, That there is, therefore, granted by the United States unto the said Lee J. Hartley the tract of Land above described: To have and to hold the said tract of Land, with the appurtenances thereof, unto the said Lee J. Hartley and to his heirs and assigns forever

In testimony whereof, I, Rutherford B. Hayes President of the United States of America, have caused these letters to be made Patent, and the Seal of the General Land Office to be hereunto affixed.

Given under my hand, at the City of Washington, the thirtieth day of [illegible], in the year of our Lord one thousand eight hundred and seventy eight, and of the Independence of the United States the one hundred and third.

BY THE PRESIDENT: [illegible] By [illegible] Secretary.

[illegible] Recorder of the General Land Office.

Recorded, Vol. 3 Page 315

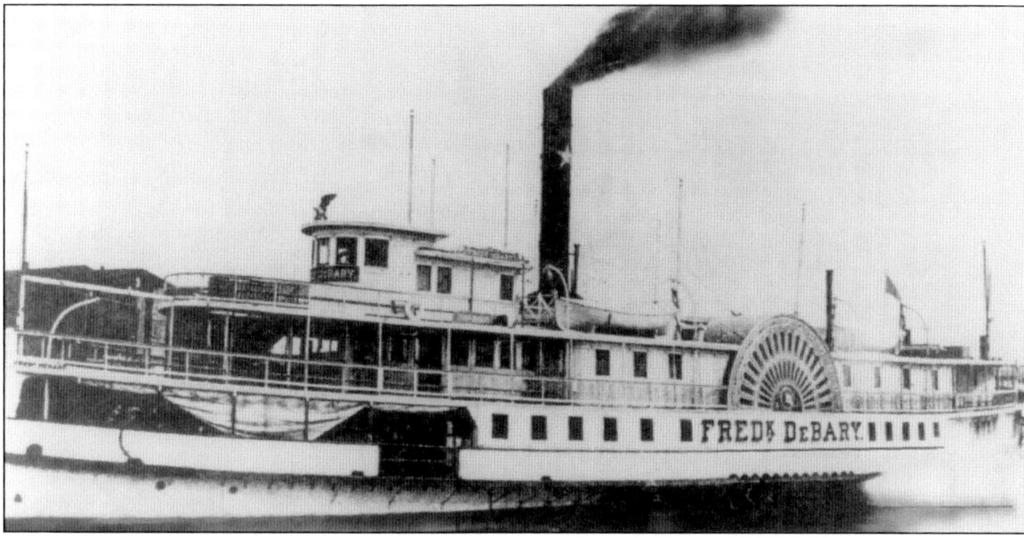

Two days after his steamboat arrived at the landing on Lake Monroe, E.W. Henck began homesteading. Henck, who later became the town's postmaster, issued the receipt pictured below to the Hartley family for rent of post office box 4 in 1891. When he first arrived, he later wrote, "There were no other inhabitants in what is now the corporation of Longwood, but on the outskirts at Fairy Lake there lived a family named Hartley of which there are now [1927] many descendants still in residence." In the beginning, mail arrived at Sanford by boat three times a week. A mail rider's route took him from Sanford through Apopka, Maitland, and Orlando. "The entire mail for all these points could have been put into an ordinary coat pocket," city founder E.W. Henck wrote. The rider was replaced by Joseph Bumby's stage line when, on May 19, 1876, the Longwood Post Office was established with Henck as the first postmaster. He was postmaster until 1885.

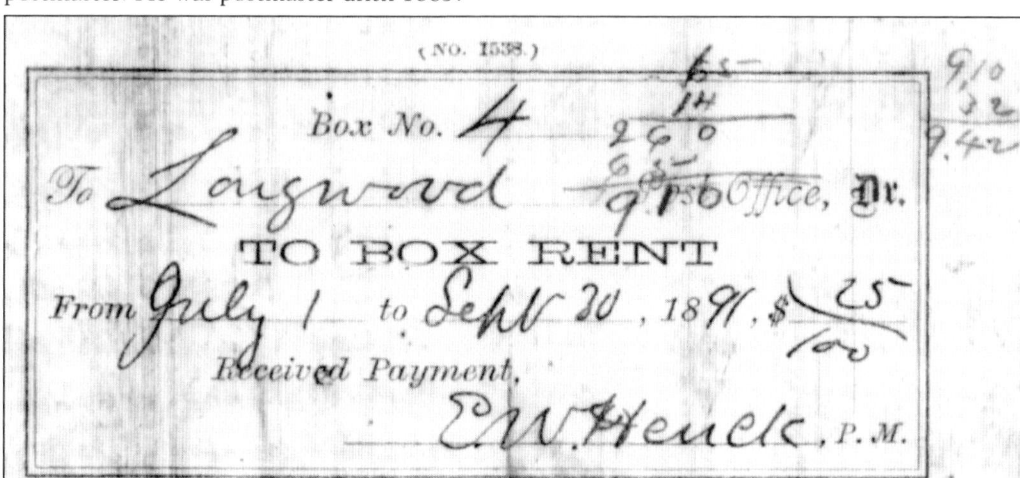
(NO. 1538.)

Box No. 4

To Longwood Post Office, Dr.

TO BOX RENT

From July 1 to Sept 30, 1891, $ 25/100

Received Payment,

E.W. Henck, P.M.

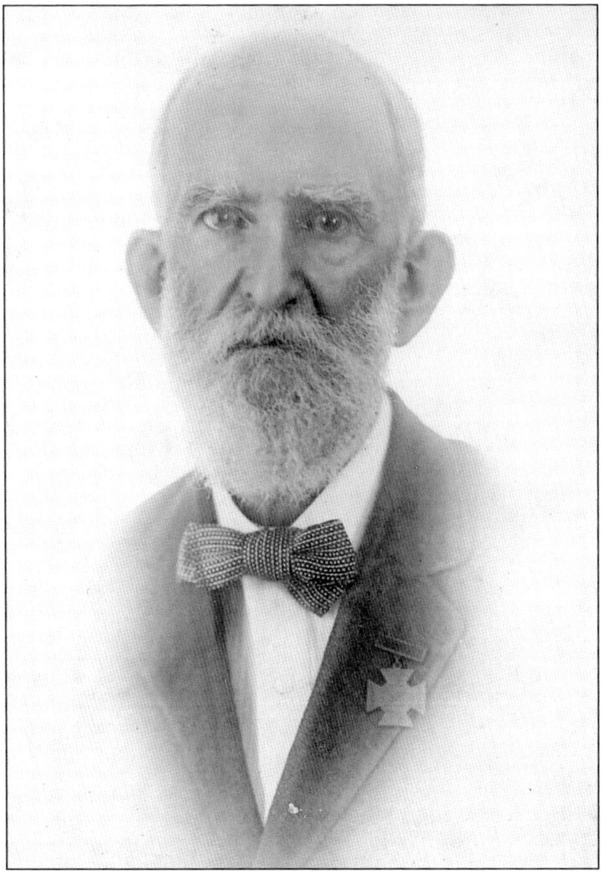

Tennessean John Neill Searcy arrived by steamer *Starlight* at the docks of Mellonville (now Sanford) on March 23, 1873. The son of a doctor and the grandson of a Nashville federal court clerk, Searcy had served in the Confederacy from May 1861 until May 1865 before coming to Florida at age 31. Entering an endless wilderness of palmettos and pine flatlands, Searcy later told his family he questioned why he ever left Tennessee.

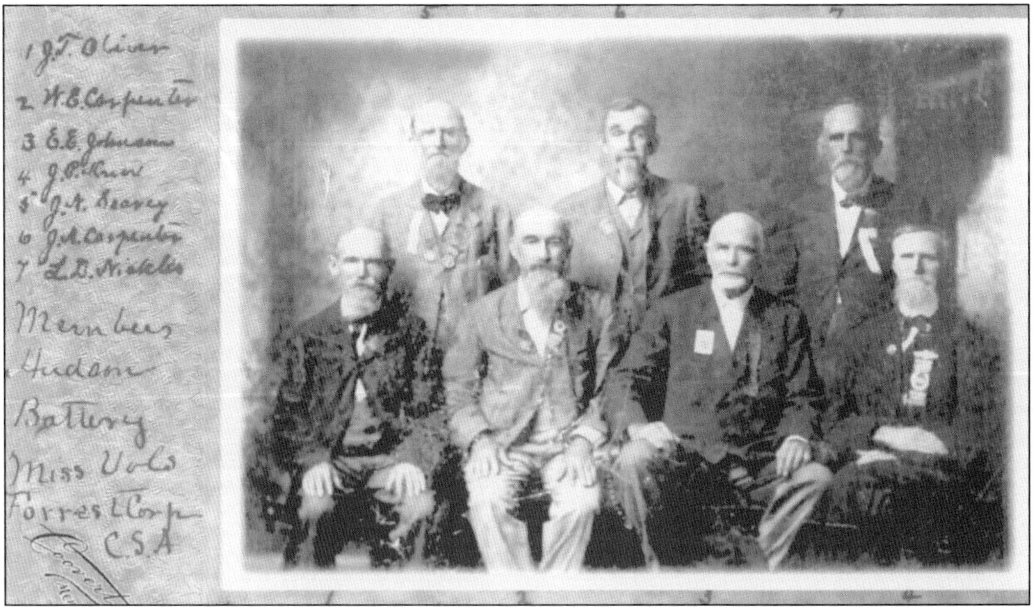

John Neill Searcy appears on the far left of the top row in this group photograph from a reunion of Confederate soldiers of the Hudson Battery, Mississippi Volunteers, Forrest Corp, CSA.

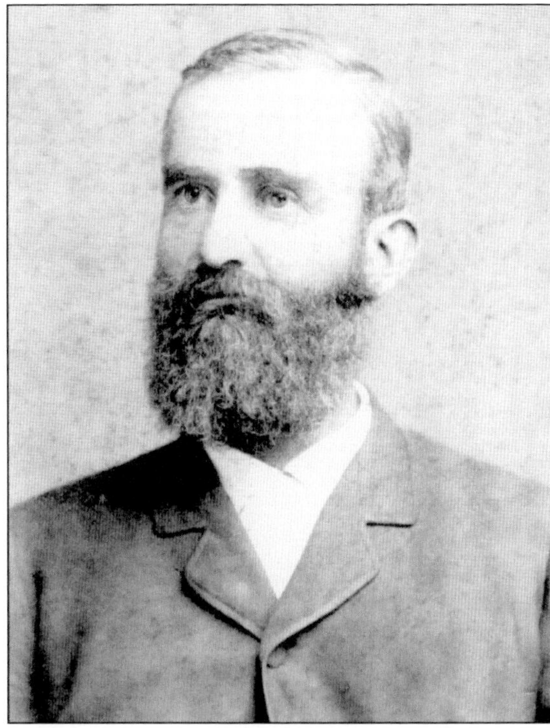

John Neill Searcy married Eva Lessie Muzzy (below) in 1885. They had three sons, but only Charles B. Searcy would live to become an adult. Charles Searcy worked as a freight and telegraph agent for the South Florida Railroad. John Searcy and his father, James, who had joined his son in Florida, helped build the Christ Episcopal Church, a Longwood landmark dedicated on Easter Sunday, April 19, 1882. By 1889, Searcy was Longwood's postmaster, a position he held for several years.

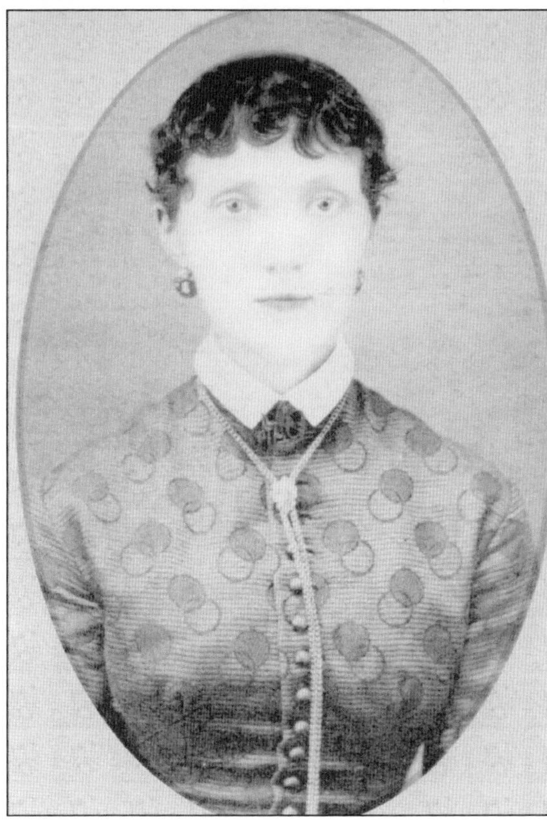

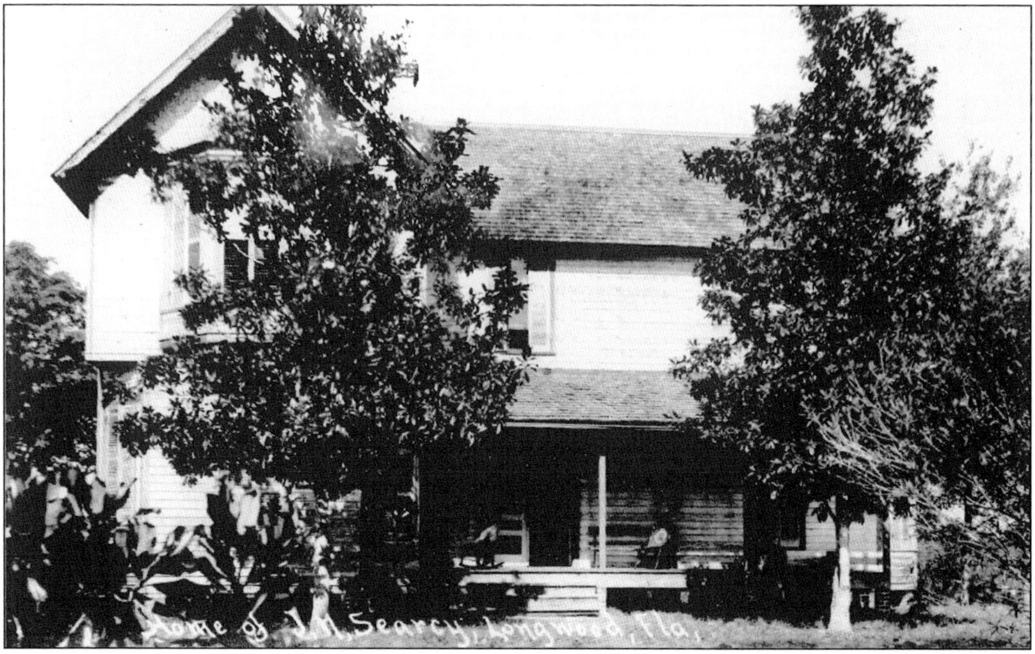

This is the two-story house John Neill Searcy built in 1888 on West Church Avenue for his family. He homesteaded in Longwood, planting groves and selling cypress cut from the land along West Lake. Searcy also was a carpenter and worked on a railroad survey crew in the late 1870s.

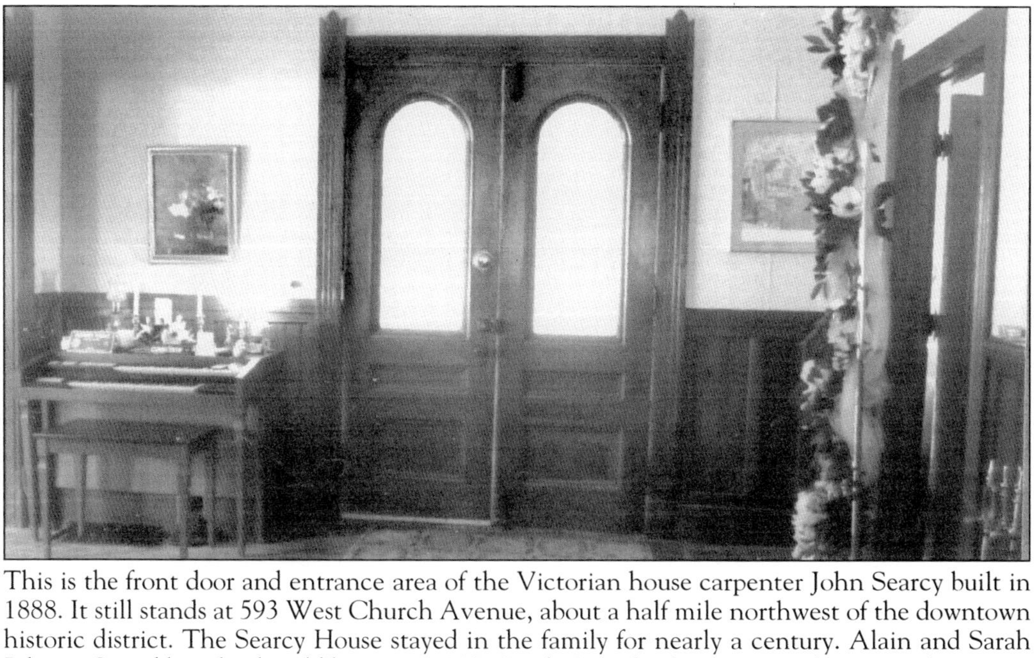

This is the front door and entrance area of the Victorian house carpenter John Searcy built in 1888. It still stands at 593 West Church Avenue, about a half mile northwest of the downtown historic district. The Searcy House stayed in the family for nearly a century. Alain and Sarah Piloian-Girard bought the old house in 1987. Sarah Girard, whose parents live next door, grew up playing along the lake and in the Searcy family's magnolia, mulberry, camphor, and palm trees. The couple, both professional photographers, renamed the property Magnolia Acres, advertising it for weddings, receptions, and other gatherings.

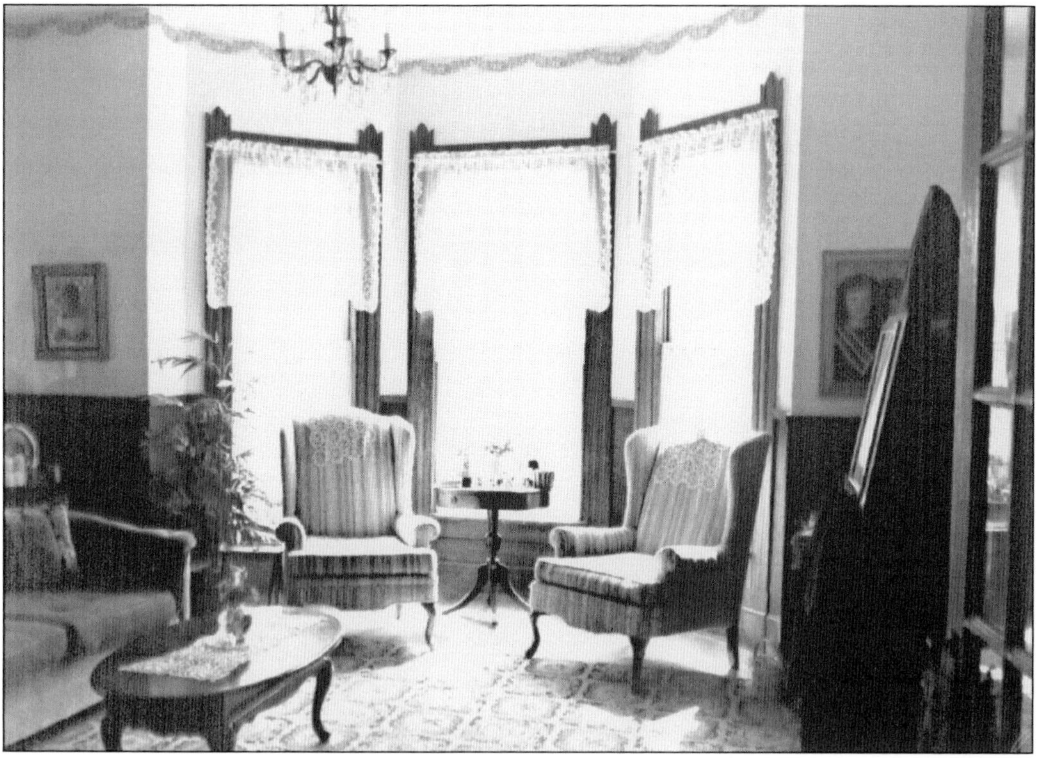

This is the bay window of the Searcy's sitting room at what now is called Magnolia Acres, a historic Victorian farmhouse in a setting reminiscent of rustic old Florida. Century-old magnolia trees surround the house.

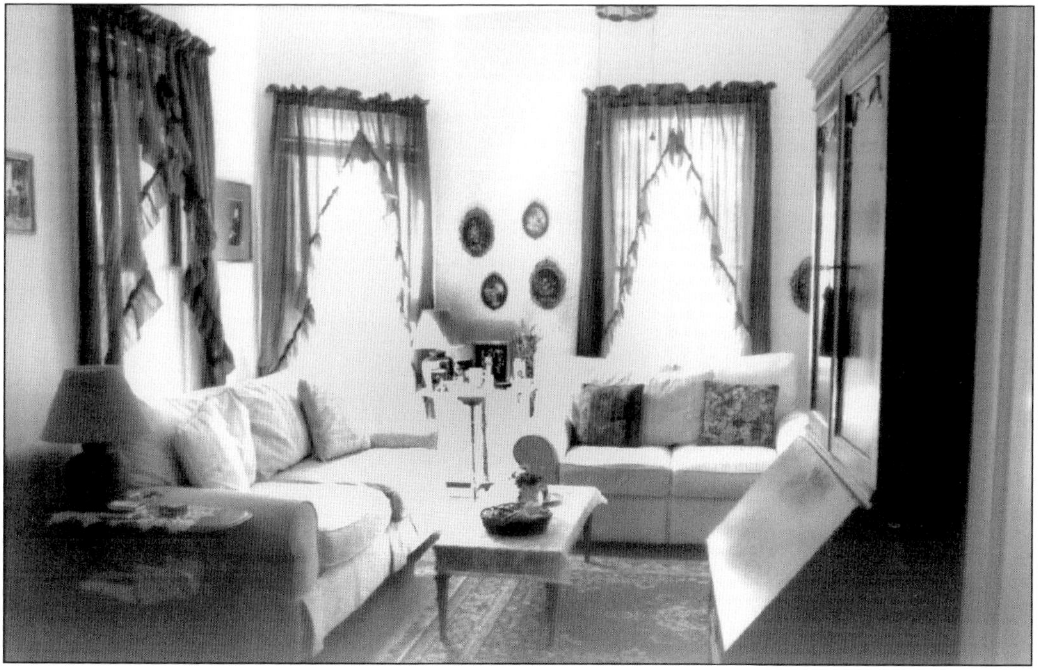

The living room is on the first floor of the Searcy House.

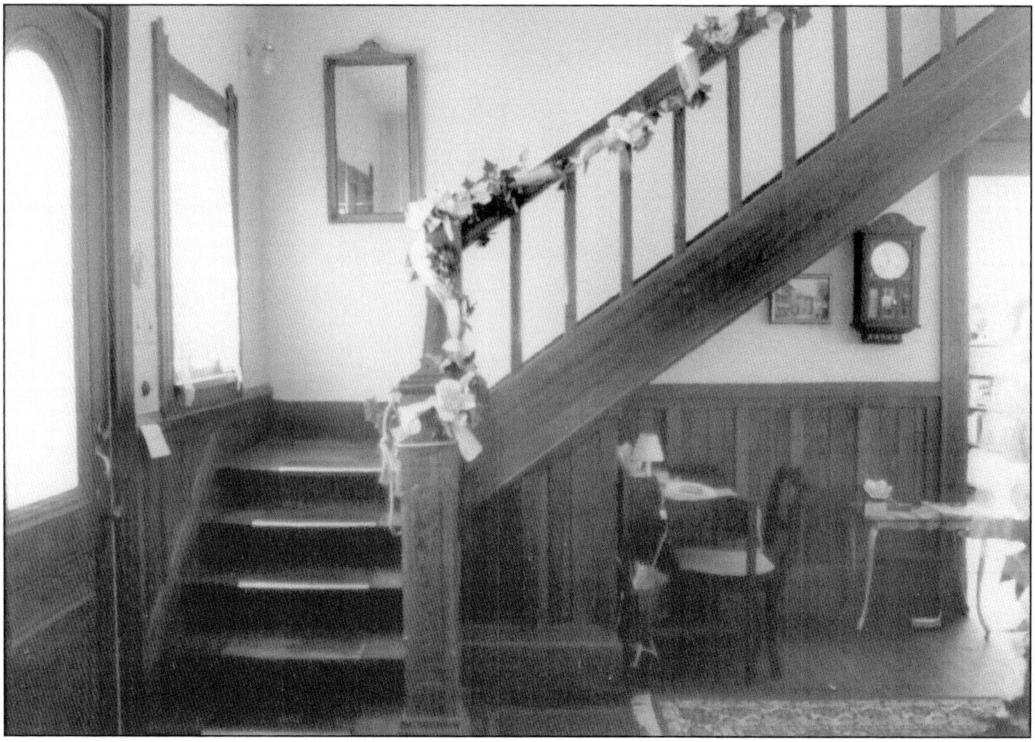

This staircase leads to the bedrooms at the Searcy House.

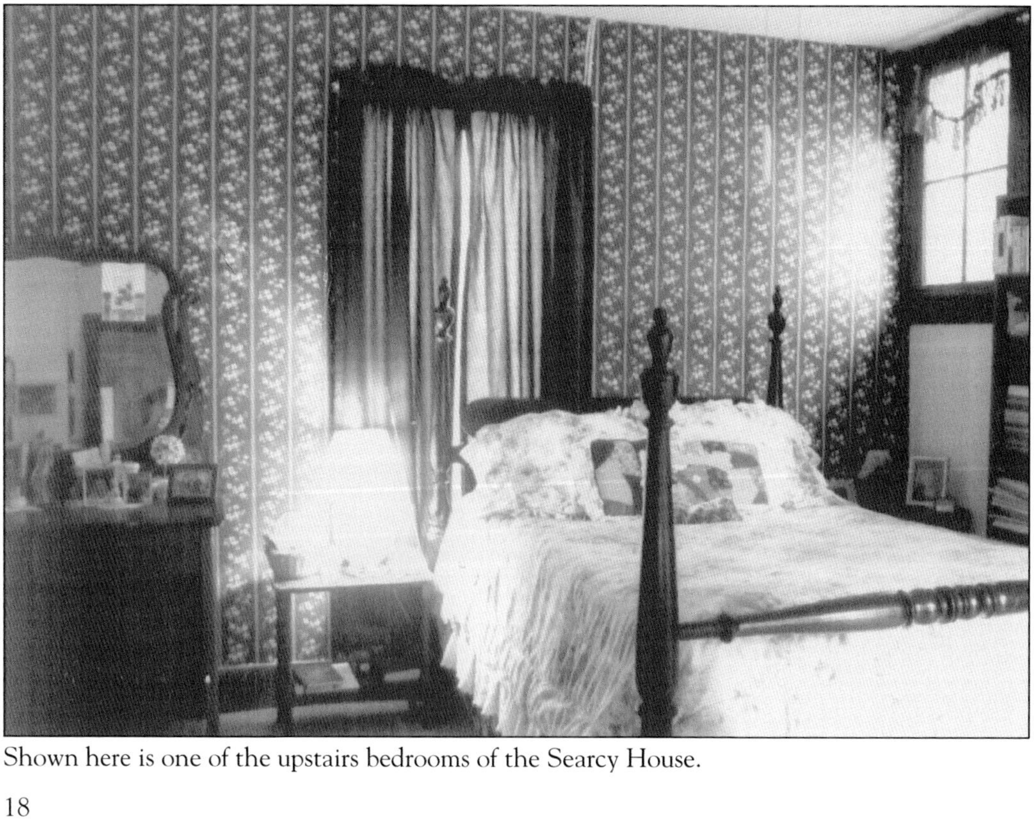

Shown here is one of the upstairs bedrooms of the Searcy House.

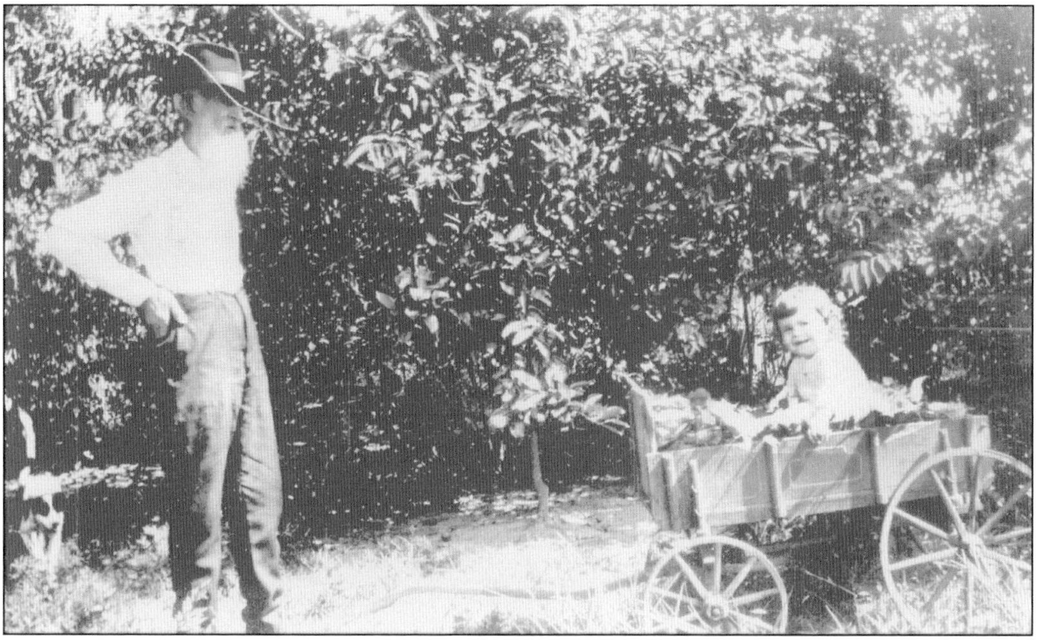

John Neill Searcy is shown here behind his home on West Church Avenue with one of his grandchildren in a wagon he built for her. The grounds are planted with huge old mulberry, camphor, and palm trees, along with tropical citrus such as orange, lemon, and grapefruit, and lovely old flowers featuring hydrangeas, plumbago, lantana, and Antique Florida roses.

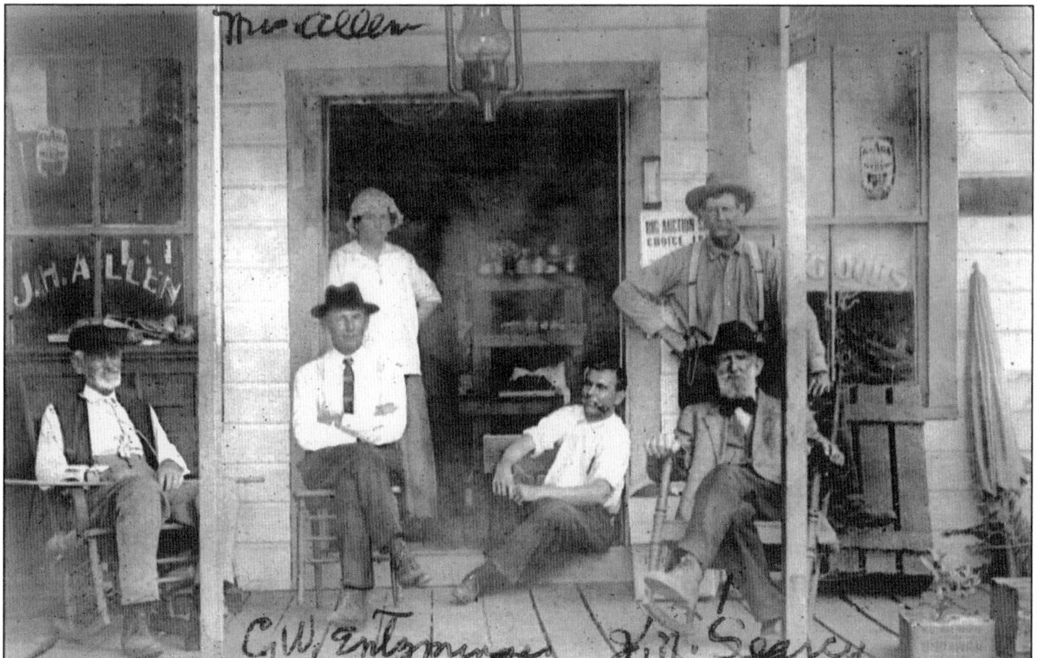

John Neill Searcy, shown seated on the right holding a cane, was one of Longwood's leading citizens. Shown with him, seated with hat and tie on the porch of the J.H. Allen Store, is C.W. Entzminger, a prominent leader of the community during the 1920s.

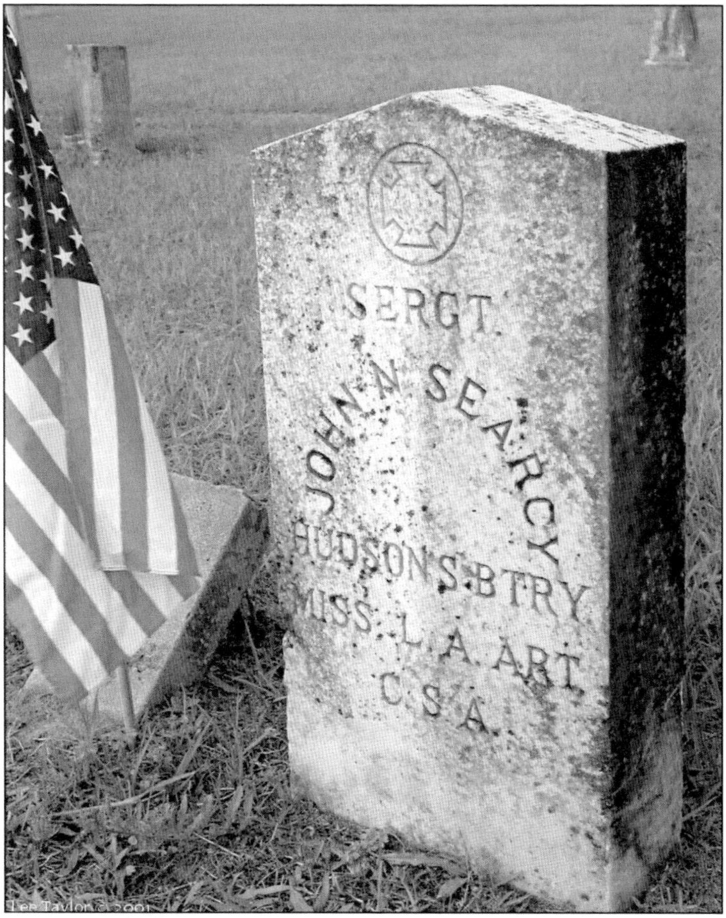

This is John Searcy's headstone at Longwood's cemetery. The Skylark neighborhood west of U.S. Highway 17-92 includes Longwood's oldest cemetery where many members of its early families are buried.

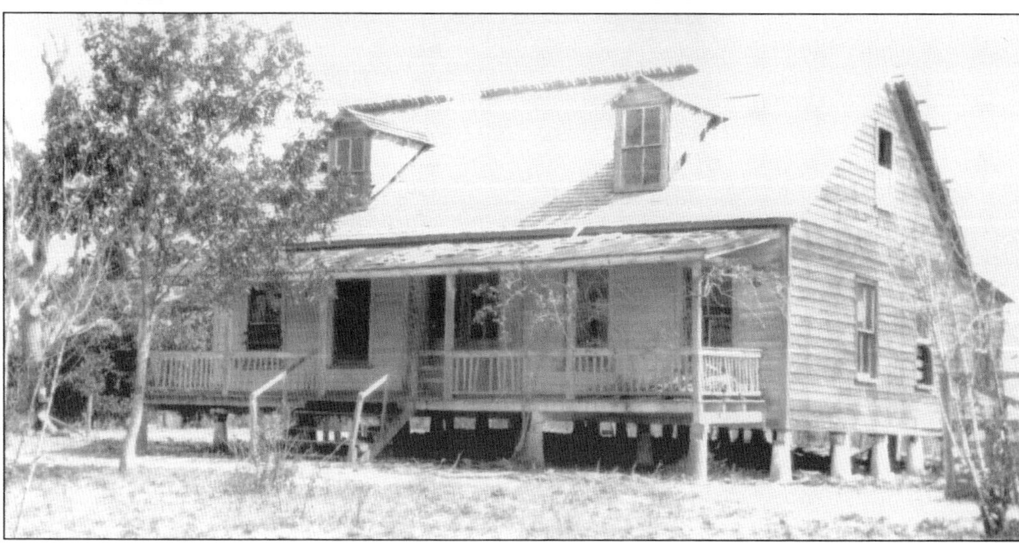

Pictured below is the Sam Dinkle family house in their grove near Stum's Corner. Stum's Corner was located at Rangeline Road at Church Avenue. Jim Dinkle built this house in the cluster of homes at what was once called West Longwood.

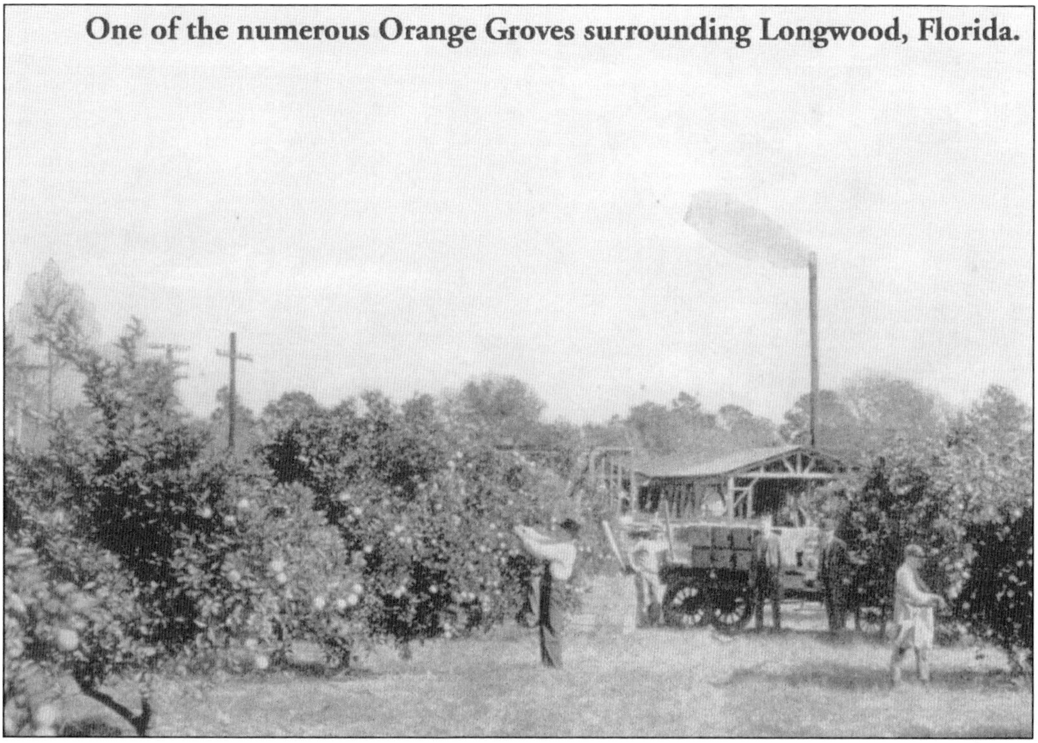

Pictured above is one of the many orange groves surrounding Longwood in the late 1800s. Central Florida's citrus industry can be traced to Capt. John R. Vinton, who, in an 1840 letter from Fort Mellon on Lake Monroe, wrote that "the orange trees are coming forward most promisingly." By 1845, steamboat lines were operating on the St. Johns River, and the business of exporting citrus and other produce was brisk.

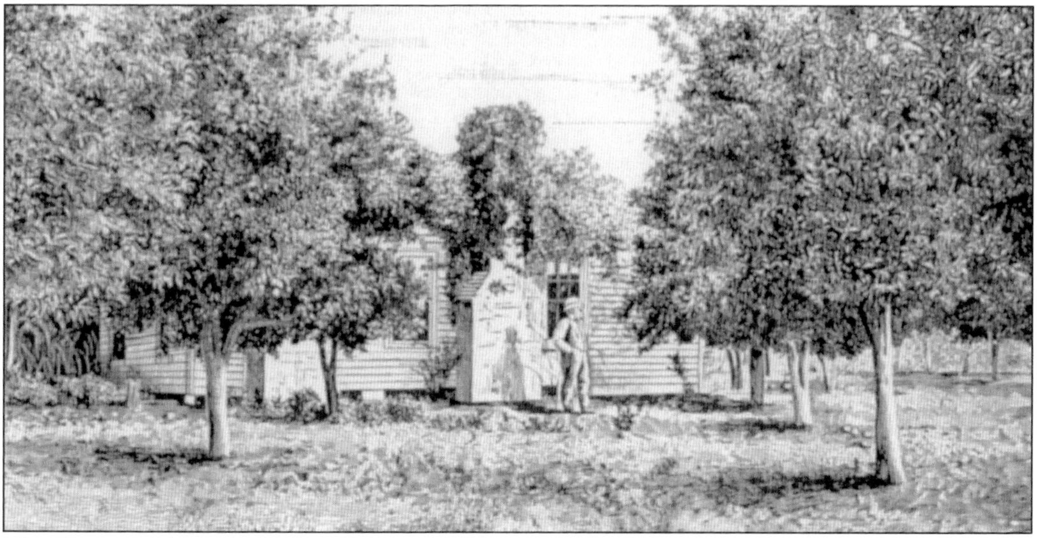

This drawing shows another of Longwood's early groves. Large-scale growing was impractical because the citrus spoiled during the long steamboat rides to northern markets. The change came in 1880 when the first railroad came to Central Florida, first reaching Sanford, then moving south to Longwood, Maitland, Winter Park, Orlando, and Kissimmee.

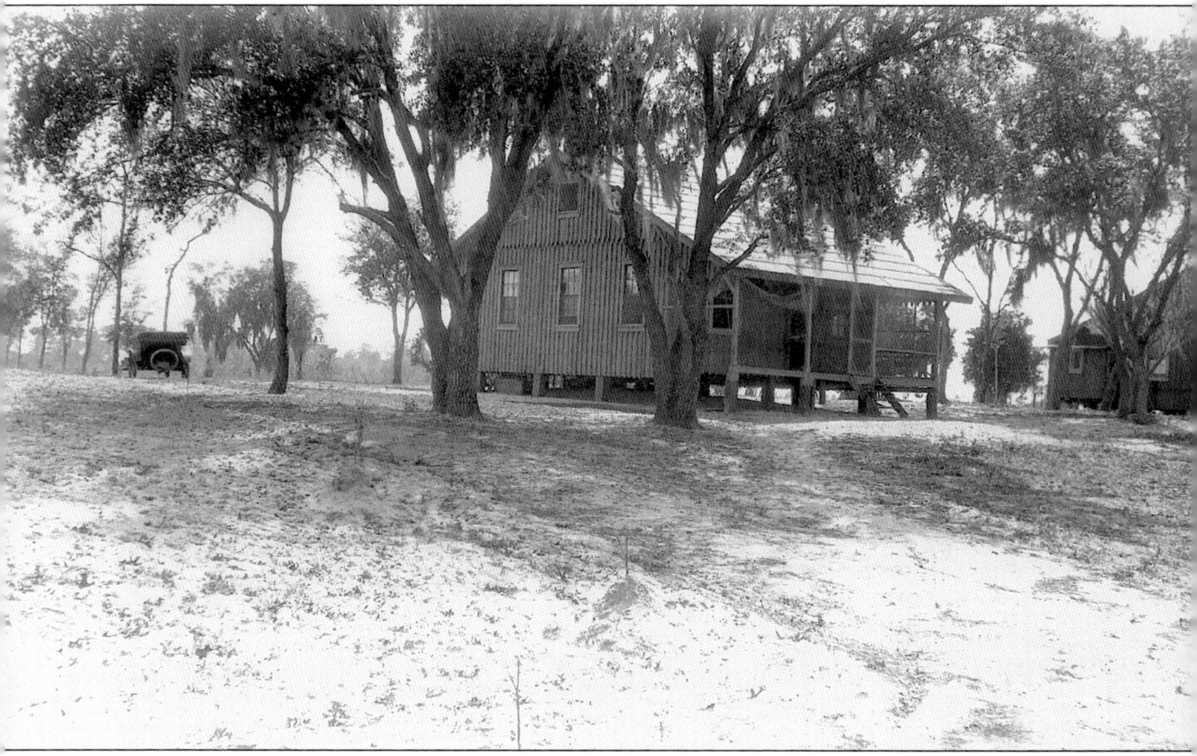

The Bickman-Phillips house was built at West Lake during Longwood's first boom era when the railroads brought in large numbers of new settlers and fueled the county's first population and business expansion. Citrus quickly overtook cotton and sugar cane as the area's premier crop. Growers began to make larger investments in their groves in an effort to satisfy the nation's demand for oranges, grapefruits, and tangerines.

Two

Railroad Builders

In the early 1880s, Longwood's founder, Bostonian entrepreneur Edward Warren Henck, began searching on horseback for a railroad route linking Sanford and Orlando, then a mere trading post. The South Florida Railroad was incorporated in 1879 by Henck, Dr. Clement C. Haskell of Maitland, and Longwood citrus grower E.T. Crafts. Longwood's other builder, Russian immigrant Peter Demens, arrived in 1881 and built the Orange Belt Railway linking Sanford (north of Longwood) to Tampa Bay in 1886. The opening of these rail lines began bringing winter visitors to Longwood's hotels and seasonal cottages. Year-round residents found investments or employment in lumbering, citrus, and turpentine businesses. Longwood's population topped 1,000 in 1887. By the end of the 1800s, Longwood had five churches, three hotels, eight stores, and a weekly newspaper.

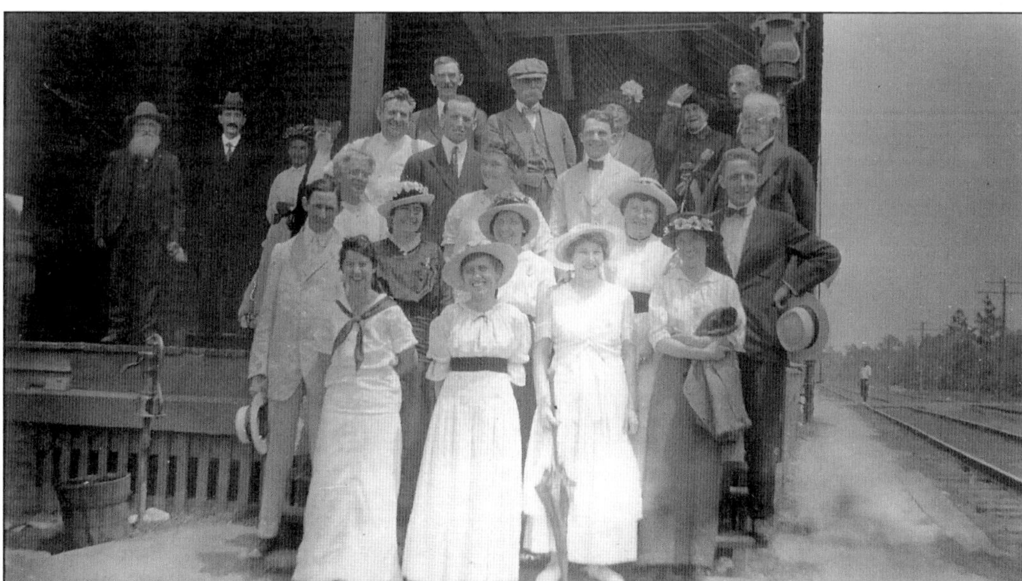

A group of winter visitors arrives in Longwood. Back then they could travel by rail from Philadelphia to Jacksonville and then on to Sanford for $30 to $35 in total fares with a quarter tip for the porter. Four meals and two nights lodging at Sanford's hotels would cost $2.50 to $4.

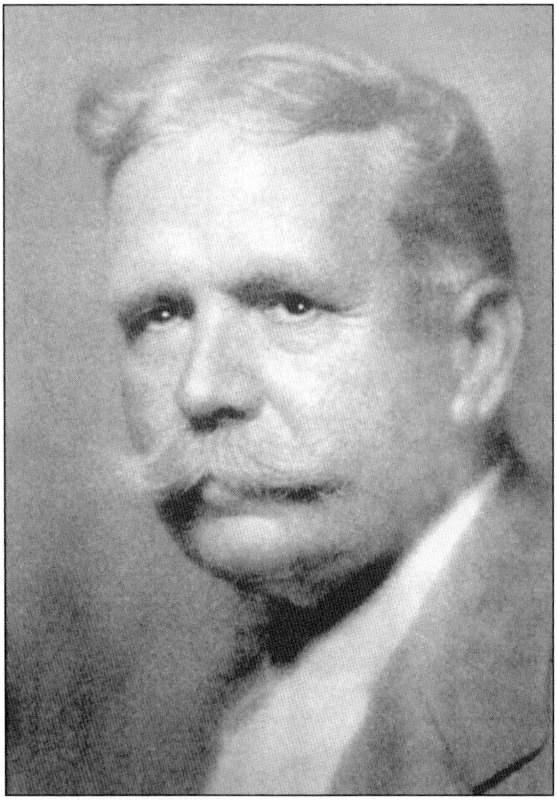

E.W. Henck, the man who would build a railroad and hotels and promote real estate, wrote, "Sanford, three quarters of a mile west of Mellonville, had one general store, one dwelling, a small board church [Episcopal], and one drugstore, the proprietor of which also kept on sale caskets in which to ship his victims North." After two days at Mellonville's "so-called hotel," Henck set out south on foot. Fifteen miles to the south, he selected his homestead on land south of what was Myrtle Lake. Longwood's founder, Bostonian entrepreneur Edward Warren Henck, who had served with the honor guard that accompanied President Abraham Lincoln's body on the train trip from Washington to Illinois, arrived in Florida by St. Johns River steamer in 1873, which at the time was the gateway to Central Florida's interior. Pictured below is the old Longwood train depot.

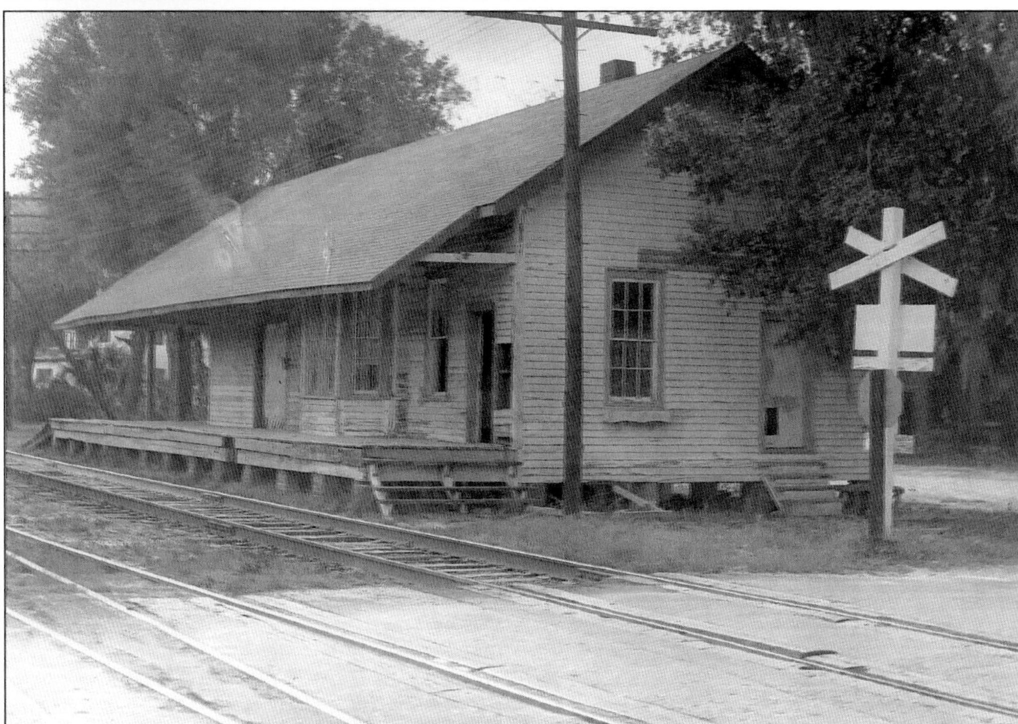

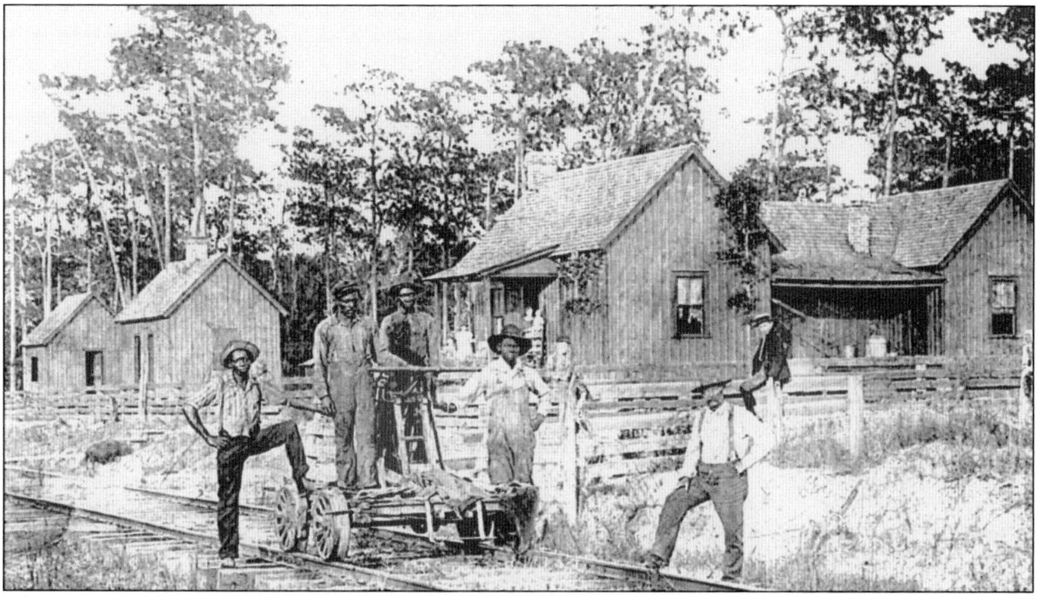

This 1880s photos shows the South Florida Railroad Co.'s maintenance crew building the tracks that would stretch from Sanford, through Longwood, and south to Orlando and Kissimmee before turning west to Lakeland and Tampa Bay.

The arrival of the first railroads brought an unprecedented wave of settlers, commerce, and development. Wealthy Northern investors looking for ways to exploit the Florida frontier would include Henck, who put together the partnership that bought the charter for the Lake Monroe & Orlando Railroad and changed its name to the South Florida Railroad. The line reached Longwood in June 1880 and Maitland a month later. On October 2, the first train left Sanford for its 23-mile maiden excursion to Orlando. By early November, the railroad was making twice daily, 10-stop trips between Sanford and Orlando. An 1880 timetable listed these stops, Sanford, Belair (Henry Sanford's estate and groves), Bents (Lake Mary), Soldier Creek (near Big Tree Park), Longwood, Snows (Altamonte Springs), Maitland, Osceola (Winter Park), Willcox (near College Park), and Orlando. Family records note that between 1893 and 1899, the South Florida Railroad paid L.J. Hartley Jr. $173.25 for cattle killed by its trains.

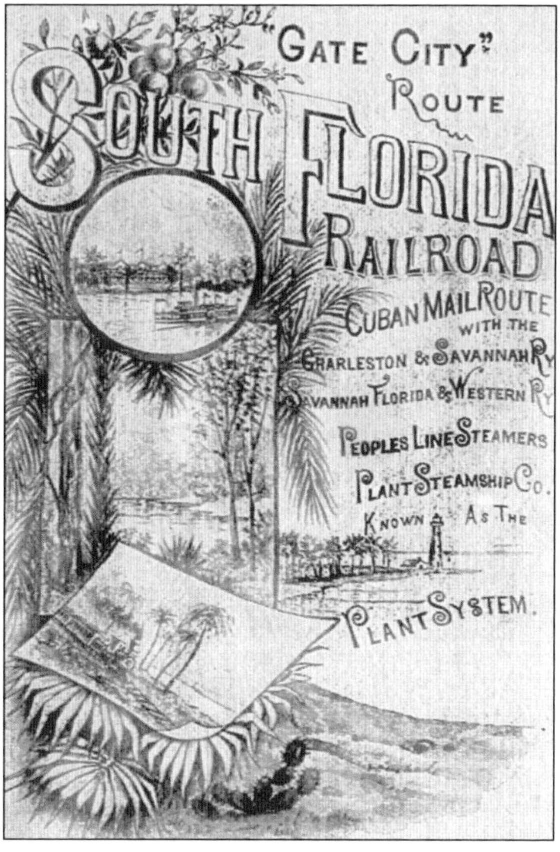

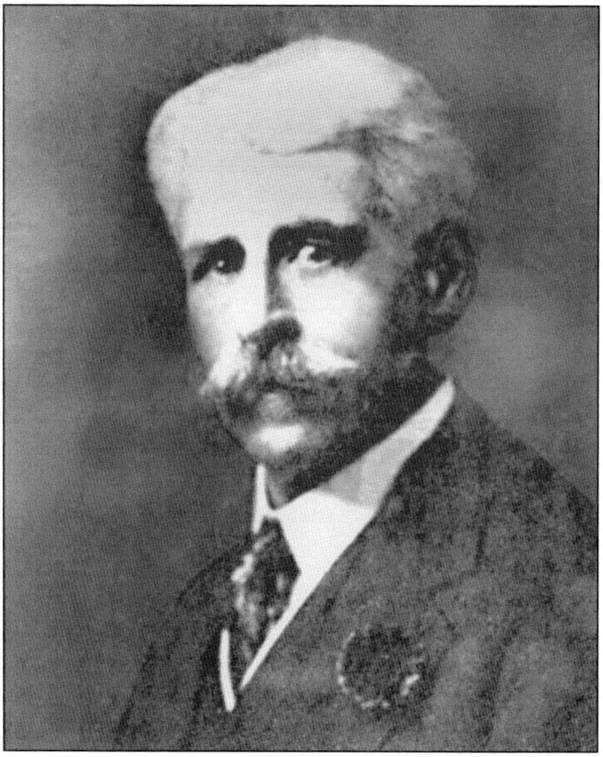

James E. Ingraham came to Florida in 1875 from Ohio, hoping the climate would cure his tuberculosis. Henry Sanford hired Ingraham as his land agent, and Ingraham helped Sanford select land to donate for the South Florida Railroad. Ingraham later joined railroad baron Henry Plant as president of the railroad, which encouraged Northern investment. Henry Flagler tapped Ingraham to run his St. Augustine-based land company, and Ingraham helped engineer Flagler's railroad entry into Miami.

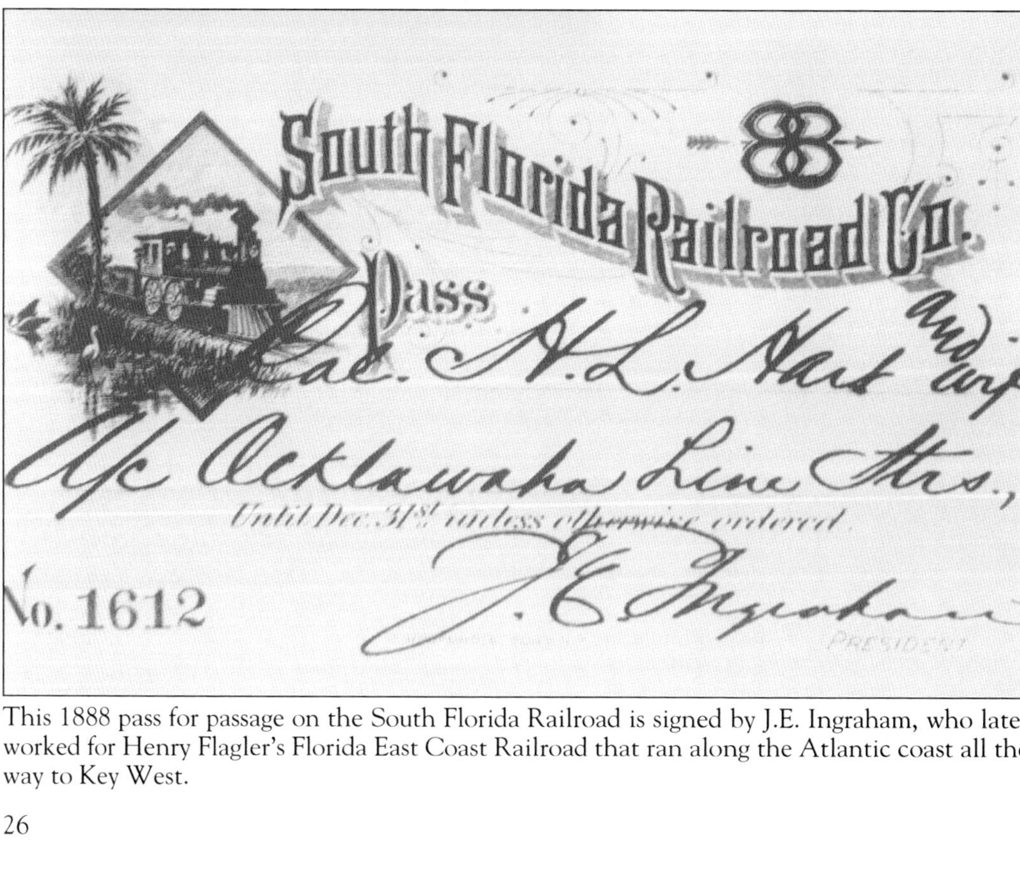

This 1888 pass for passage on the South Florida Railroad is signed by J.E. Ingraham, who later worked for Henry Flagler's Florida East Coast Railroad that ran along the Atlantic coast all the way to Key West.

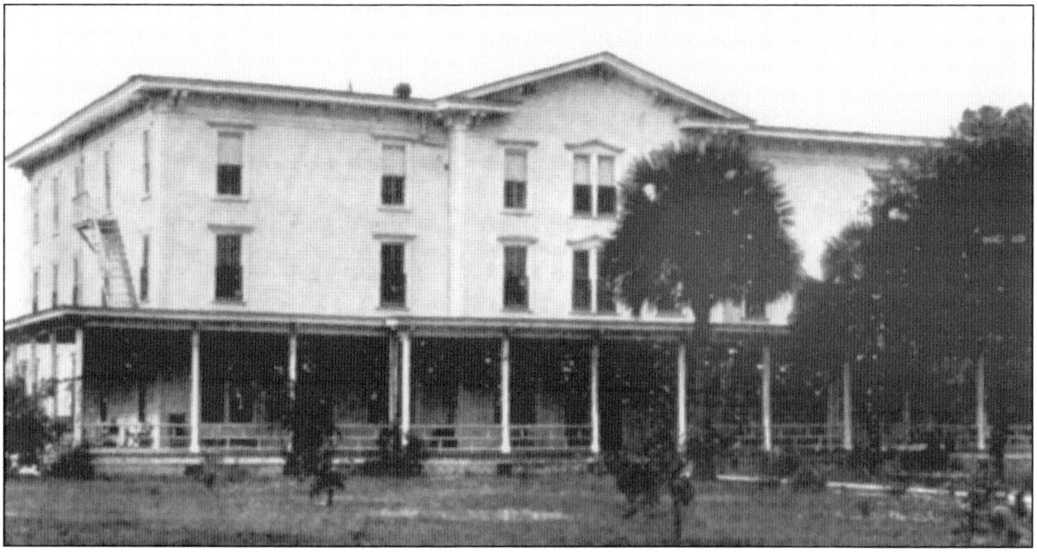

Two years after he laid the first railroad line from Sanford to Orlando, E.W. Henck built a two-story hotel in Longwood. That hotel burned, but Henck built this rambling 38-room hotel, completed in 1886, on County Road 427. The Longwood Hotel would survive the severe freezes of 1894 and 1895 that wiped out citrus groves and forced settlers to pull up stakes. Henck sold it in 1910. Other large wooden hotels were built along the railroad line, but only the one in Longwood remains today. Construction on the resort hotel began in 1883. A newspaper in 1886 reported that Carlos Cushing, a wealthy New England businessman who built a large home on Lake Brantley, bought Henck's largest hotel before it was completed. Henck invested about $15,000 in the three-story hotel before he quit and decided to sell it at a loss. It opened as The Waltham, a name selected from a district of Boston. Cushing was listed as proprietor, but many believe Peter Demens's money paid for the hotel's completion.

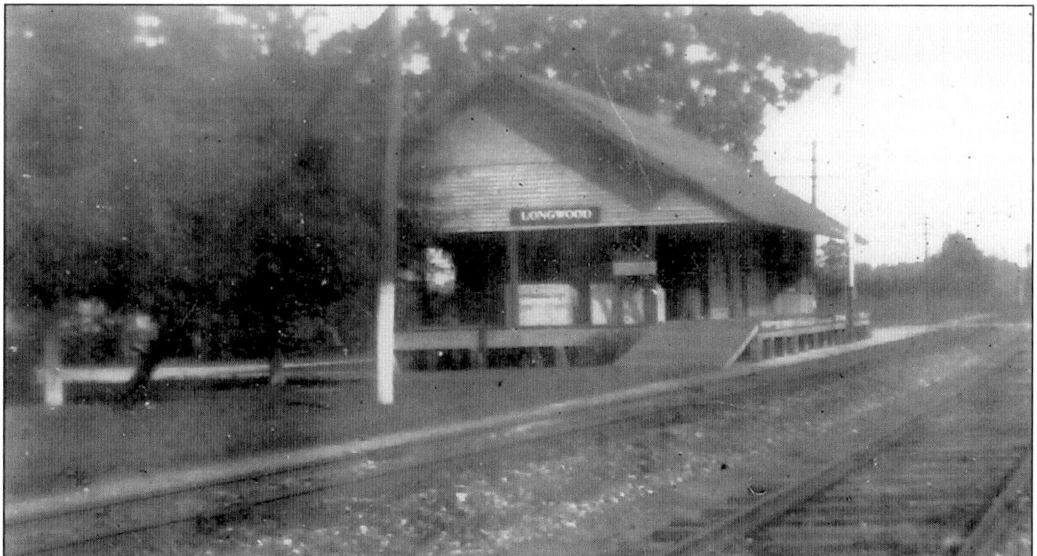

Longwood's railroad station, seen here in the early 1900s, is pictured before it was moved to the north Florida town of Hilliard. This view is looking north along the railroad tracks. Church Avenue runs behind the depot.

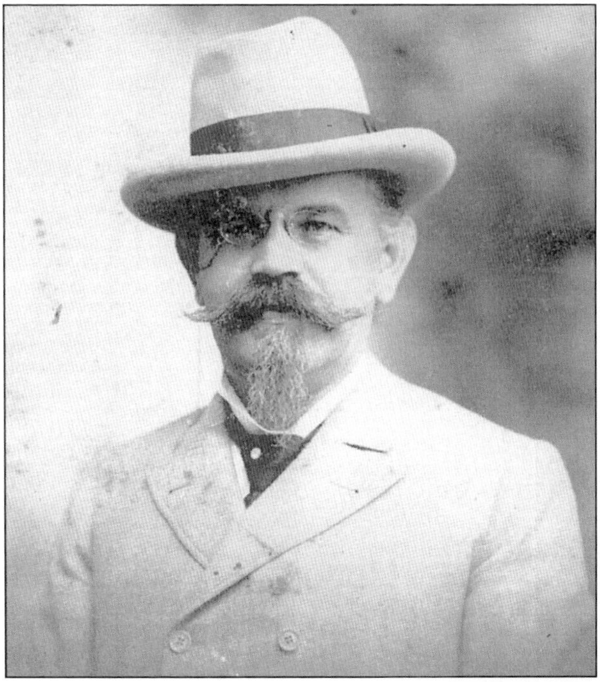

On April 20, 1885, Longwood sawmill owner Peter Demens, shown here, became owner of a charter for a railroad to run from the community of Lake Monroe to south of Lake Apopka when its owners couldn't pay a debt. He completed the line to the new town of Oakland and later to the Tampa Bay area. The town at the end of the line became St. Petersburg, a name selected by one of his partners to honor Demens's hometown. By 1889, though, Demens sold his railroad to get out of debt and moved to North Carolina. Eventually, he moved to California.

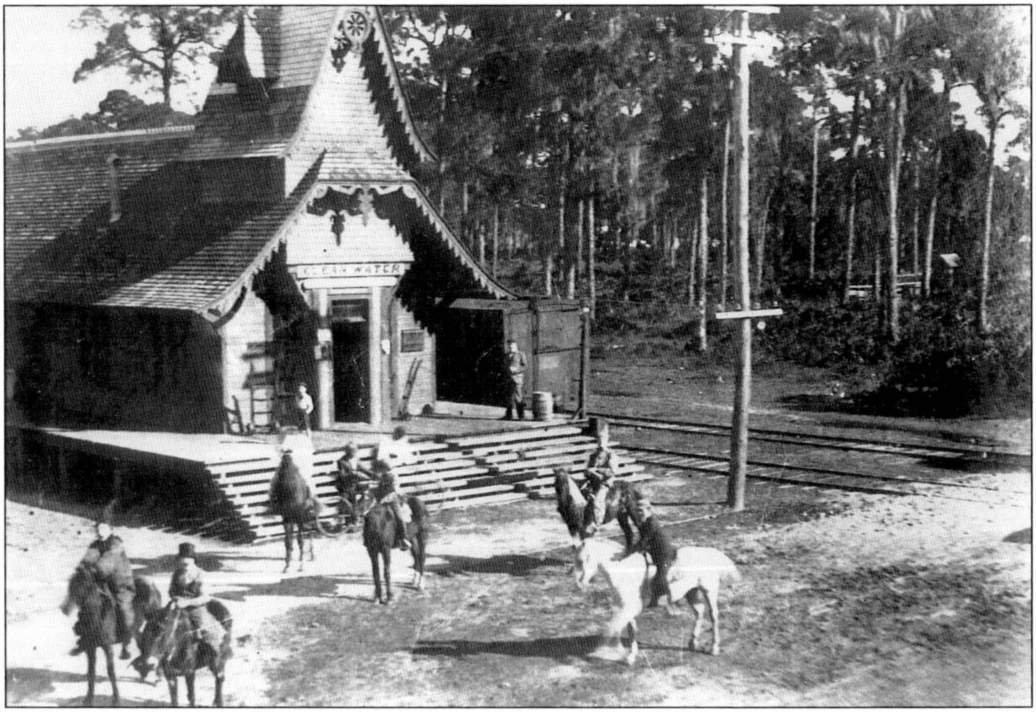

Peter Demens's expansion plans included a contract to build railroad station houses from Lakeland to Dade City. This photo of the Demens-built depot for Clearwater shows the Russian-influenced style he also used for the depot at Upsala, the Swedish colony north of Longwood. Demens also supplied labor and material for buildings at Rollins College in Winter Park.

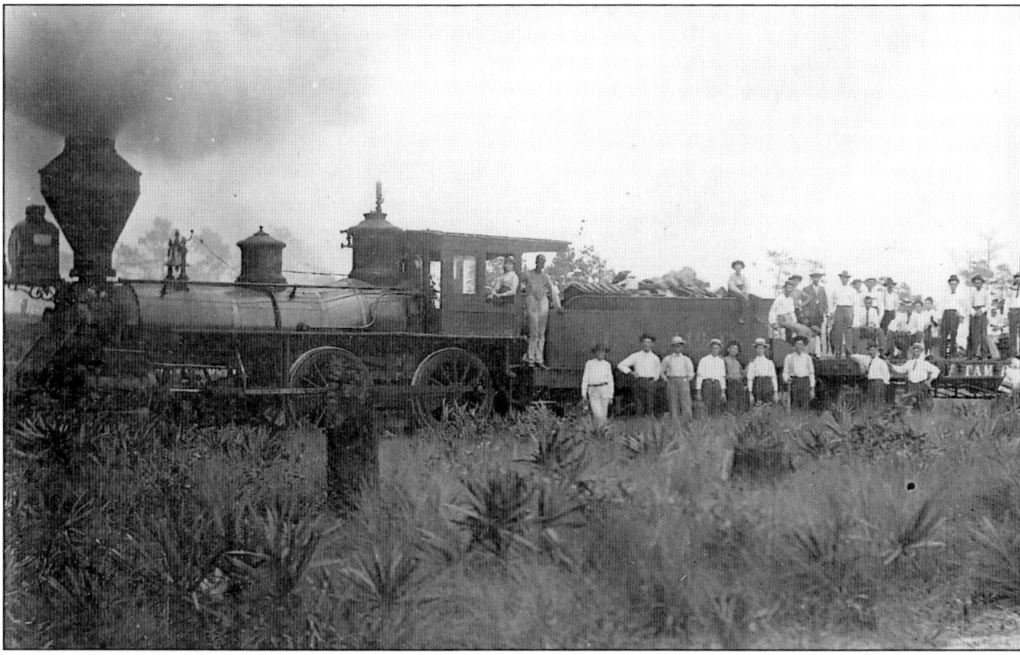

The crew and guests pose here for a 1880s photograph of the Orange Belt Railway Co., built by Longwood's Peter Demens to link orange-growing regions of Central Florida with the Gulf Coast.

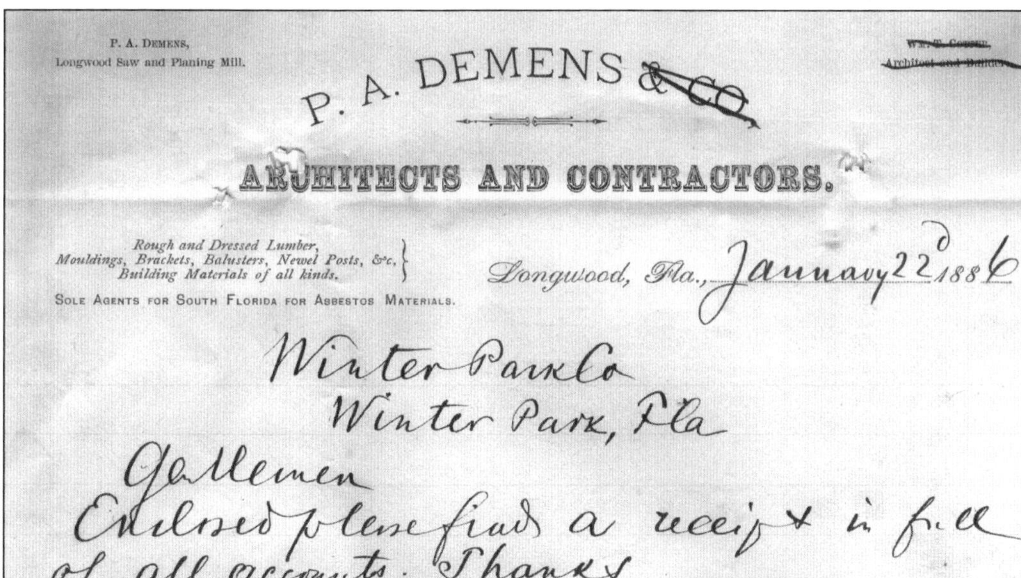

P. A. DEMENS,
Longwood Saw and Planing Mill.

P. A. DEMENS & CO

ARCHITECTS AND CONTRACTORS.

Rough and Dressed Lumber, Mouldings, Brackets, Balusters, Newel Posts, &c., Building Materials of all kinds.

SOLE AGENTS FOR SOUTH FLORIDA FOR ASBESTOS MATERIALS.

Longwood, Fla., January 22d 1886

Winter Park Co
Winter Park, Fla
Gentlemen
Enclosed please find a receipt in full of all accounts. Thanks.

The 1884–1885 State Gazetteer and Business Directory lists Longwood's chief industry as the P.A. Demens & Co. sash, door and blind factory. In those days, it was the major supplier of lumber and building materials for much of the area. The company's owner was Pyotr Alekseyevich Dementyev, who shortened his name to Peter Demens when he came to America. He was 31 when he came to Florida in June 1881 as an expatriate nobleman who probably had been on the losing end of a political feud in czarist Russia. In Longwood he bought 30 acres of groves and a 30 percent interest in a sawmill, later buying out his partners.

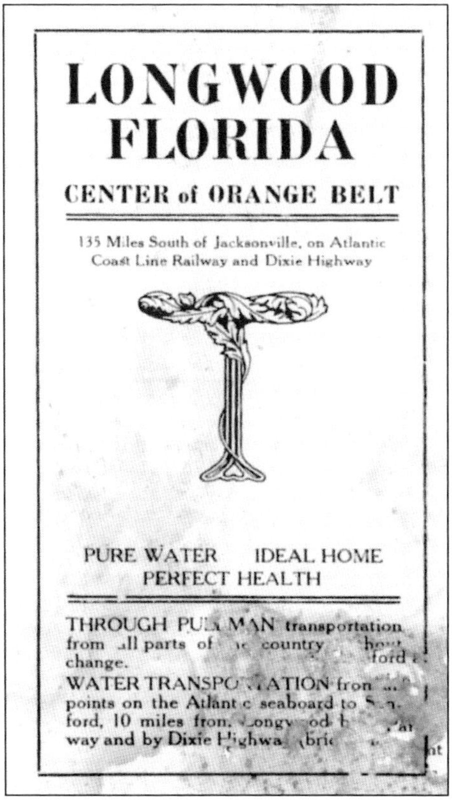

This Longwood advertisement promotes the city as the "Center of Orange Belt." Longwood offered "pure water, ideal homes sites, and perfect health. Longwood is an incorporated town with churches, schools, electric lights, cement walks, Masonic hall, public library, and everything for a perfect home."

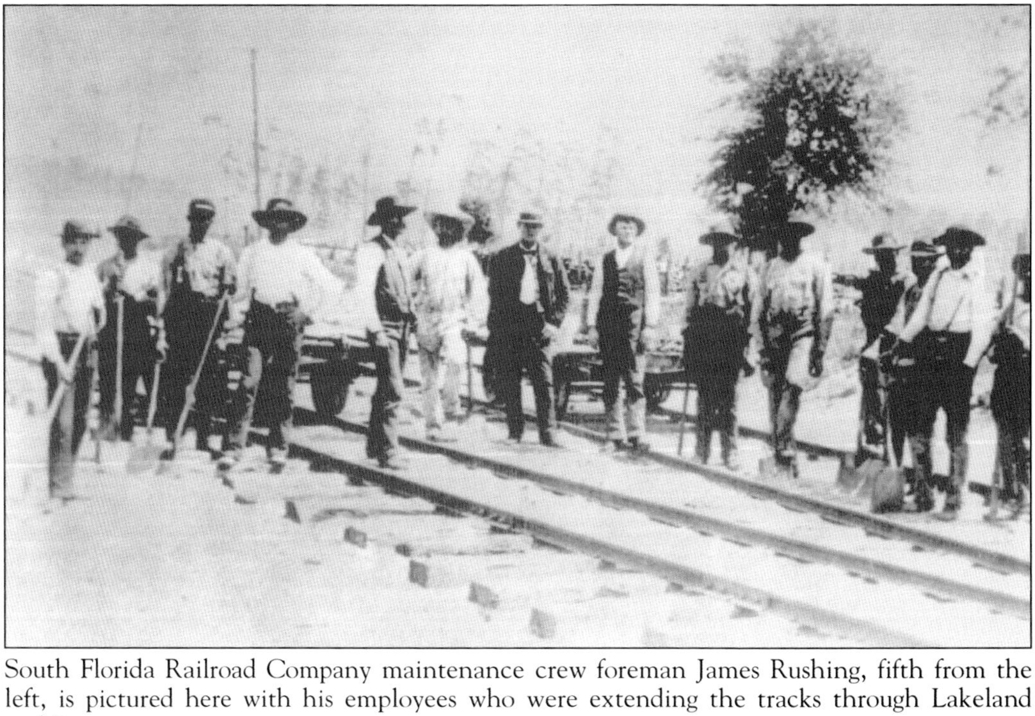

South Florida Railroad Company maintenance crew foreman James Rushing, fifth from the left, is pictured here with his employees who were extending the tracks through Lakeland and Bartow.

Ben J. Overstreet is shown here with his wife, Bessie, and their son B.J. Overstreet Jr. The Overstreets were major landowners during the lumber and turpentine eras. Besides the Overstreet Turpentine Co., other companies included the Spencer Sawmill, the Zachary Lumber Co., and the Wilson Cypress Co.

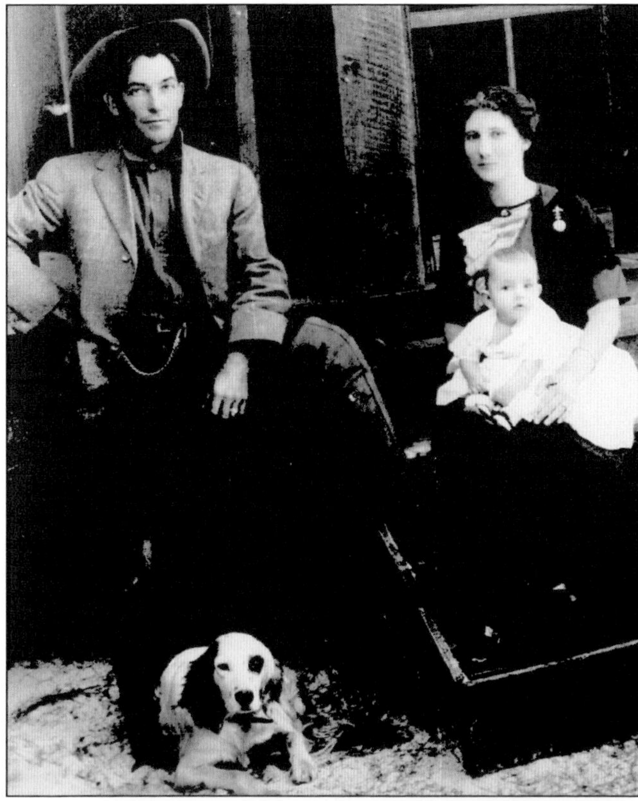

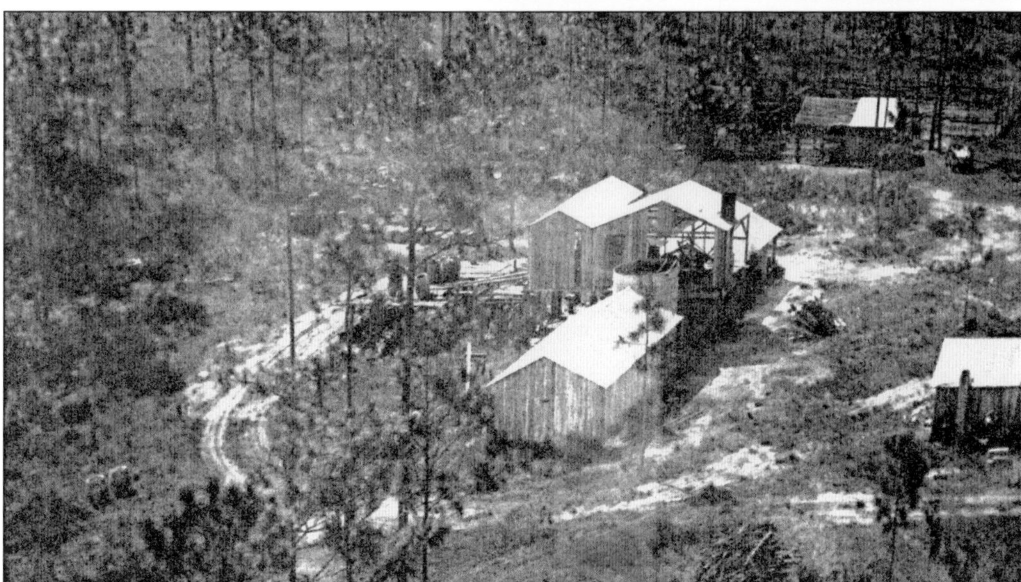

This photo shows one of the many sawmills and turpentine factories that dotted the pine and palmetto forests in and around Longwood and the Wekiva River. The remote flatlands provided work for black settlers throughout the 1880s after the construction of the railroads. A historic marker just east of the sharp bend where Longwood-Markham Road becomes Markham Road honors the early settlers at the community of Markham.

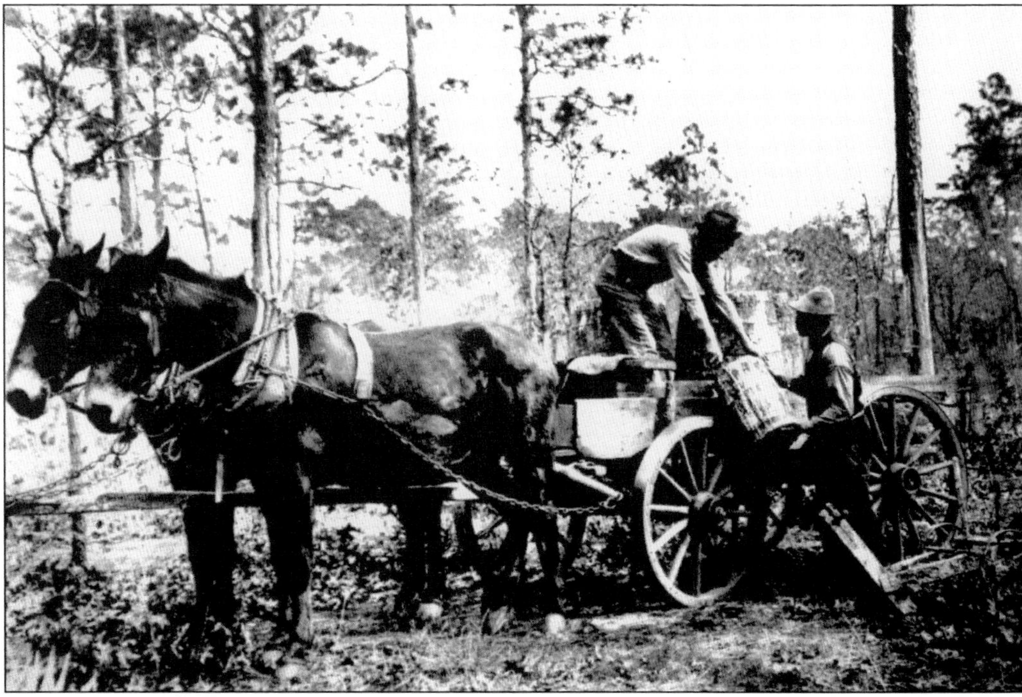

Turpentine workers load barrels of sap. Maybelle Thomas Glover's family worked in turpentine trees. "Men would chip bark, collect the sap in clay cups, transfer it to wooden barrels, and take it by mule and wagon to Mr. Hagan's distillery and later to the Markham train station," she writes in a family history. "There was a commissary and little houses for the workers there near the train station."

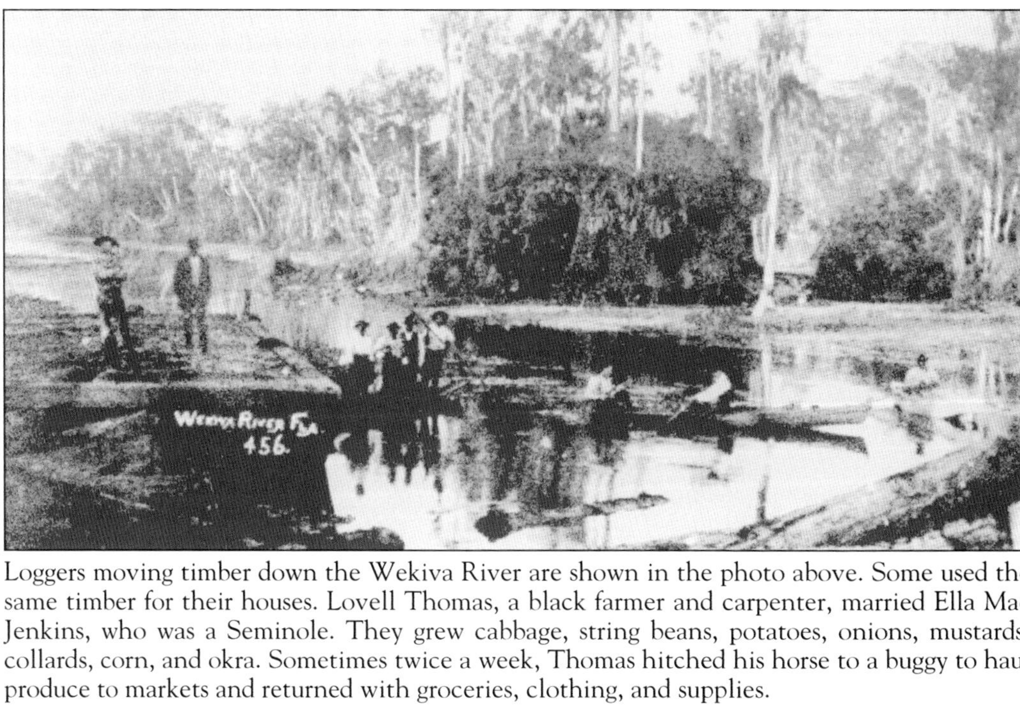

Loggers moving timber down the Wekiva River are shown in the photo above. Some used the same timber for their houses. Lovell Thomas, a black farmer and carpenter, married Ella Mae Jenkins, who was a Seminole. They grew cabbage, string beans, potatoes, onions, mustards, collards, corn, and okra. Sometimes twice a week, Thomas hitched his horse to a buggy to haul produce to markets and returned with groceries, clothing, and supplies.

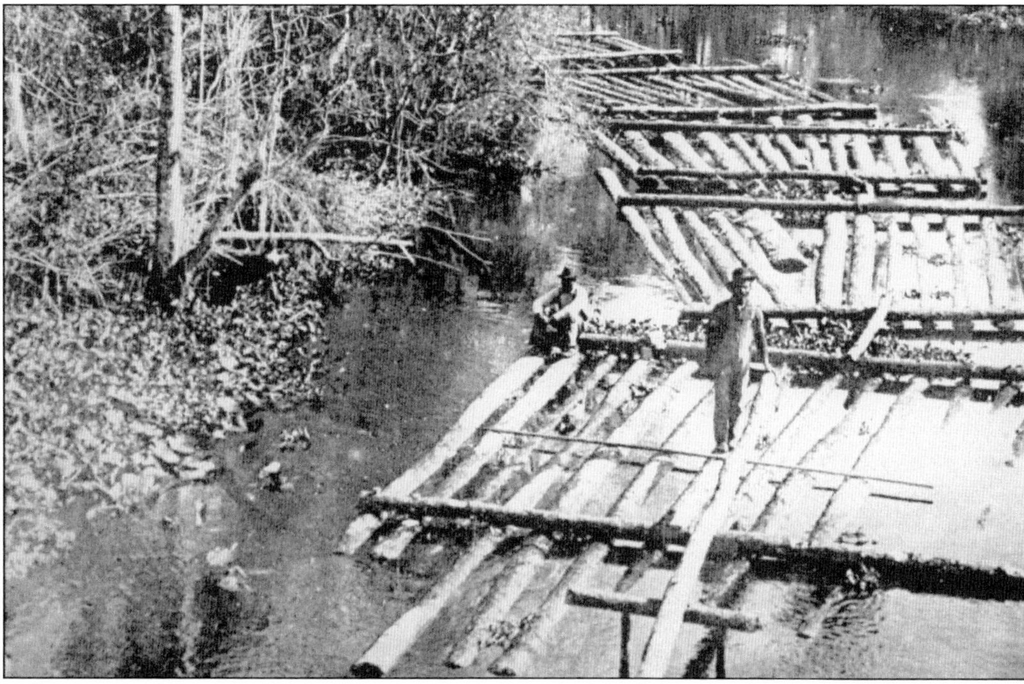

A logger stands on a makeshift raft used to move timber downstream. The planks and timbers used to build the first bridge over the Wekiva River were milled at Markham. Florida's vast first-growth forests made the men who owned the timber and turpentine rights rich. The companies, though, kept the men who worked the trees in poverty and near slavery.

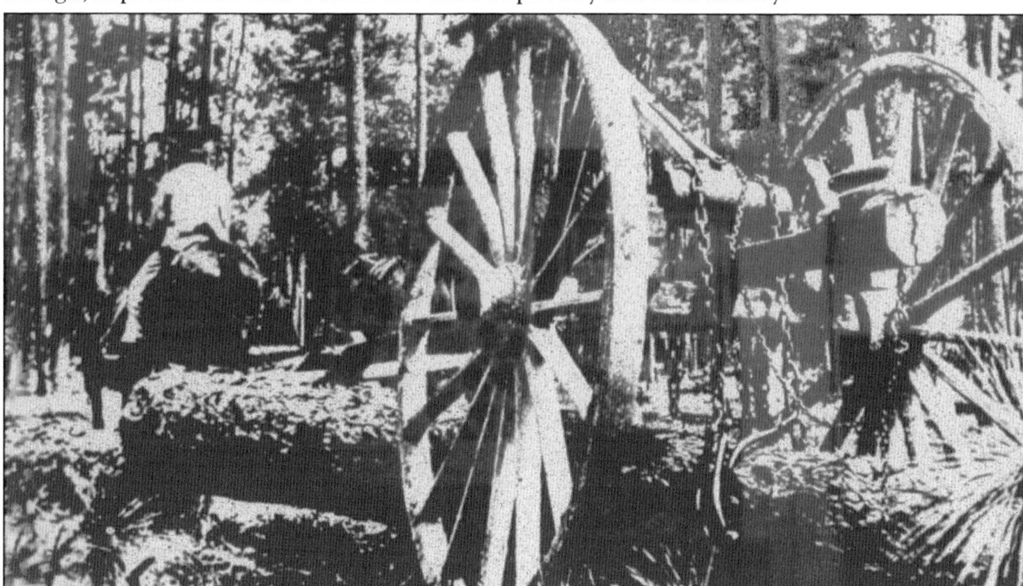

A logger on horseback drags timber from the woods to the riverfront. Throughout North and Central Florida, the living and working conditions of the lumber and turpentine men were primitive and harsh. Crews and their families were crowded into isolated shanties. The food and wages were miserable. Many were forced to trade the scrip they earned for overpriced goods at company stores. In most areas, the laws were made and enforced by labor contractors.

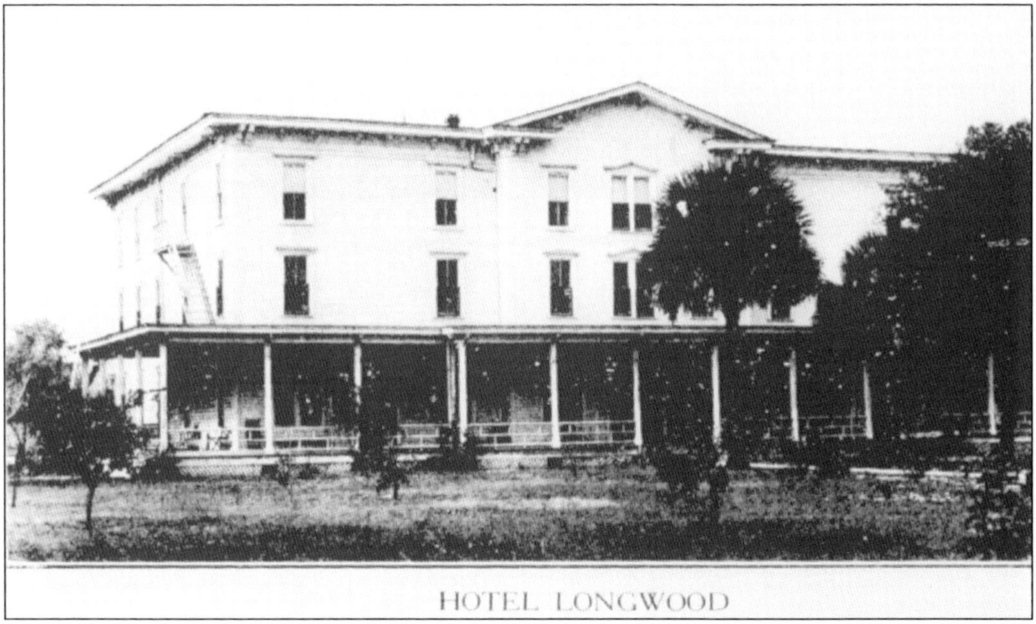

Timber made at the Longwood area sawmill was used to build the Longwood Hotel during the early railroad years. By the 1940s, 70 years of turpentine and logging operations had stripped Florida of its old slash and longleaf pines. After the pines dried up from the turpentine operations, loggers moved in, cutting every tree and replanting none. Once the logging stripped the land of pines, ranchers, citrus growers, and farmers cleared out palmettos for cattle, groves, and fields.

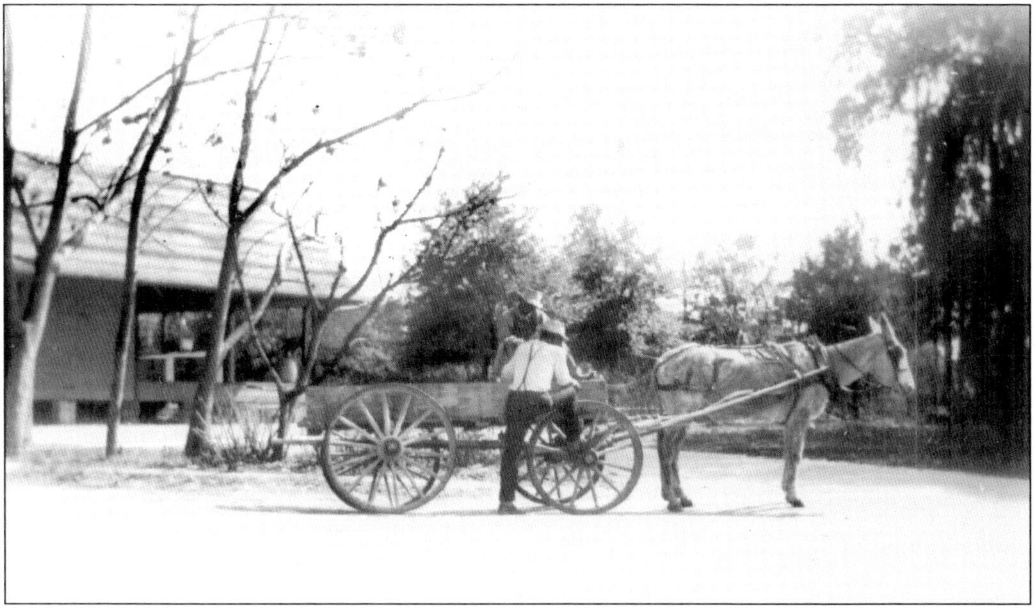

This scene shows George Jones, one of Longwood's pioneer black settlers, climbing into a farm wagon. The photo was taken from the post office on what is now Church Avenue. In the background is the railroad depot. Jones, shown with John McQuigg, owned farmland west of Rangeline Road and on both sides of what today is State Road 434.

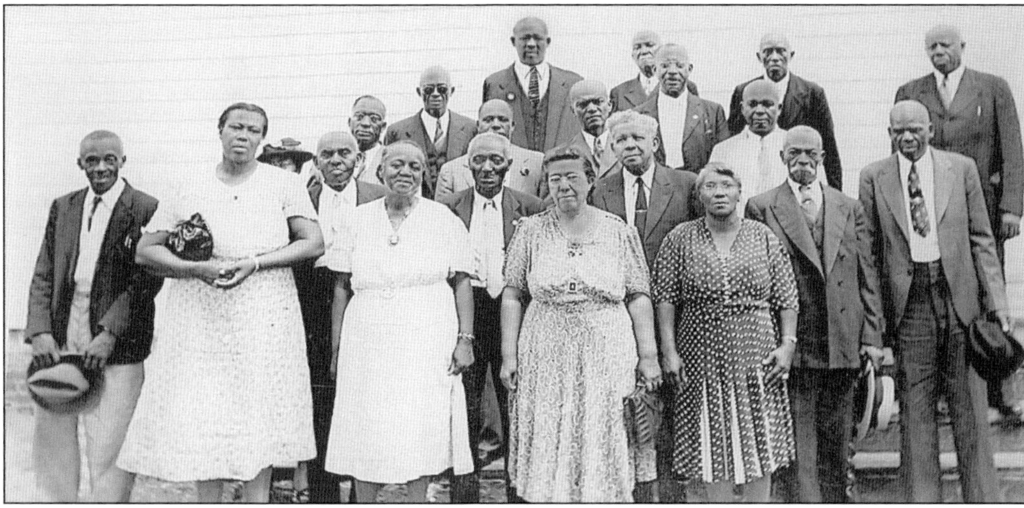

Thomas Shepherd, pictured here (second row, right) with a group of Baptists at a convention, homesteaded in Longwood after coming to Florida to work for the railroad. Shepherd, born into slavery on a Georgia plantation, was 19 when emancipated. He was still a young man seeking a better living when Longwood founder E.W. Henck went to Georgia to recruit laborers to build the South Florida Railroad. At Montezuma, Georgia, he hired Shepherd and others. Henck helped Shepherd file his homestead claim on 77 acres that today straddle State Road 434 through Longwood.

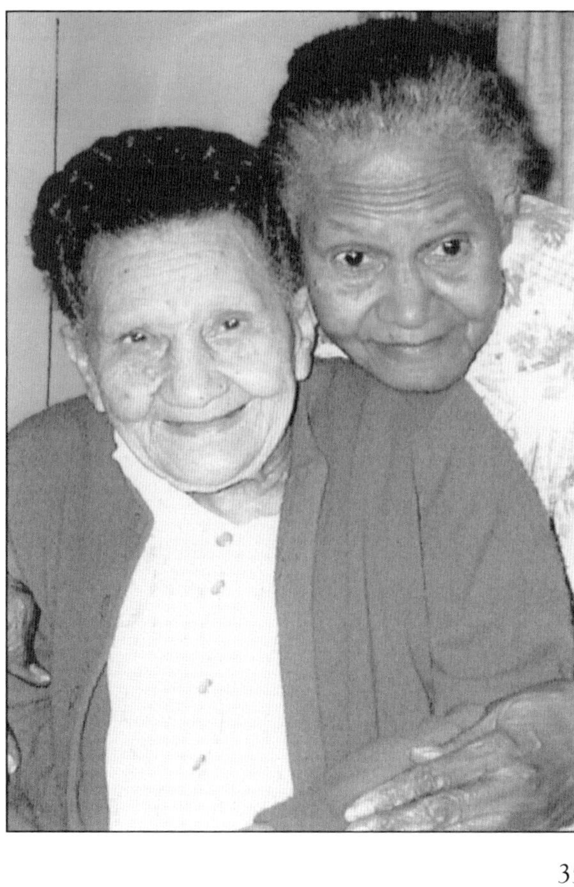

Stella Fleece, shown here seated in front of her sister Annabelle, said her great-grandfather Thomas Shepherd went back to Georgia for his family, including his father, Nathan Shepherd; his sister Millie Shepherd, who married Henry Patterson; and his brother Peter Shepherd, who would become the first pastor at Corinth Baptist Church, founded in 1883 on land given by E.W. Henck. Shepherd had four daughters and a stepson. One of Shepherd's four daughters, Annie, married Augustus Bell. They would have two daughters in Longwood, Willie and Eulah, while living on Shepherd's farmland. Annie Bell was 15 when she had Eulah, Stella Fleece's mother, in 1887.

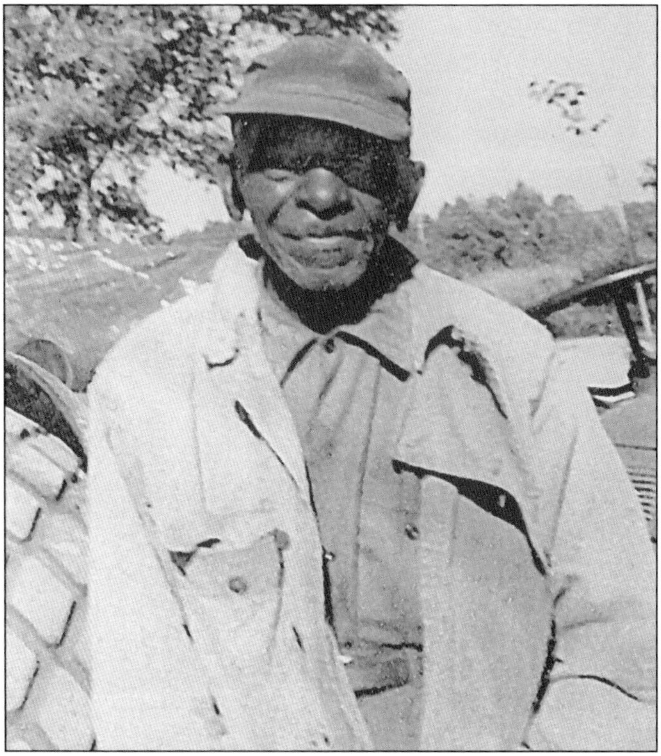

George Jones was one of the early settlers in the Longwood area. The Jones and Shepherd farms and groves covered much of the land on both sides of State Road 434 in the Rangeline Road area.

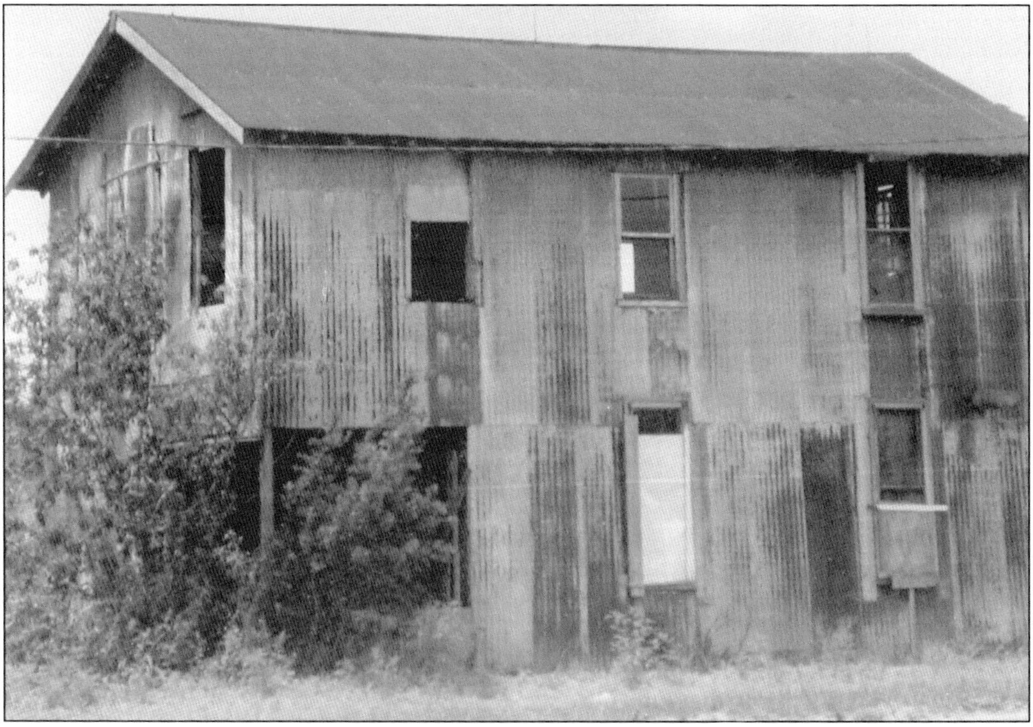

This is George Jones's barn, which was on the south side of what is now State Road 434. The barn was demolished in the 1980s when commercial property was developed in the area.

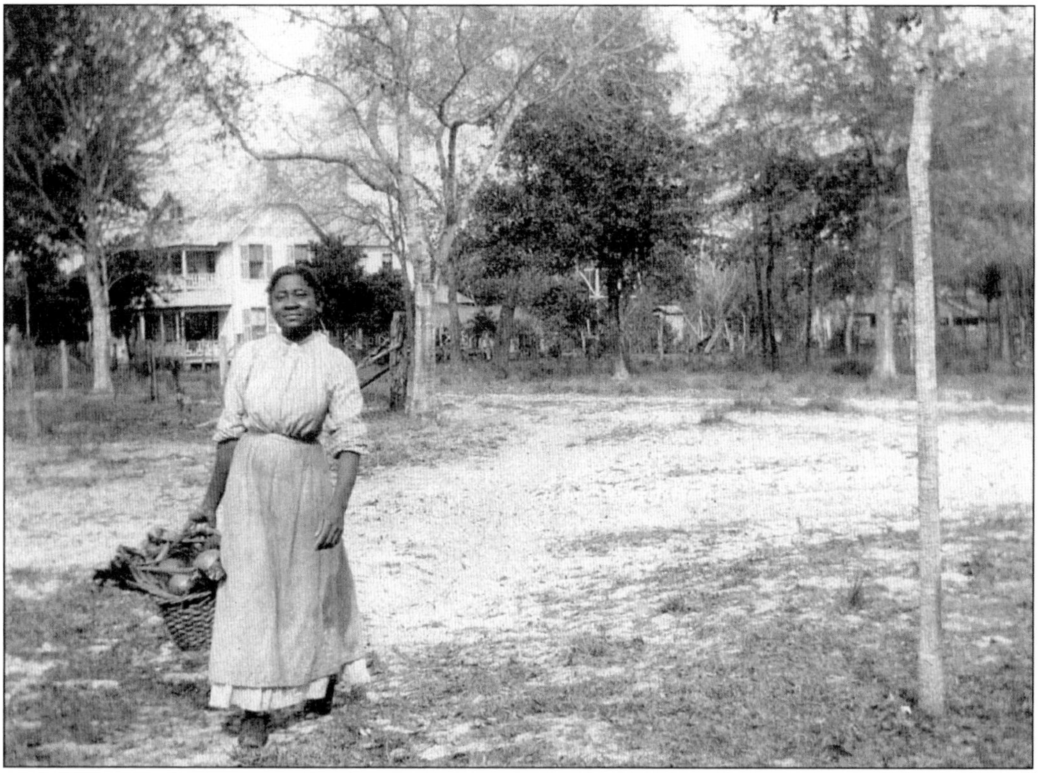

One of the Niemeyer's domestic workers carries a basket of fresh-picked vegetables from the family garden.

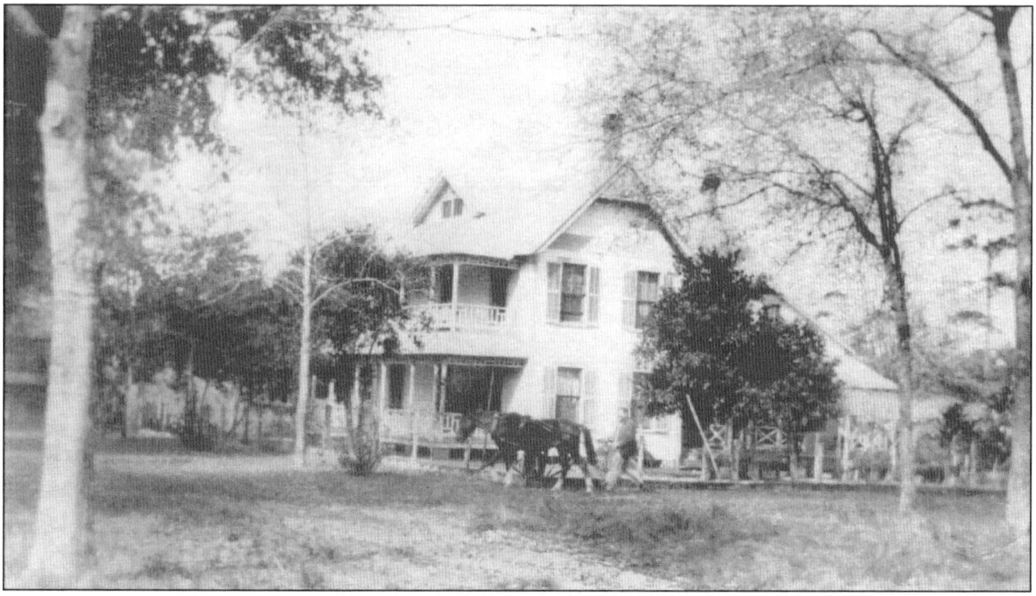

In the foreground of this photo of the Clouser House in the early 1900s is one of the family members plowing a garden. In the 1880s Longwood's larger houses were built along Warren, Church, and Bay Avenues. Others were built along the lakes and in the orange groves and farms.

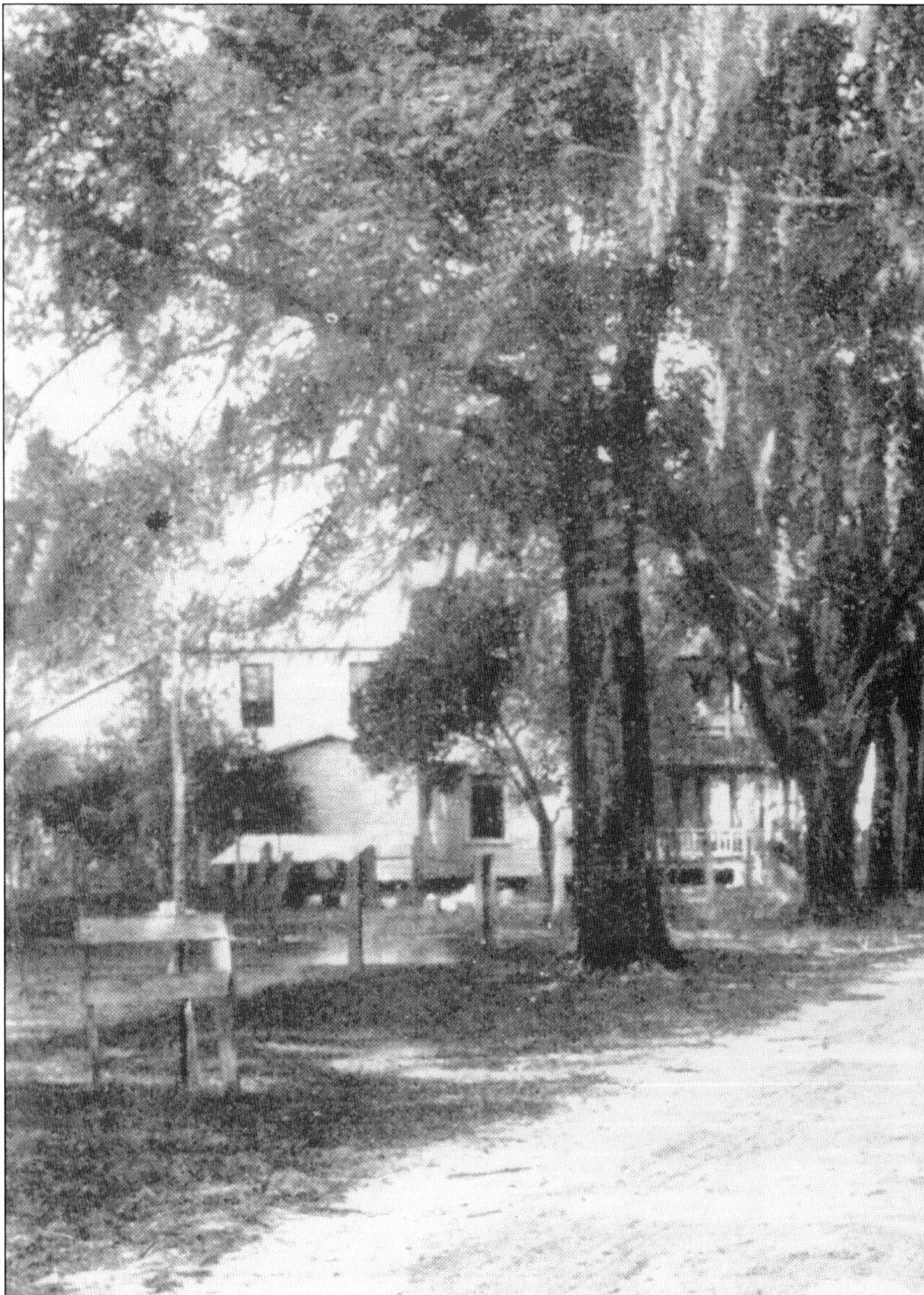

This photograph shows the view looking east in the early 1900s. Warren Avenue and the Josiah

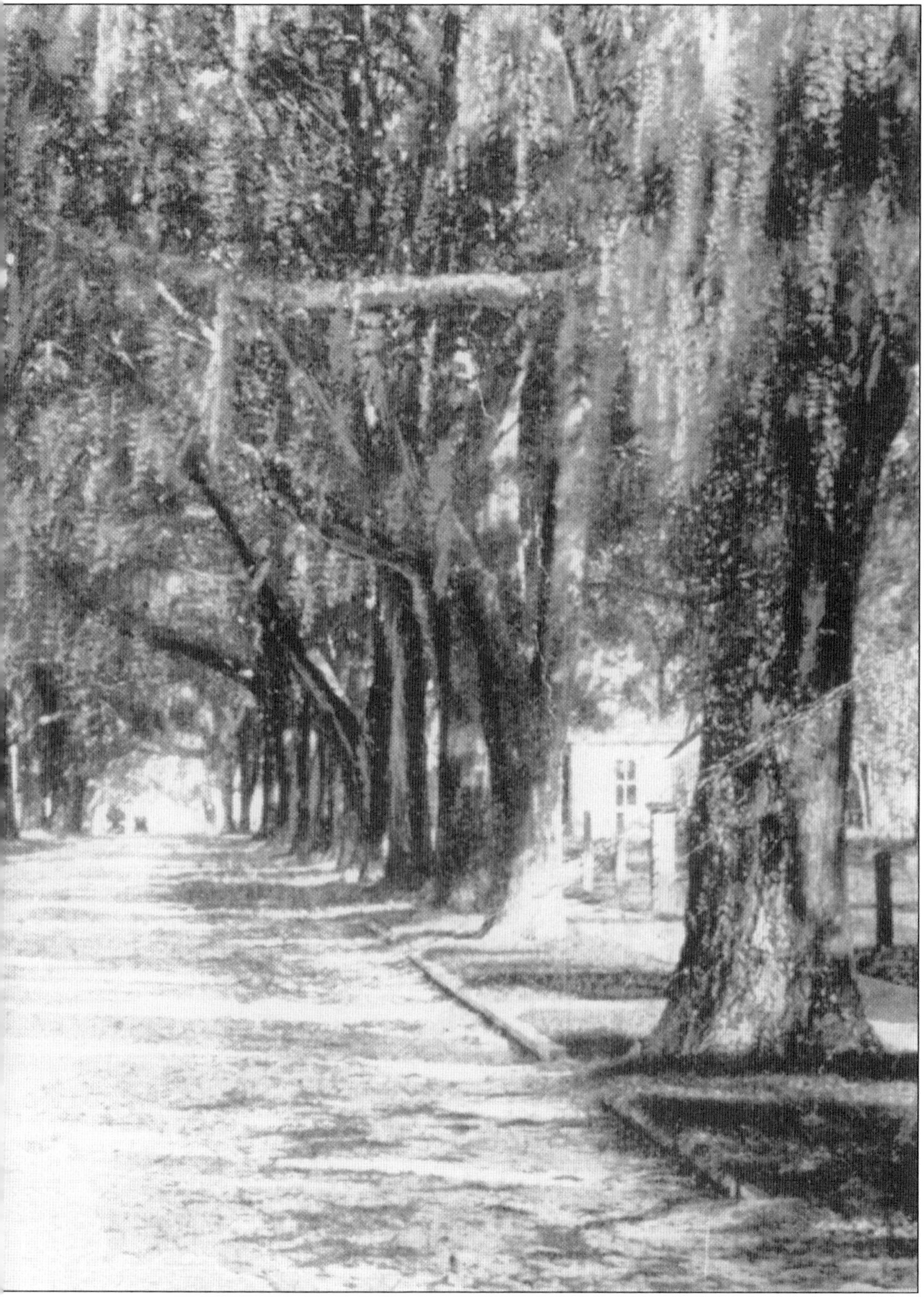

Clouser House, built by Clouser, can be seen.

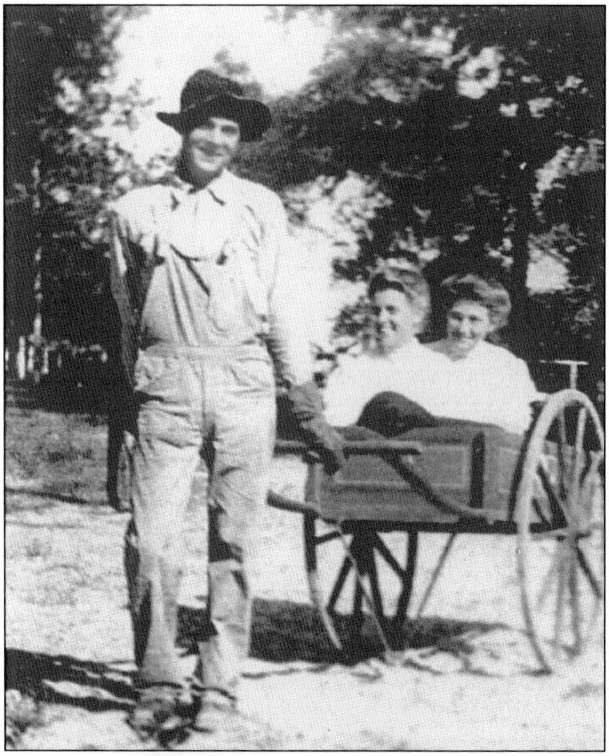

Members of the Niemeyer family take a break for a joyful ride in a farm wagon. Even in town, homeowners had enough land around them for stables, a cow, chickens, a few citrus trees, and a garden. Nearby, the public buildings included five churches, one of which is still in use. In addition, the town had three hotels, eight stores, and a weekly newspaper.

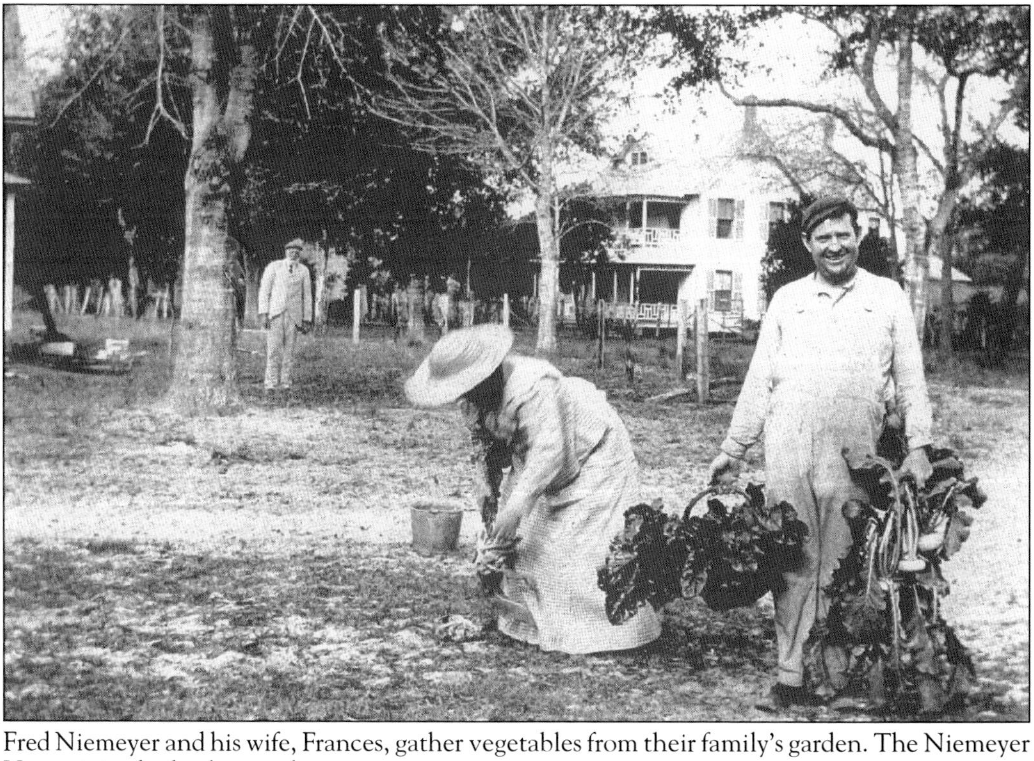

Fred Niemeyer and his wife, Frances, gather vegetables from their family's garden. The Niemeyer House is in the background.

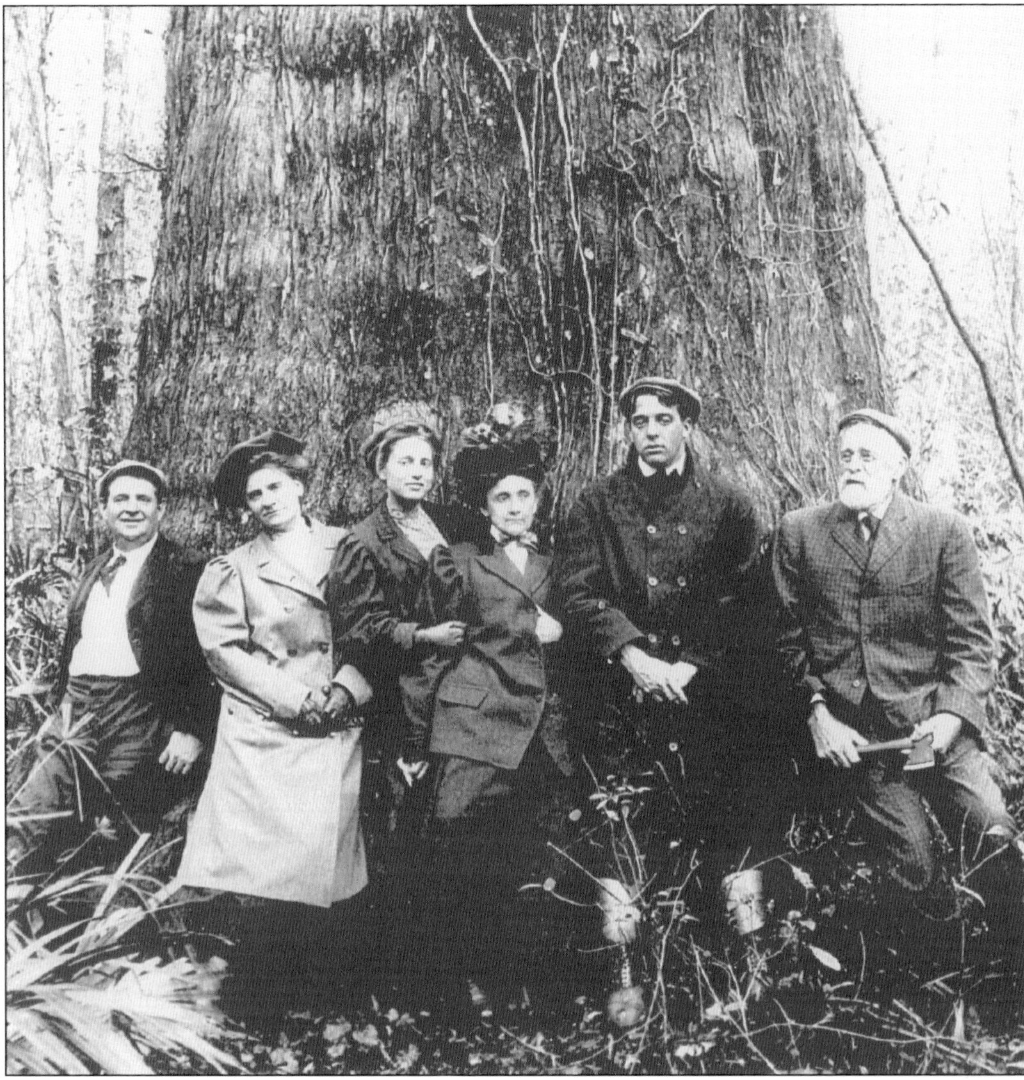

Pictured on a trip to The Senator are, from left to right, Fred Niemeyer, his sister Clara Niemeyer, his daughter Adeline "Addie" Niemeyer, an unidentified winter visitor, local schoolteacher T.W. Lawton, and "Pappy" Dunbar. This photograph was taken in the early 1900s. Lawton rented a room from the Niemeyers while teaching in Longwood. In 1917, T.W. Lawton became Seminole County's second school superintendent.

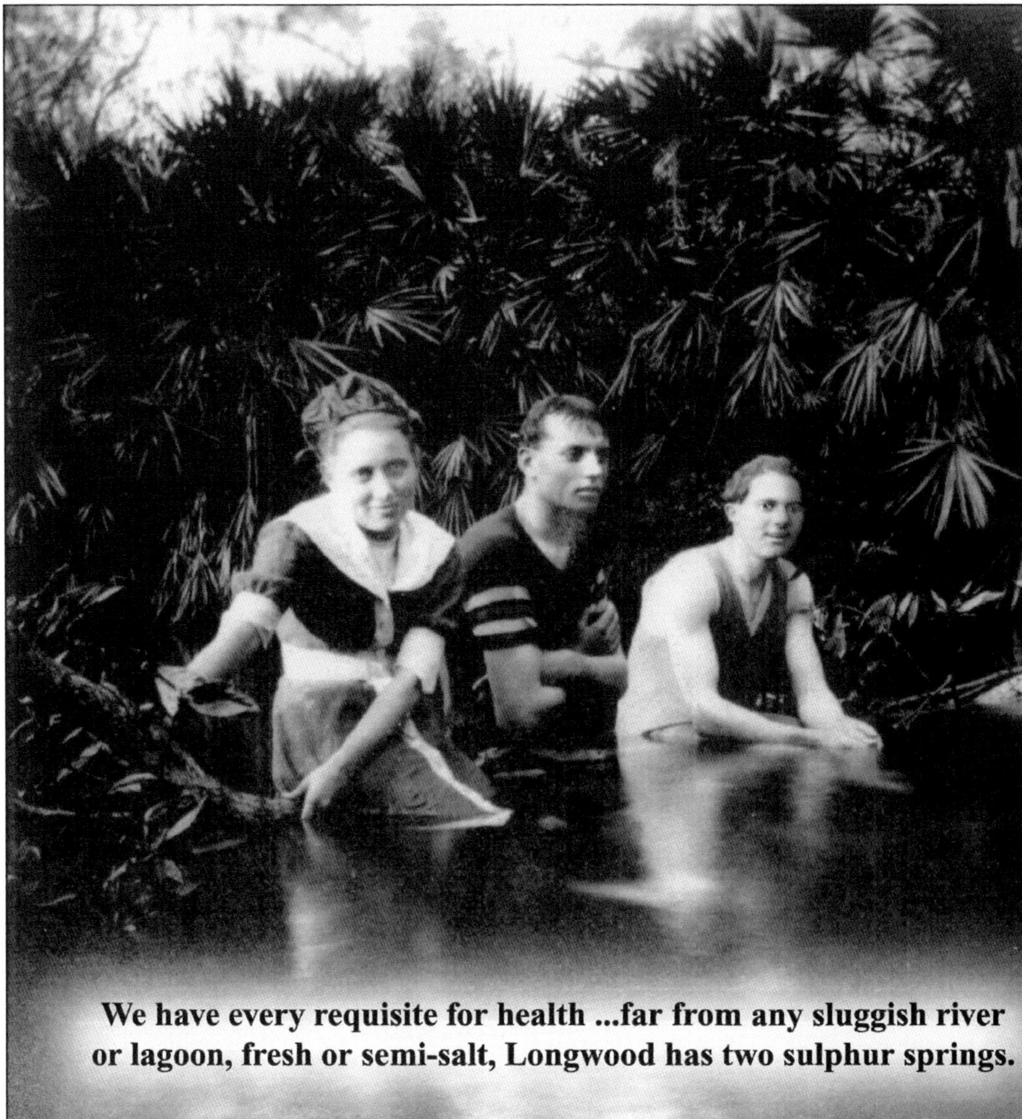

Addie Niemeyer is shown here with Aaron Bistline and Dan Clouser as they enjoy the cool water of Sanlando Springs. Addie Niemeyer Bistline, the granddaughter of Josiah B. Clouser and the mother of John and Fred Bistline, was born in Longwood in 1889 when the town advertised the healing benefits of the natural springs in the area.

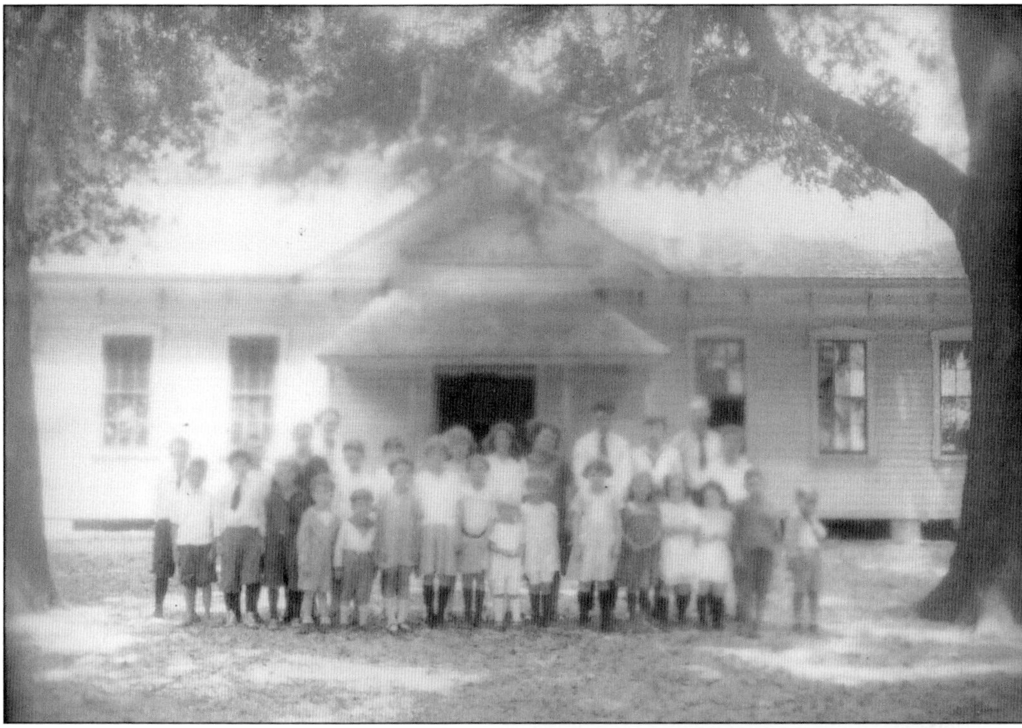

Above is the Longwood School, a two-room building on Wilma Avenue that also served as City Hall.

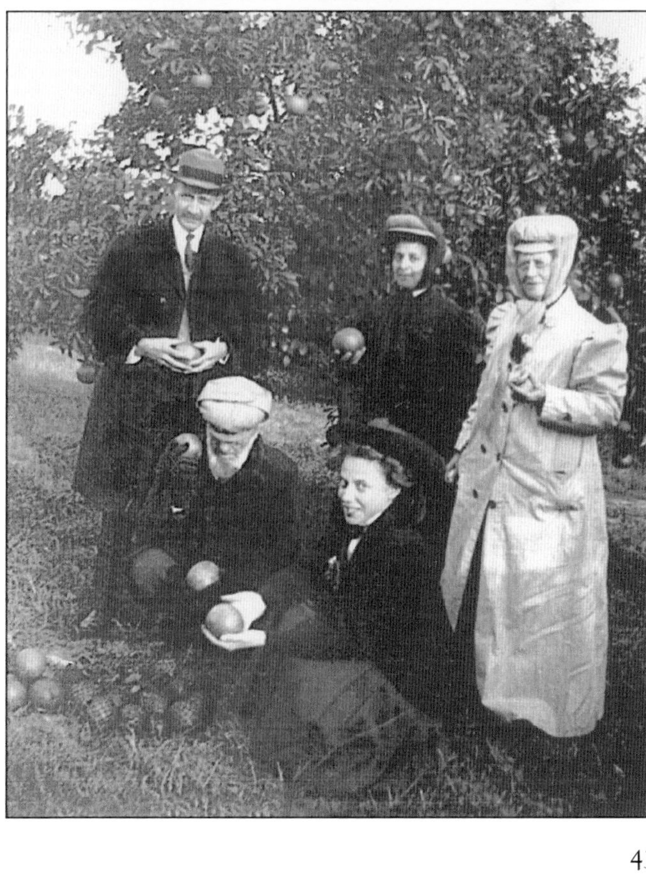

Out on a driving tour of Longwood's orange groves, Addie Bistline, kneeling, shows off some just-picked citrus to some winter visitors. Elsie Dunbar is on the right.

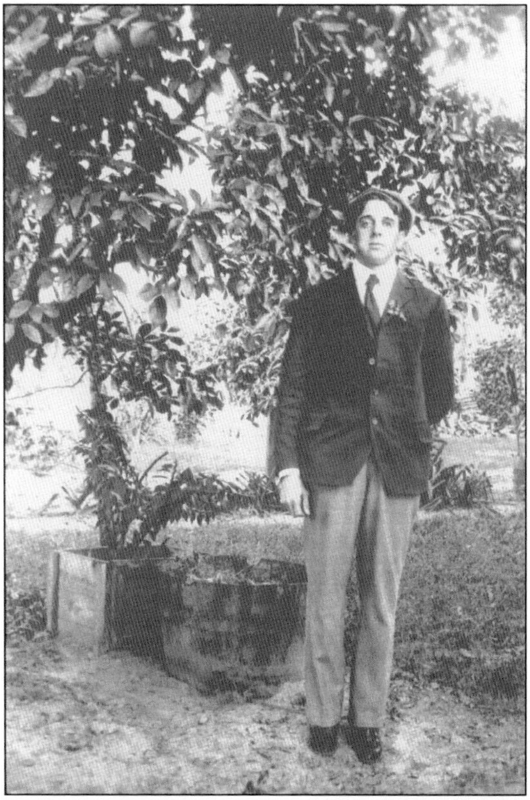

T.W. Lawton is shown in an orange grove in the years he was a schoolteacher in Longwood. Oviedo's Lawton Elementary is named for him. Originally, the elementary school was at the site of today's Oviedo High School. Thomas Willington Lawton became the dean of public education in Seminole County for nearly four decades. A member of one of Seminole County's oldest families, Lawton graduated as a class of one from Rollins College in 1903, later earning a master of arts degree from a Boston college. He retired in 1952.

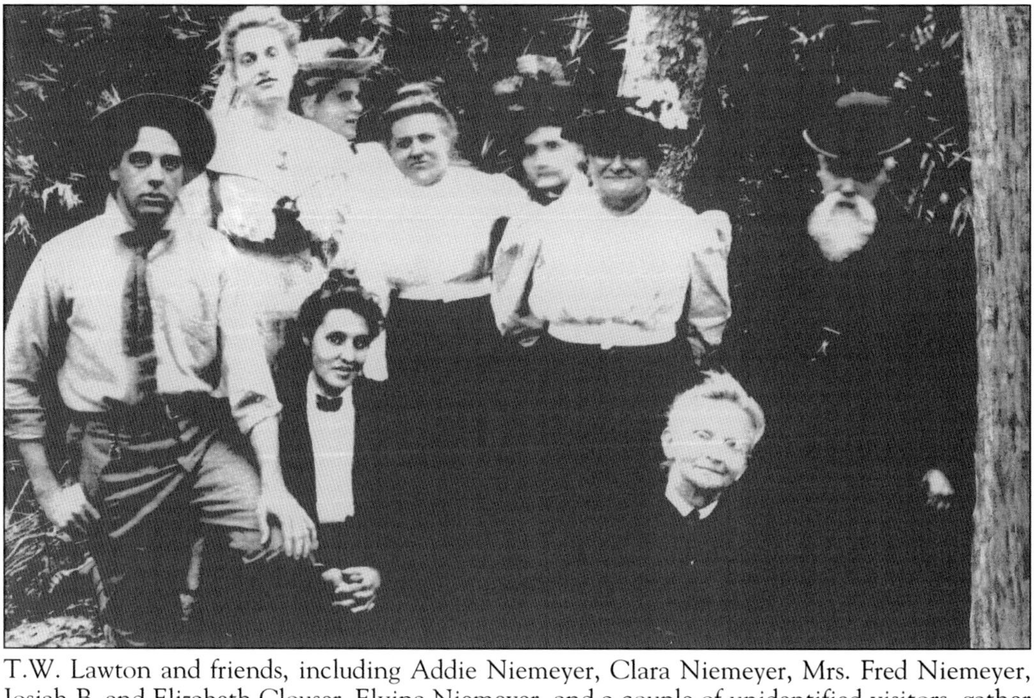

T.W. Lawton and friends, including Addie Niemeyer, Clara Niemeyer, Mrs. Fred Niemeyer, Josiah B. and Elizabeth Clouser, Elvina Niemeyer, and a couple of unidentified visitors, gather for a photograph after a picnic.

Addie Niemeyer poses here on the day she graduated from Rollins Academy, a high school on the campus of Rollins College in Winter Park.

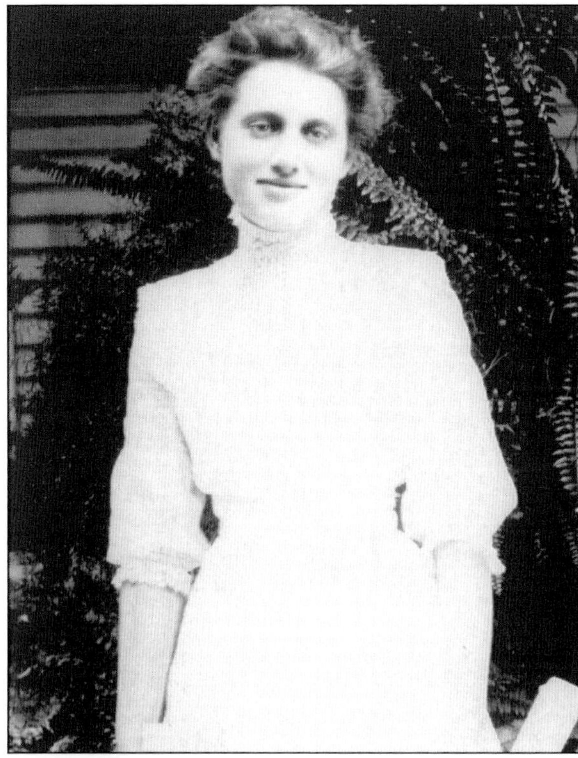

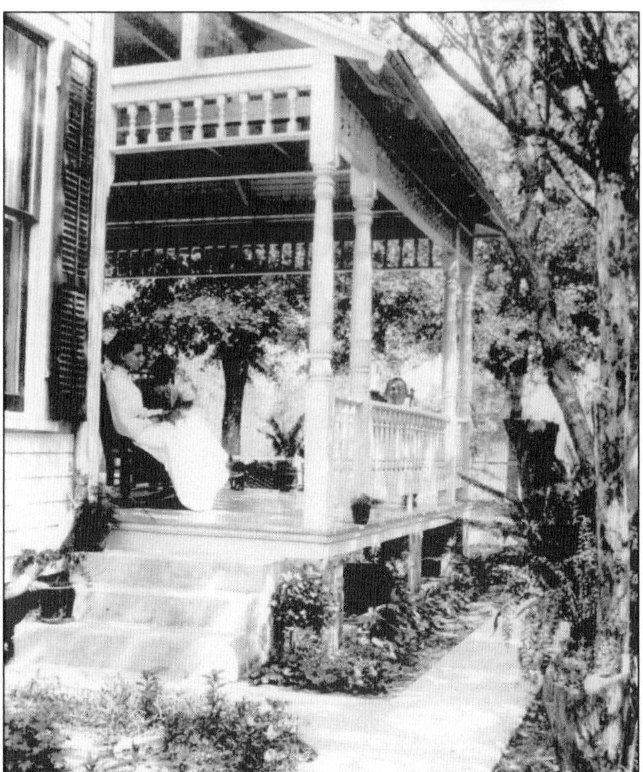

Addie Niemeyer relaxes on the front porch of her parents' beautiful house.

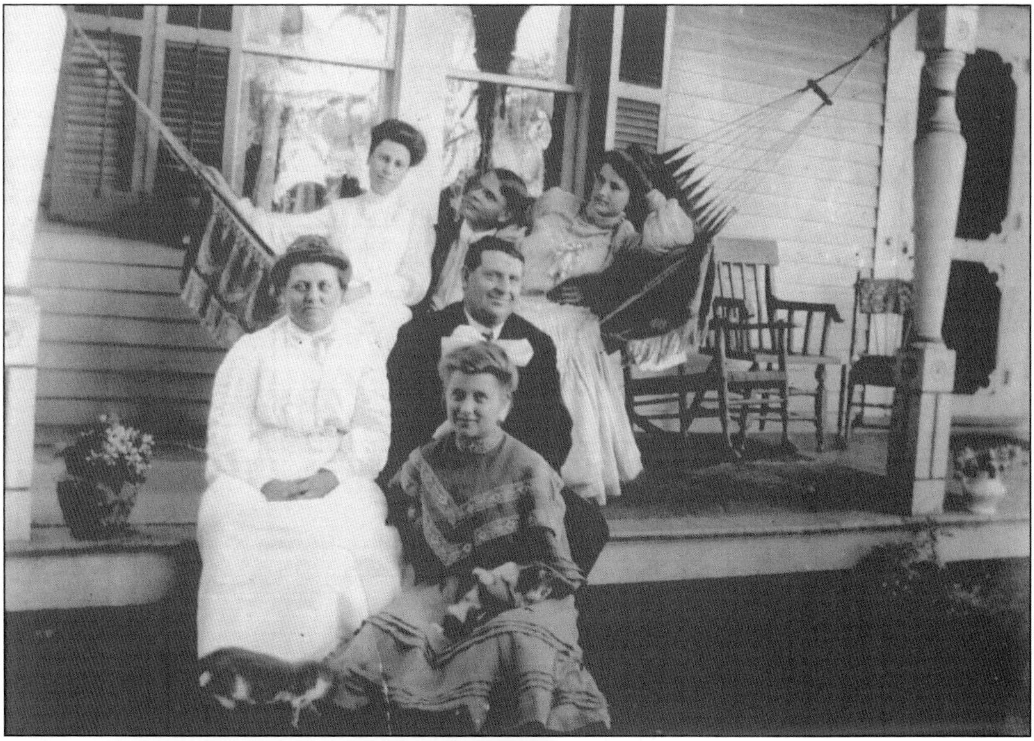

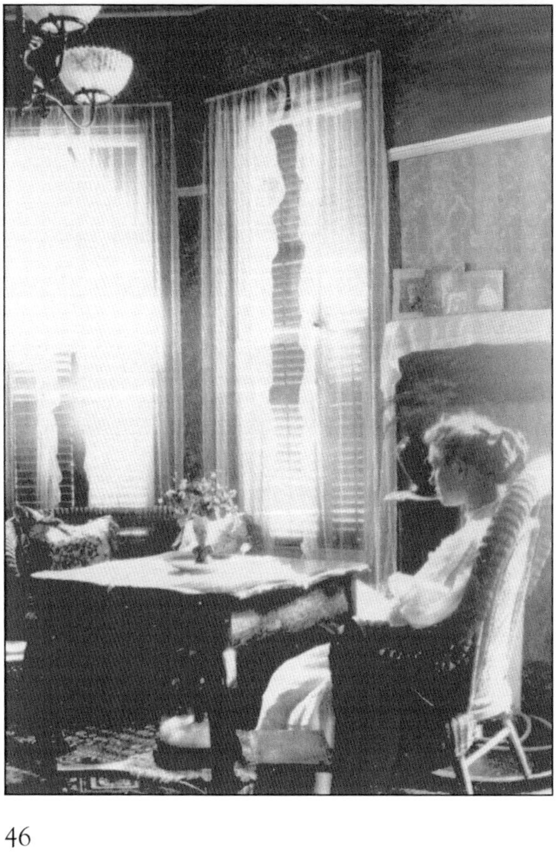

The Niemeyers frequently traveled to Scranton, Pennsylvania to visit relatives. This photo shows them lounging on the front porch and swing.

Addie Niemeyer, left, reposes in the study of her parents' home.

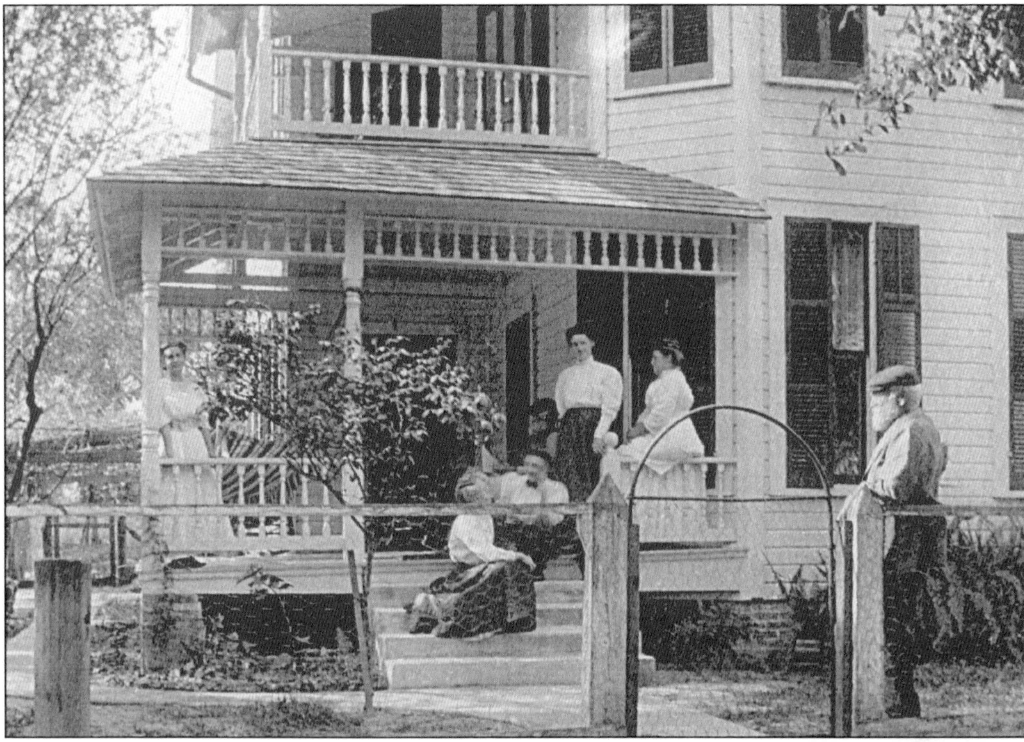

From left to right, Addie Niemeyer, Elsie Dunbar (seated on steps), an unidentified friend, Frances Niemeyer, and Pappy Dunbar relax in front of the Niemeyer home.

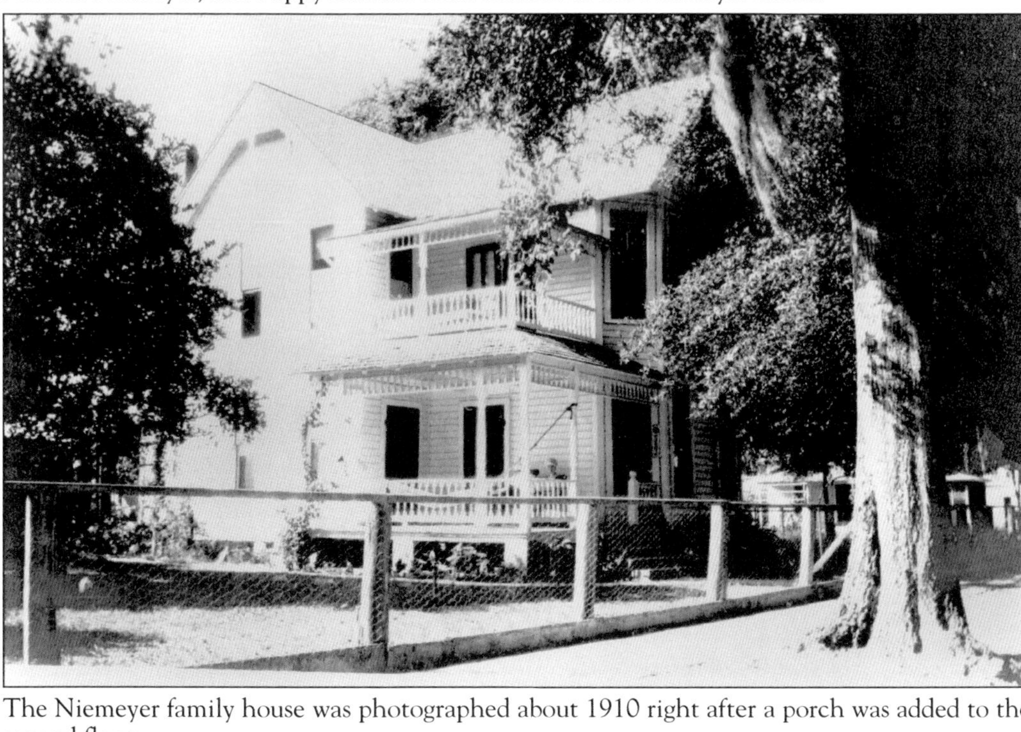

The Niemeyer family house was photographed about 1910 right after a porch was added to the second floor.

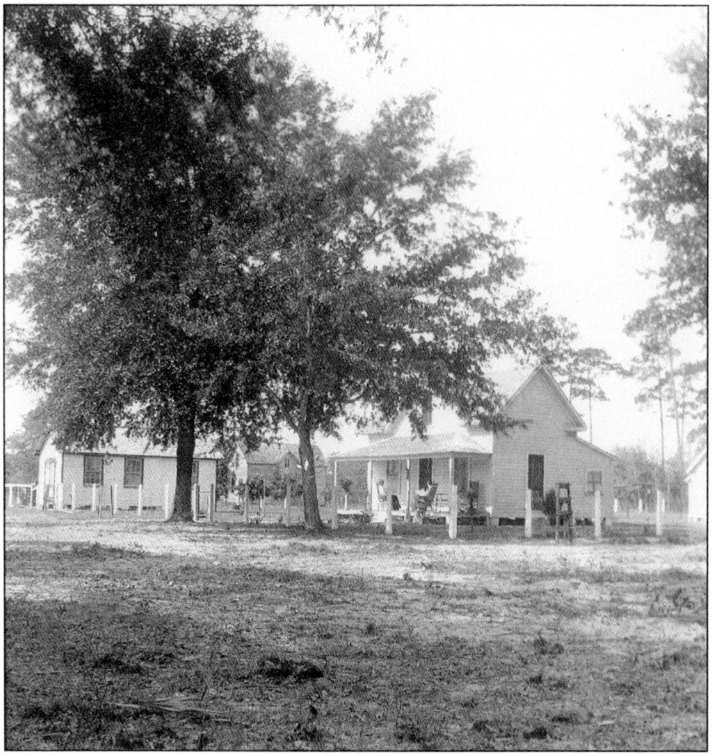

Two brothers, J.D. and N.J. Lewis, both attorneys, constructed this house. During the 1920s and 1930s, the house was owned and occupied by John "Pappy" Dunbar and Elsie, his daughter. The one and one-half story core of this house, with its metal shingle roof and two-over-two double hung windows, is the original portion of the structure. The one-story porches and asbestos shingle siding are later additions. The Dunbar House was on the southwest corner of Wilma Street and Warren Avenue. The house was torn down in the mid-1990s and the Longwood Community Building is planned for that site.

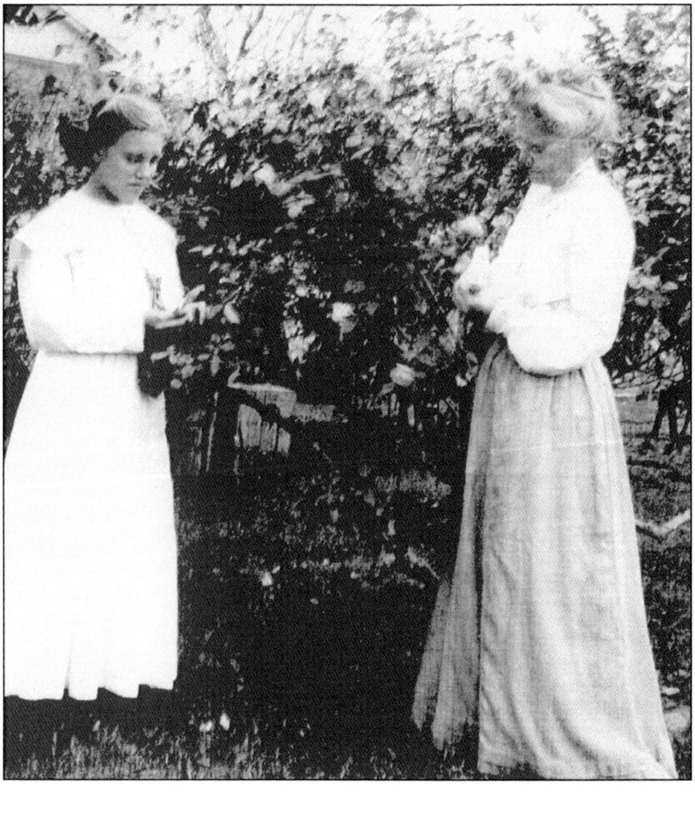

Addie Niemeyer and Elsie Dunbar pick roses in the Niemeyer garden.

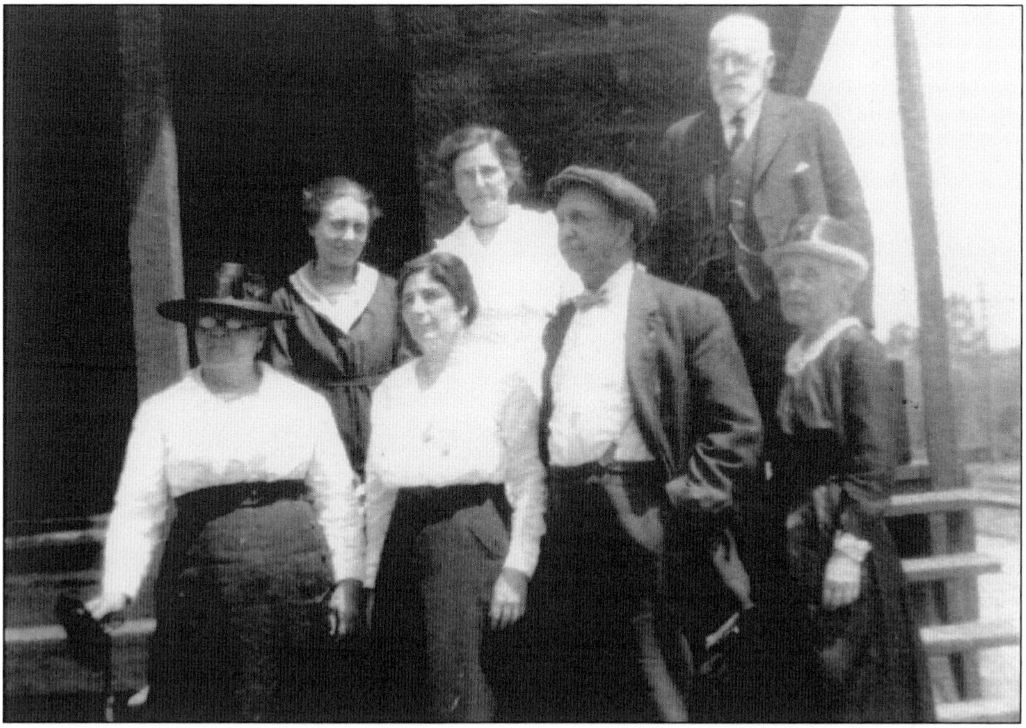

This photo of people waiting for the train shows early Longwood resident John "Pappy" Dunbar (top right) with friends at the Longwood depot for the South Florida Railroad. From left to right are (front row) Mrs. Hardaway, Mr. and Mrs. Hardy, and Elsie Dunbar; (back row) two unidentified women and Dunbar.

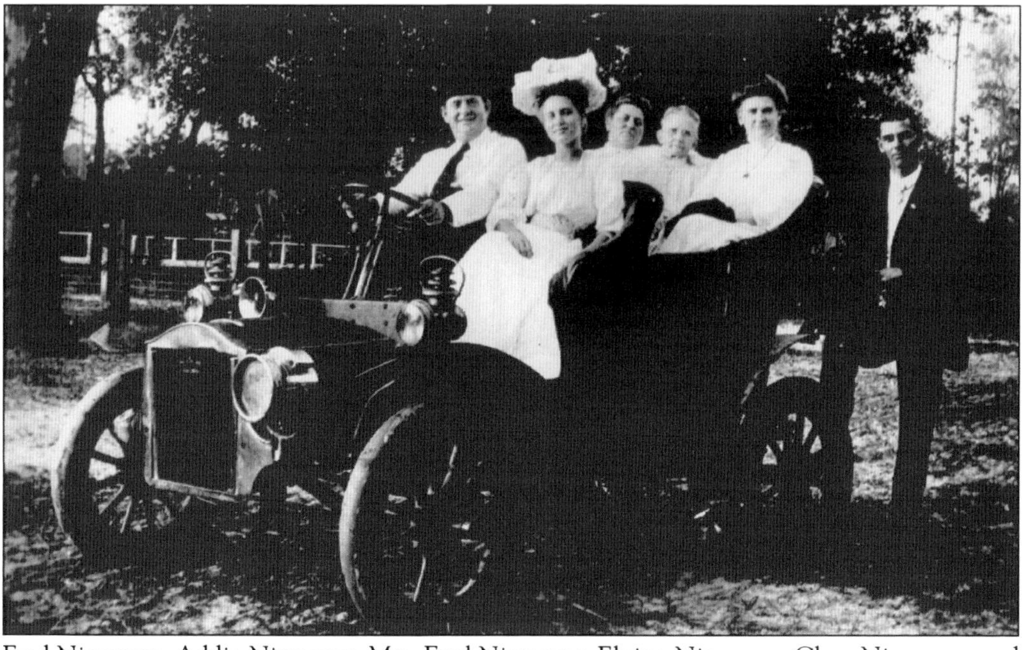

Fred Niemeyer, Addie Niemeyer, Mrs. Fred Niemeyer, Elvina Niemeyer, Clara Niemeyer, and an unidentified gentleman pose on a car before setting out for a Sunday drive.

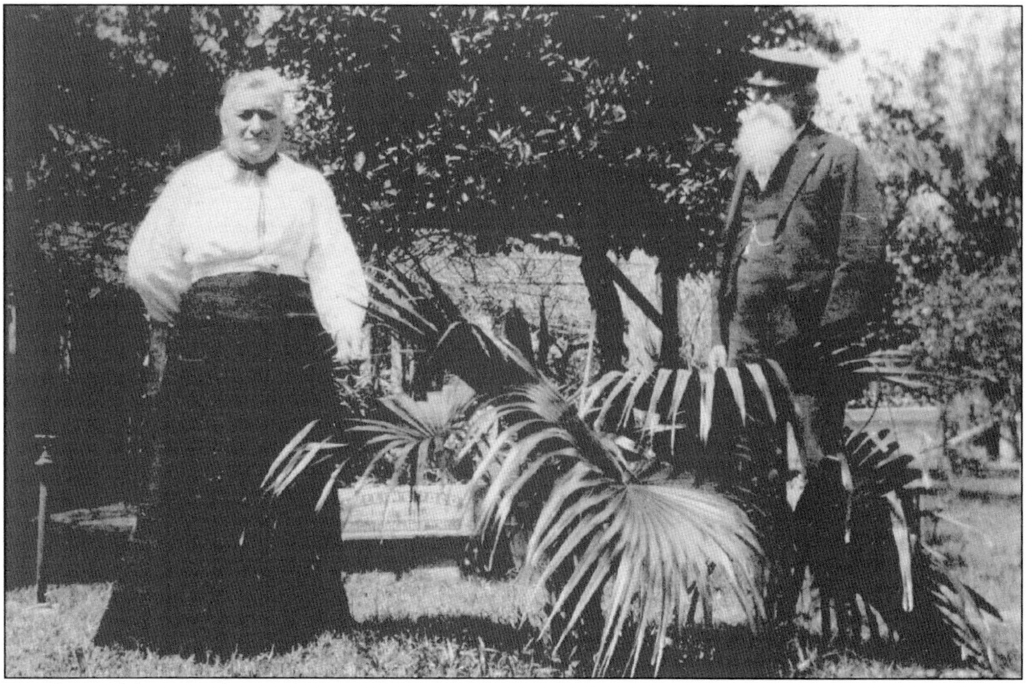

Josiah B. Clouser, shown here with his wife, Elizabeth, outside their home, brought family, including two children, to Longwood in November 1881 from Pennsylvania. Clouser, according to family history, first saw the South while stationed here with Northern troops during the Civil War. Henck later hired him to supervise construction of the Longwood Hotel. He is also believed to have worked for sawmill owner and railroad builder Peter Demens.

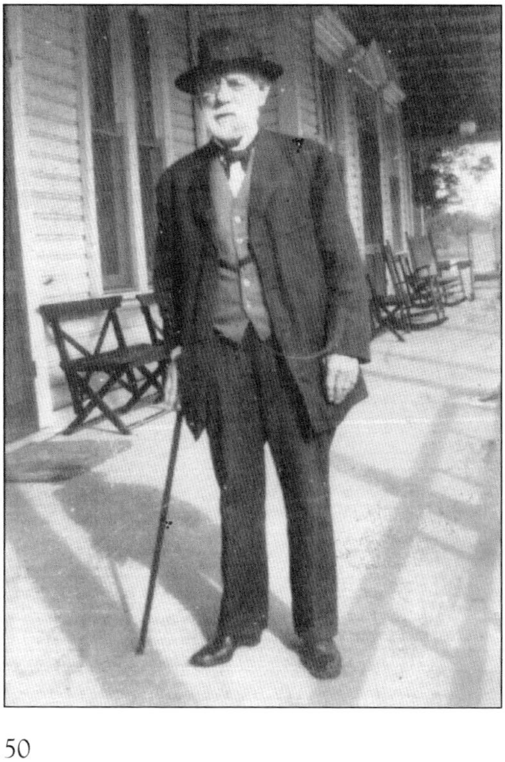

Josiah B. Clouser, with cane in hand, is shown on the porch of the Longwood Hotel. Besides building E.W. Henck's second home and the Longwood Hotel, the master cabinetmaker and stair maker was one of Longwood's first aldermen, taking office soon after the town's first election on December 3, 1883. He served several terms as alderman and was mayor in 1889, 1895, and 1912. During this period he also ran a general merchandise store with his son and Fred J. Niemeyer, his son-in-law.

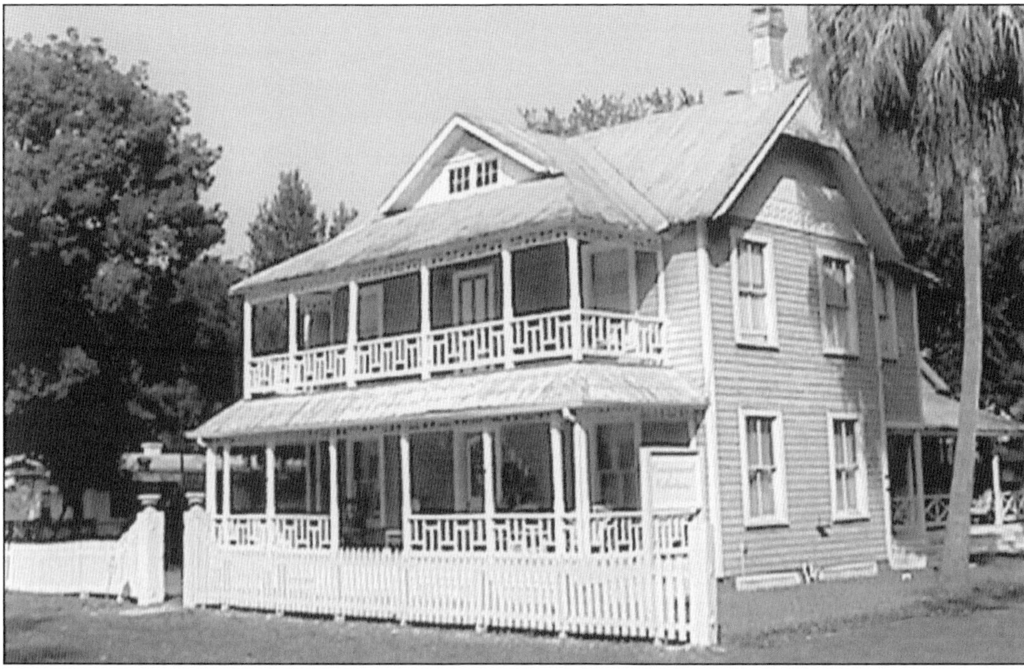

Josiah B. Clouser built several homes for his own family, including this large house on West Warren Avenue, and many other businesses during the 1880s and 1890s. Josiah B. Clouser opened his own shop at Wilma Street and West Bay Avenue. The workshop originally faced Bay Avenue and was located behind the house at 216 West Warren Avenue.

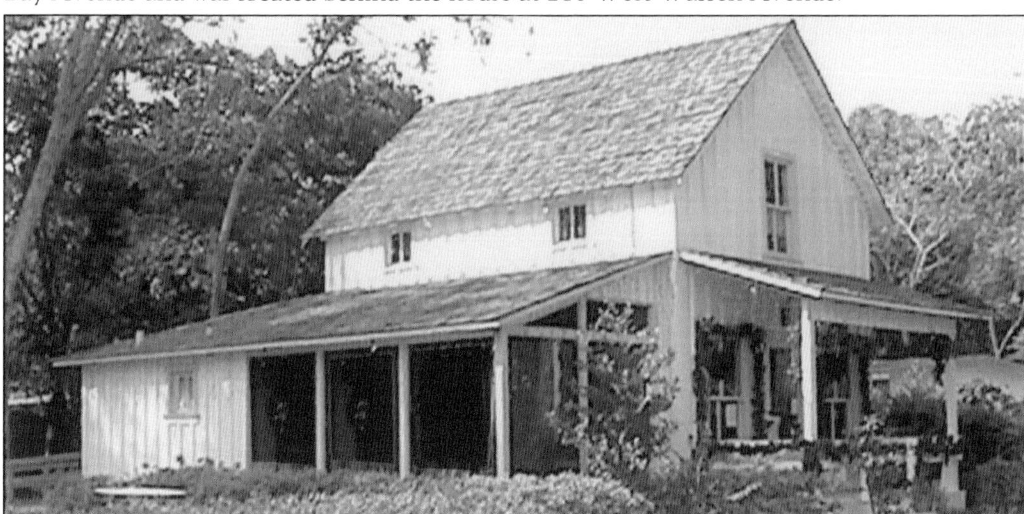

The Clouser Cottage, built in 1881, is the oldest house built in Longwood that still stands. Clouser built the cottage soon after he came to Florida from Pennsylvania with his wife, Elizabeth, and their teenage son and daughter. They arrived at Sanford's wharfs aboard a St. Johns River steamer in November 1881. The only place they could find to stay was "a bale of hay and an old blanket in the upper story of a box board shanty," according to family history. That night, they shared their tight quarters "with a lot of fleas and wild hogs who lived in the sand under the building." Clouser set out immediately to build a suitable house, this cottage, which remained the family home for two years.

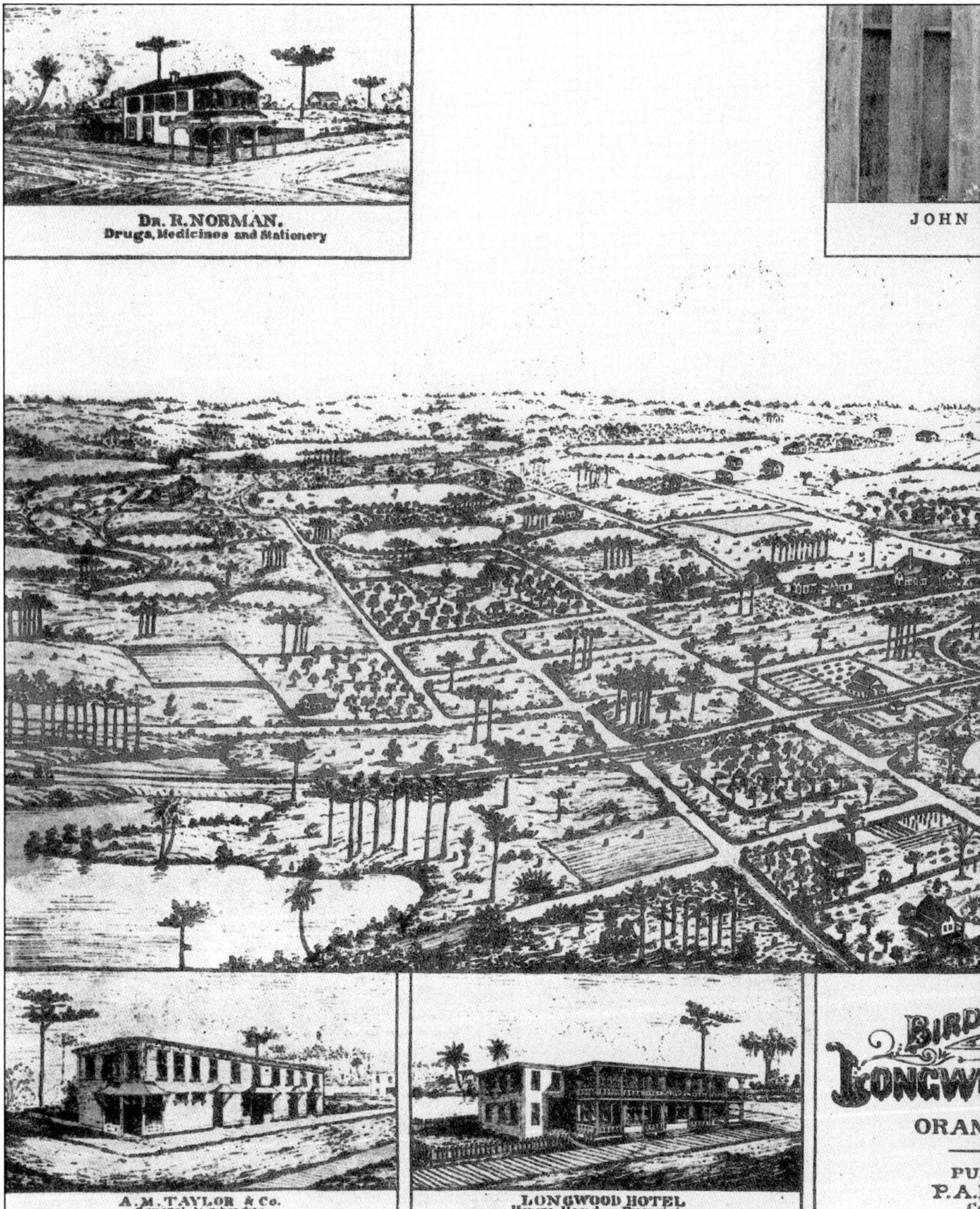

Not long after settling at what is now called East Lake in 1876, E.W. Henck named Longwood after an attractive suburb of Boston. Local lore suggests Henck changed the community's name to Longwood because he feared "upper crust New Englanders" would be skeptical of the rustic sounding "Myrtle Lake." Boston's Longwood took its name from a 600-acre estate owned by David Sears. About 1840, Sears acquired his estate at Brookline, naming it Longwood. The community Henck helped develop on the estate land adopted the name linked to Napoleon Bonaparte. Longwood was the exiled French emperor's home on the island of St. Helena, an

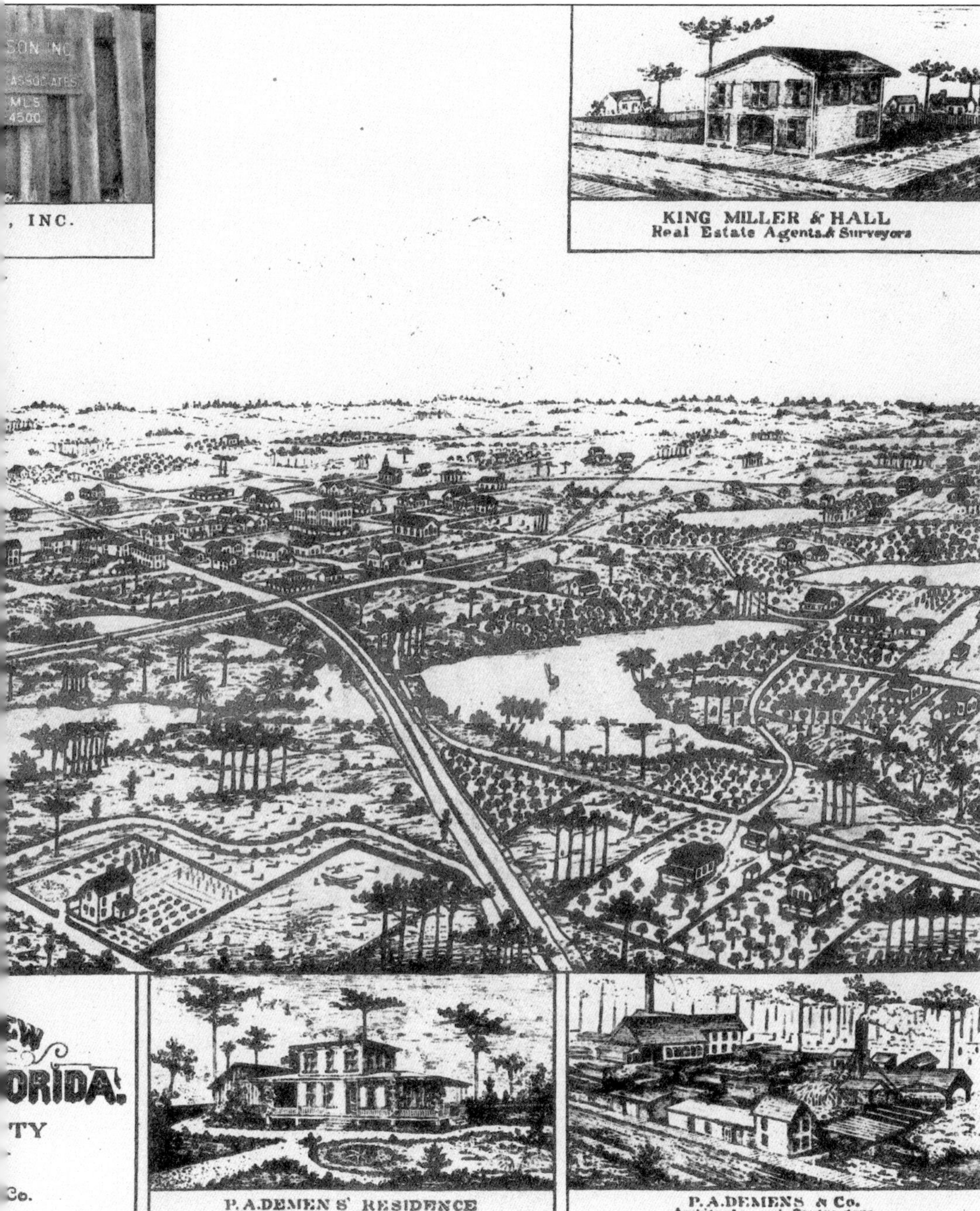

English colony more than 1,100 miles off the African coast, after his defeat at Waterloo. Sears in 1811, when at 25, visited Paris when Napoleon was still emperor and later incorporated Napoleon's empire style into the décor of his home on Boston's Beacon Street. The island of St. Helena included a forest of gum trees. As early as 1678, people on the island called it the Great Wood. When some of the trees were cut down, the area was called Dead Wood. When a large area of the island was enclosed with a long stone wall, the area was named Longwood.

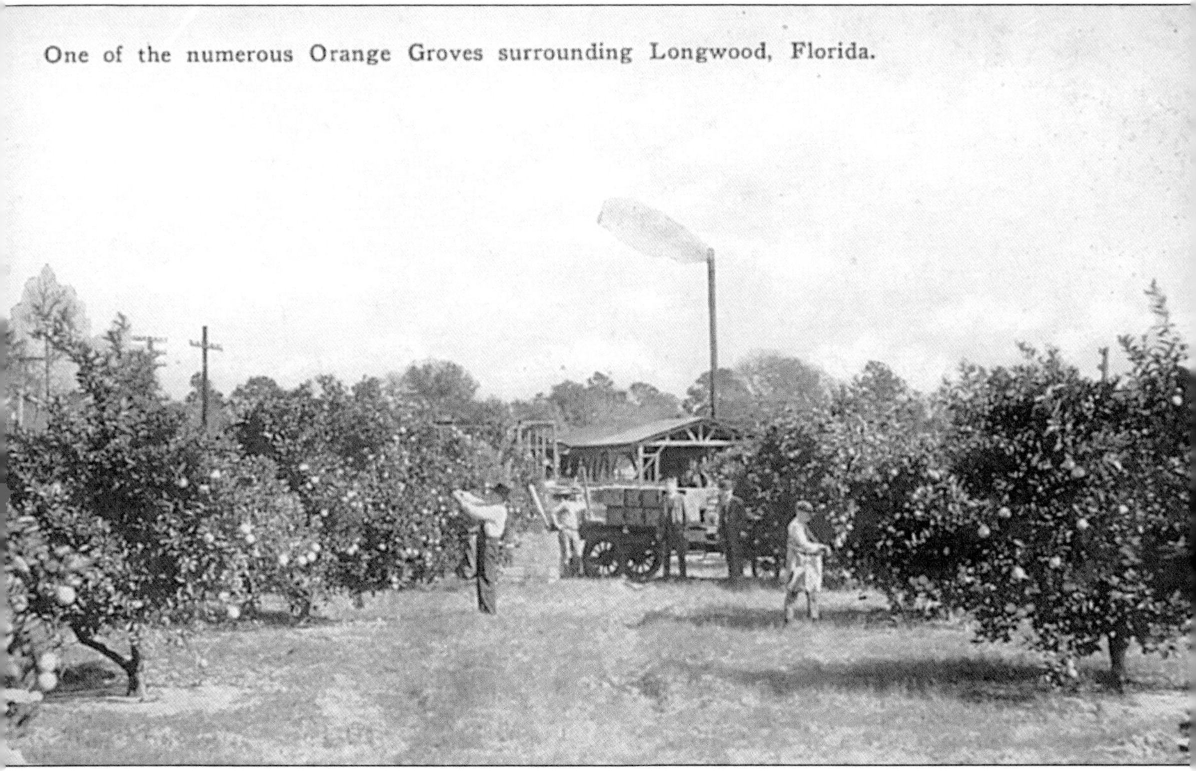

One of the numerous Orange Groves surrounding Longwood, Florida.

By the mid-1800s more than 1,000 people lived in Longwood, many working in area citrus groves and lumbering operations. Soon, though, lumbering ravaged the land and many people left as logging companies moved to more luscious forests. Even worse times were approaching. Central Florida's citrus industry suffered a devastating blow during a six-week period between December 29, 1894, and February 7, 1895. An 18-degree freeze on the first night killed the season's crop while it was still on the trees. But the worst possible thing happened next—January brought warm, wet weather, which encouraged trees to produce sap and new growth. This made them extremely vulnerable to the second freeze. People said they heard the trees pop like pistol shots as freezing sap split the bark. More than 90 percent of Central Florida's trees were killed. It would be 15 years before the citrus industry fully recovered. Land values plummeted, and growers with mortgages were forced to sell at a loss. Family after family in Longwood—and throughout the region—left. People with money were able to scoop up large tracts at bargain prices. Many growers diversified into other crops so they would not be so vulnerable to a freeze again, and the citrus industry slowly climbed back out of its hole. But it would be 1919 before orange production in Orange County again reached 6 million crates a year—the level it was just before the freeze. The Great Freeze struck when the lumbering business was declining after stripping the area of old pine growth. Orange groves were replanted and several squab farms were established, supplying area hotels in the winter and shipping to the New York City markets the rest of the year. By the early 1900s, though, the opening of a turpentine distillery fueled the city's rebirth.

Three

Boom and Bust Eras

Between 1920 and 1925, Longwood's population grew from 106 to 600 residents, and the city was incorporated in 1923. Real estate interest in Longwood and in much of Florida created a two-decade boom as Florida thrived on winter tourism and land development. But then the second of two killer hurricanes in a decade hit Florida in 1928; flooding left 2,300 people dead. Florida's boom was over, and the Great Depression began in 1929. Longwood's population dropped to no more than 350 residents in 1930. The city's only bank failed. A move to allow the city government to dissolve reached the Legislature. Many of the subdivisions planned in the 1920s were never developed, leaving the wilderness to reclaim the abandoned home sites. Longwood was surrounded by small farms and groves during the 1930s and 1940s, but things changed substantially mid-century. Aerospace and defense industries established a major presence in Central Florida in the 1950s and an interstate highway linked the region to points northeast and southwest in the mid-1960s. Walt Disney forever changed the landscape by opening the first of many theme parks in Orlando, and the 1990s saw a tremendous expansion of the high-tech industry in Central Florida.

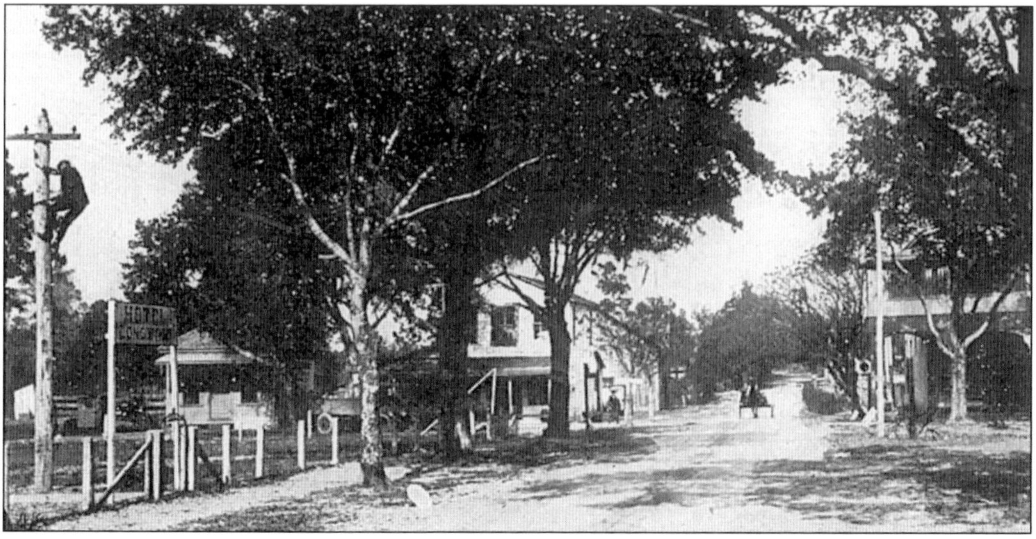

This scene shows a carriage and driver on the "Dixie Highway" at Longwood in the early 1900s.

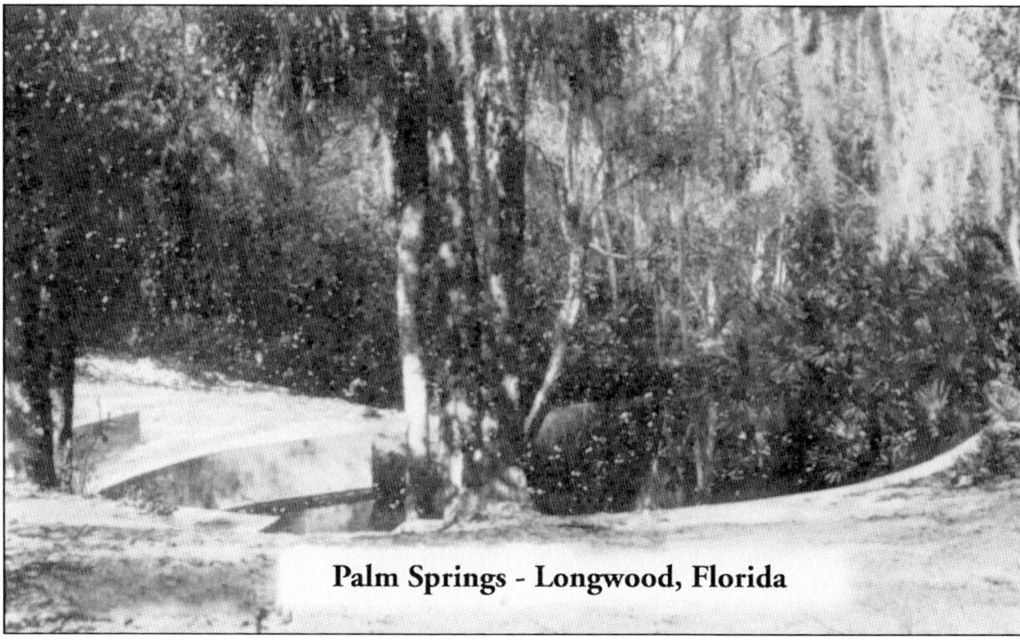

E.W. Henck, who had a lot of land to sell, offered Sanlando Springs, mislabeled on this advertisement as Palm Springs, and its 152 acres of "rolling fruit land" for $11,000. "A few fine lots are left on the Dixie Highway and are offered at $350 to $500 per lot, $50 down and balance at $20 per month. On other streets corner lots are from $200 to $350 per lot, $20, $30 down and $20 per month. Other lots $100 up, $10 down and $5 per month. Buildings on Dixie Highway cost no less than $2,500 and on other lots $1,500. Fruit and vegetable lands $20 per acre and up according to location."

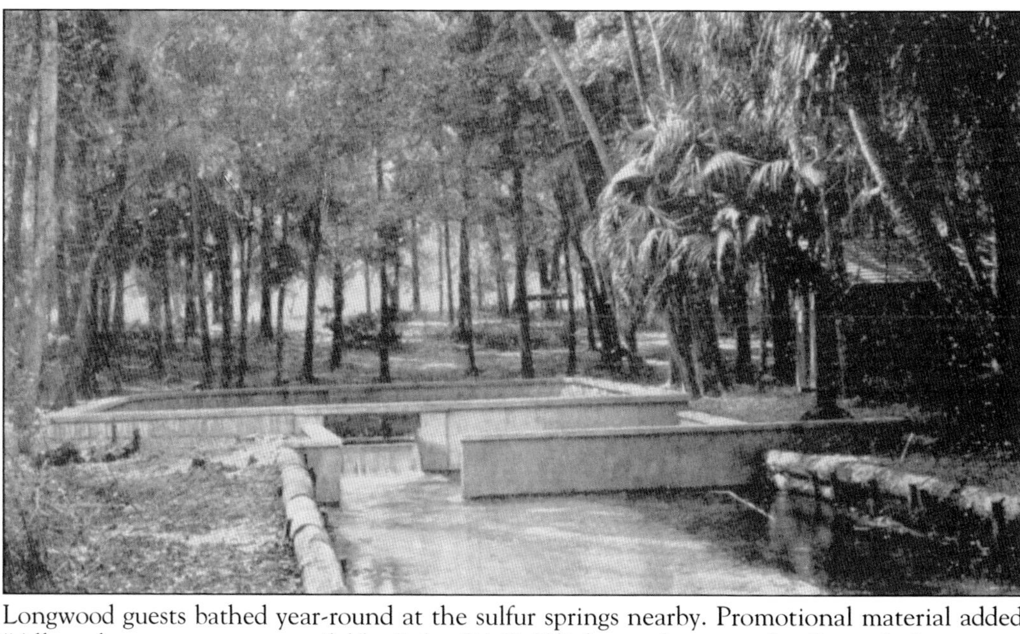

Longwood guests bathed year-round at the sulfur springs nearby. Promotional material added, "All outdoor amusements available. Splendid Golf links nearby are at the disposal of guests . . . Fresh fish, game, vegetables and milk are always available."

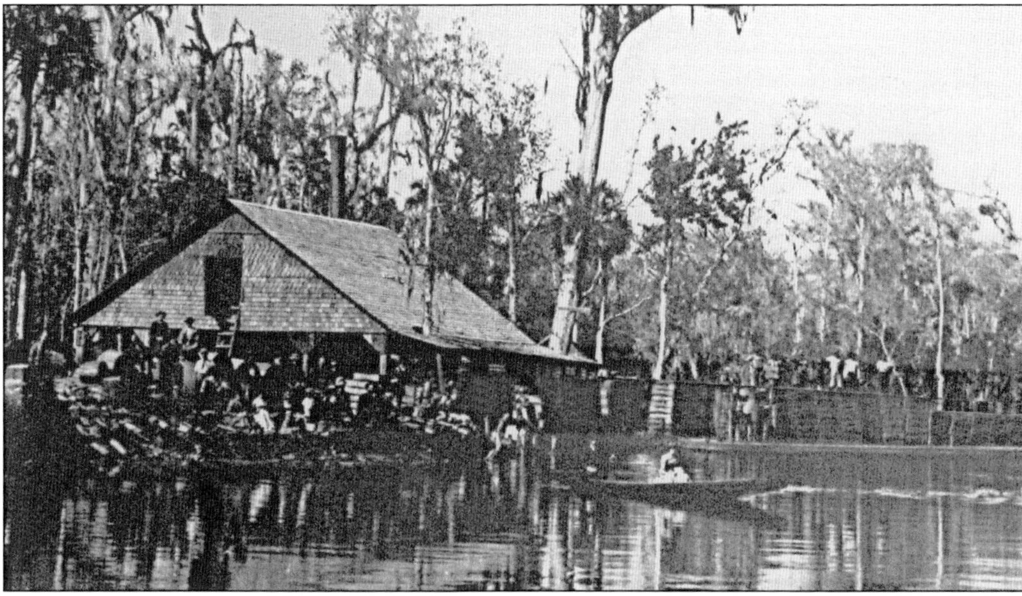

This scene shows the bathhouse at Wekiwa Springs. Longwood promoted itself as "one of the healthiest places in the state," offering "pure, invigorating, piney air, such as a pure water supply . . . No malaria is ever known at any section at any season, a consideration of importance to those who make a long sojourn to the South . . . Why shiver with Cold?" Northerners were told of the opportunities to buy winter cottages or bungalows in or near orange groves. They also could buy citrus and farmland; "Land may be had for every variety of crop at reasonable prices. A fine place for chicken, turkey and squab farming with the best of markets close at hand."

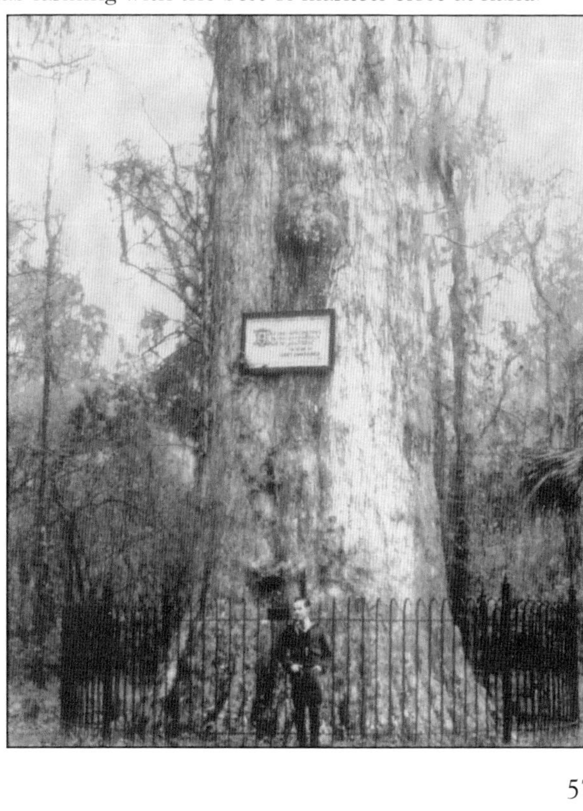

This photo from the early 1900s shows people taking a walk at Big Tree Park, home of The Senator. Alice Bryant Cole, born April 12, 1908, recalls that the cypress tree was a popular family and community gathering place. "I use to walk to the Big Tree and have a picnic. One or two families would go. You'd cut an old cabbage palm down and momma carried that old wash pot in the wagon. Us kids would just walk or run through the woods to the Big Tree and then they'd build a fire and we'd cut up that cabbage. The men would go fishing and we'd cook up that cabbage and fry the fish. That was a picnic. School and church picnics were held at the springs at Palm Springs."

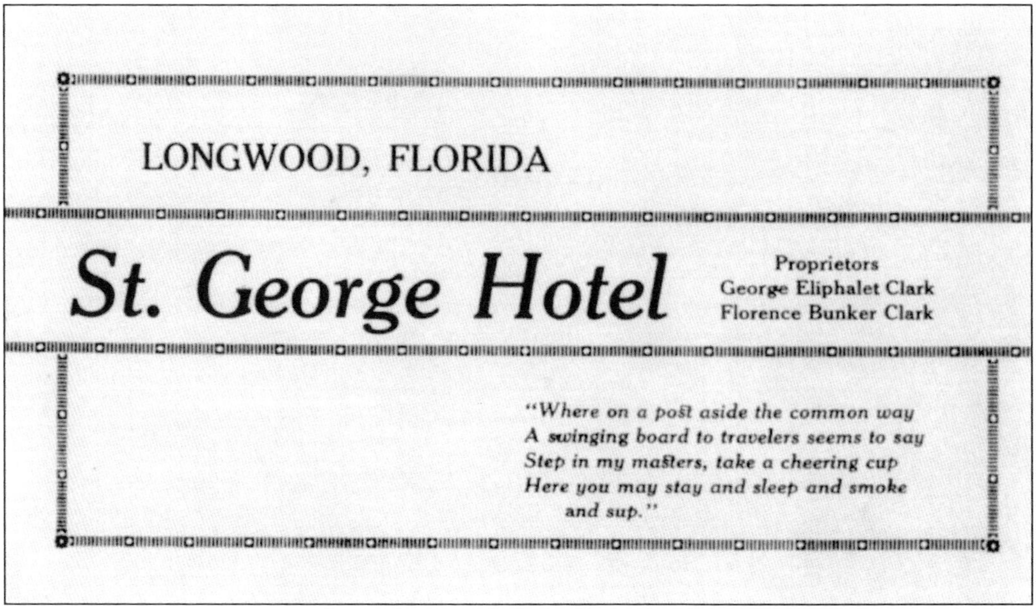

Advertising for the St. George Hotel, with proprietors George Eliphalet Clark and Florence Bunker Clark, who also ran Kineowatha Camps in Wilton and Farmington, Maine, included this poem: "Where on a post aside the common way, A swinging board to travelers seems to say, Step in my masters, take a cheering cup. Here you may stay and sleep and smoke and sup." The owners of the St. George Hotel advertised, "We make a specialty of chicken dinners during winter months." The St. George Hotel's owners advertised that more people wanted to stay at Longwood than could be accommodated. They offered free land for builders of another hotel and apartments and manufacturers.

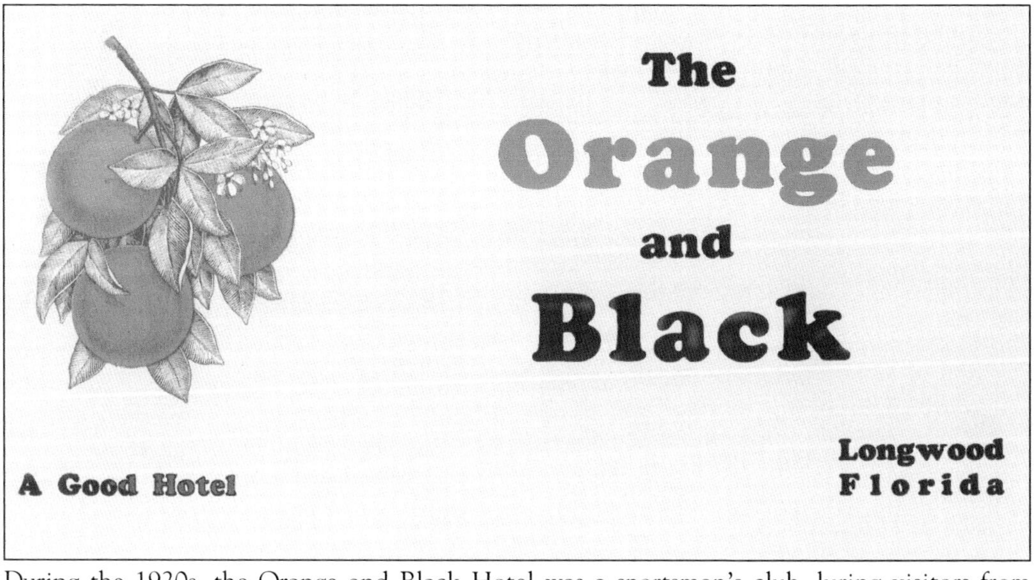

During the 1920s, the Orange and Black Hotel was a sportsman's club, luring visitors from throughout the state. New paved roads between Sanford and Orlando made it possible for men from the cities to slip away for some gambling and rip-roaring adventures that kept the townsfolk talking.

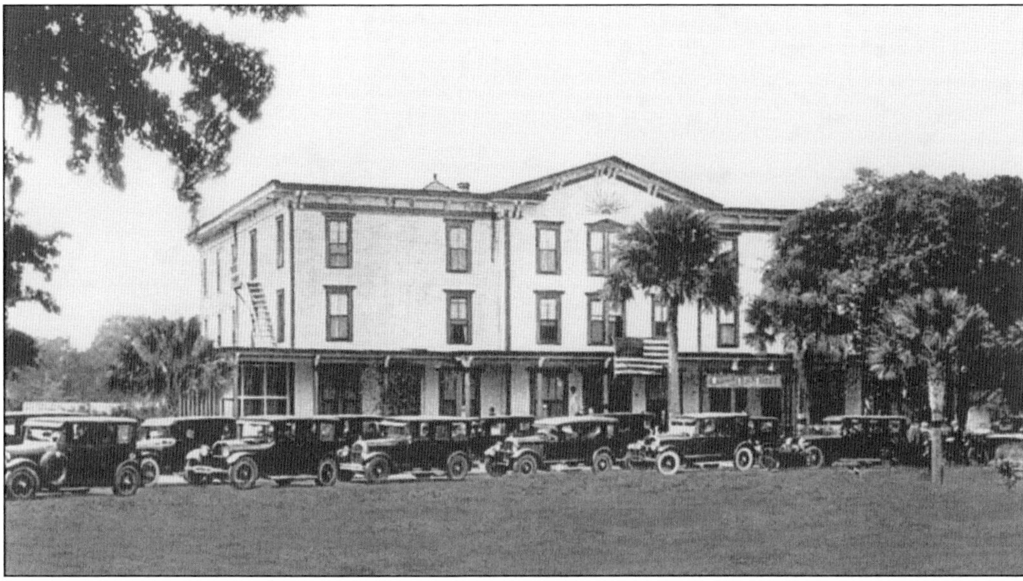

This November 17, 1924 photo shows the Orange and Black Hotel when the governors of 20 states gathered here for a conference. The official visit gave the hotel a chance to spread the word about Longwood's "high rolling ground, beautiful lakes and stately pines, flowers in profusion, bountiful orange groves and lovely palms . . . [with] an abundance of pure, soft water, and nearby two sulfur springs where one may bathe throughout the year . . . A boom town with large crate mill, turpentine plant, and novelty wood working shop and saw mills."

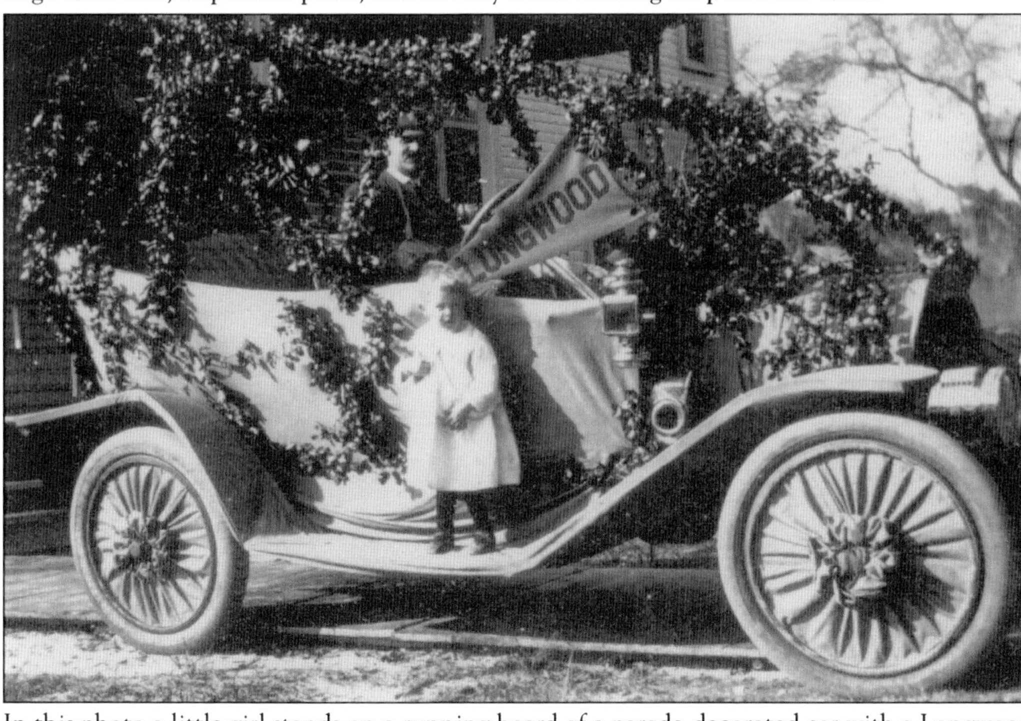

In this photo a little girl stands on a running board of a parade-decorated car with a Longwood banner. This photo was taken in 1927 in front of the landmark hotel when it was the site of a governors' conference.

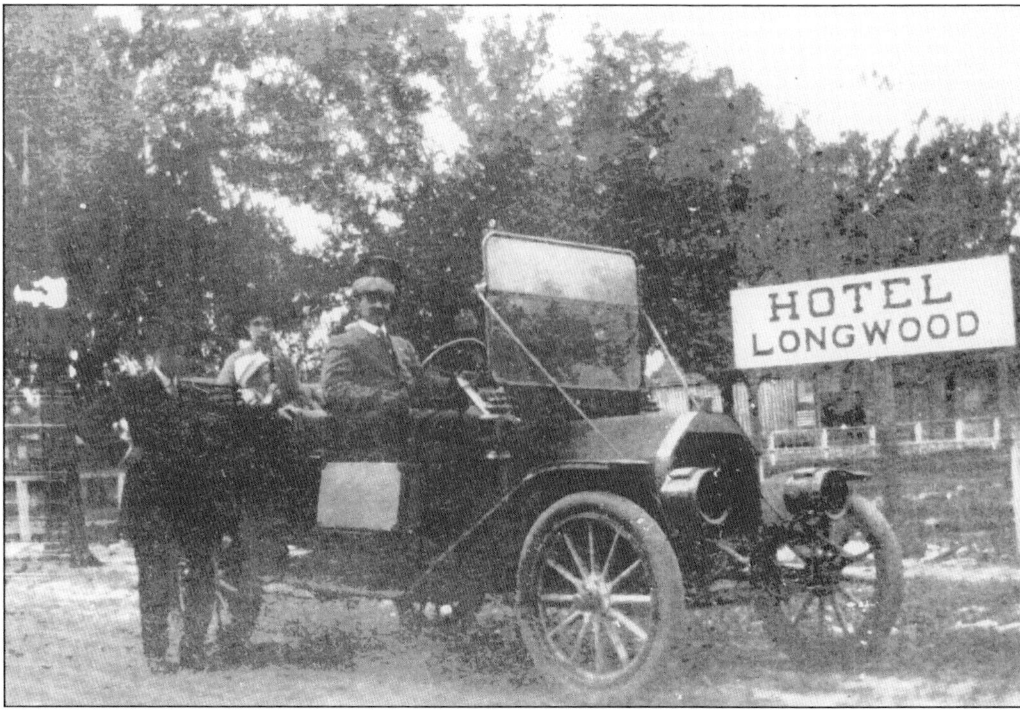

Longwood Hotel is pictured here in 1924 with the hotel sign visible and an old Ford driven by a guest at the entrance to the hotel property. E.A. Whitcomb, owner and manager of the Newfane Inn in Newfane, Vermont, managed the hotel.

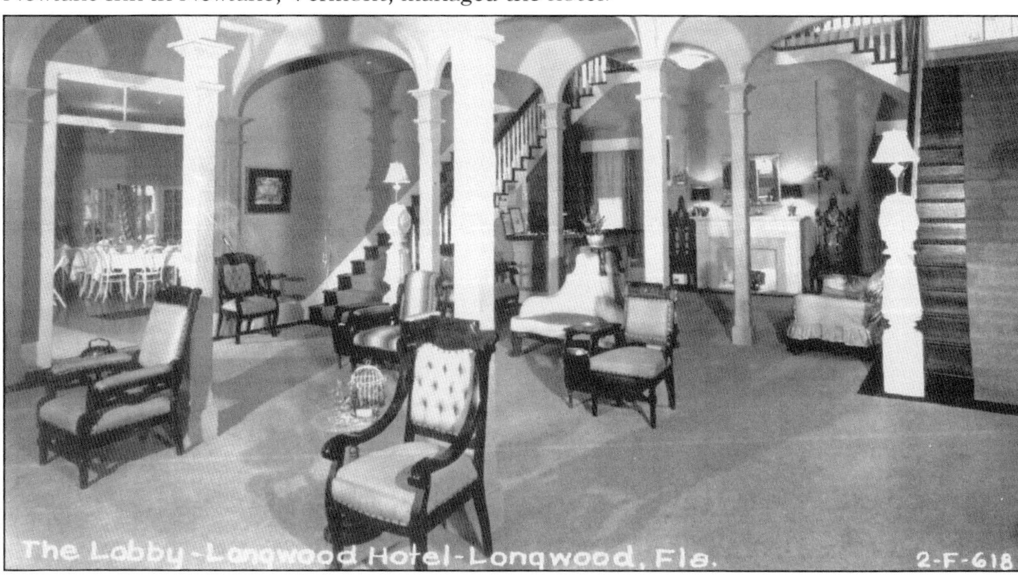

This is how the lobby of the Longwood Hotel looked in the 1920s when it boasted electric lights, running water, private baths, comfortable beds, large public rooms, and ample porches. Guests arrived at the hotel along the Dixie Highway on the Atlantic Coast Line and the Clyde Line Steamers. The Dixie Highway, a fine brick road from Jacksonville to Tampa and from coast to coast, runs through the center of the town, providing 1,000 miles of perfect road for automobiles and other vehicles.

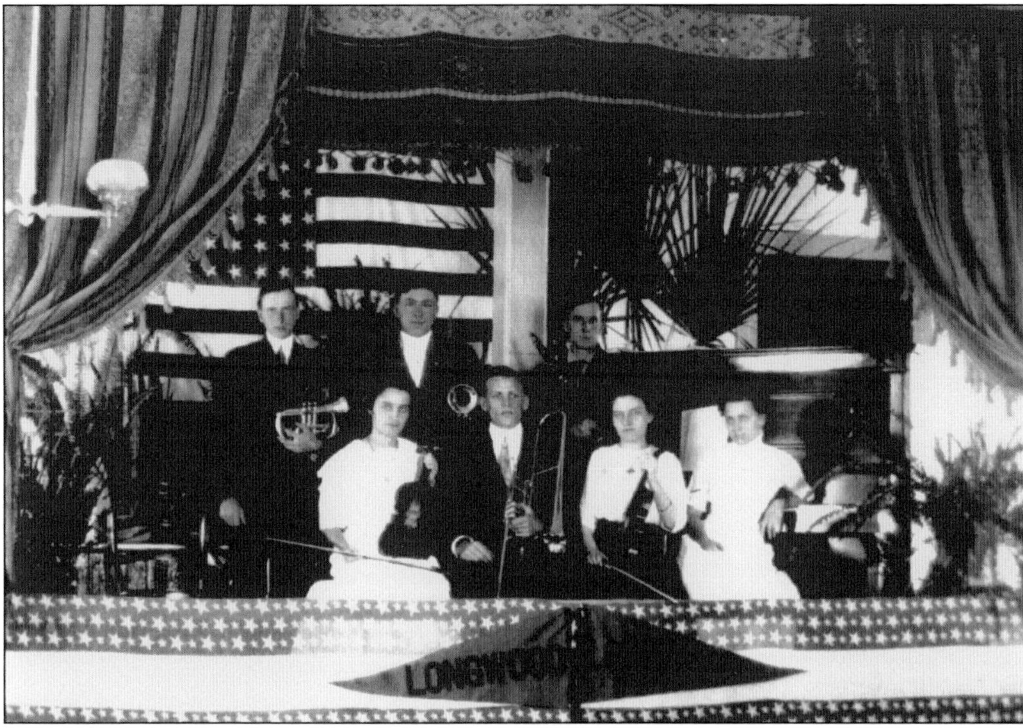

A Longwood band is shown inside the Longwood Hotel, which was the centerpiece of social gatherings and remains one of the top landmarks in the historic district.

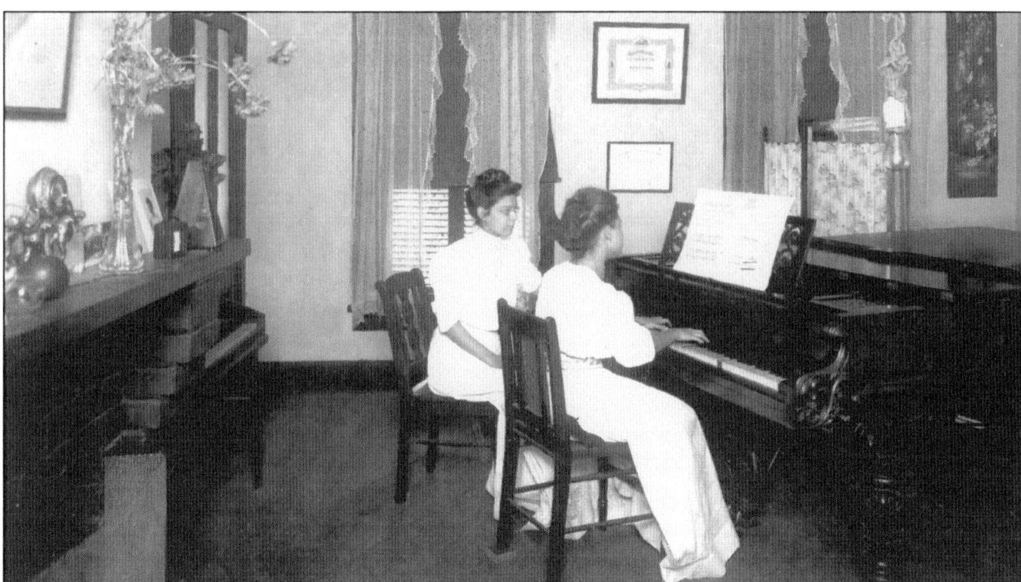
Addie Niemeyer and her teacher prepare for a recital at Rollins Academy. Real estate and hotel promotions said Longwood offered, "A good graded village school where you can send your younger children, while Rollins College at Winter Park, seven miles away, with over 400 students, affords first class educational advantages to more advanced pupils, and is easily reached from Longwood."

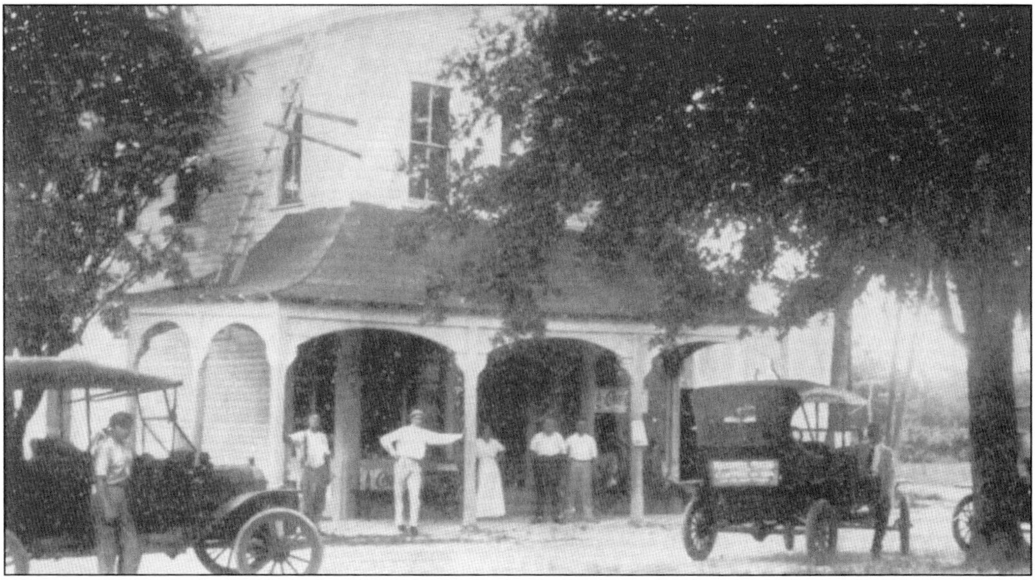

This is another view of the Allen Store after a garage was added in the early 1900s. J.H. Allen and George E. Upchurch operated stores on the same block of County Road 427 at Church Avenue but on opposite sides of the main road. The Niemeyer store was across Church from the Upchurch store. The railroad station was between the Niemeyer store and the tracks. Residents also bought roasted peanuts on Saturday nights at another store at County Road 427 and Warren Avenue.

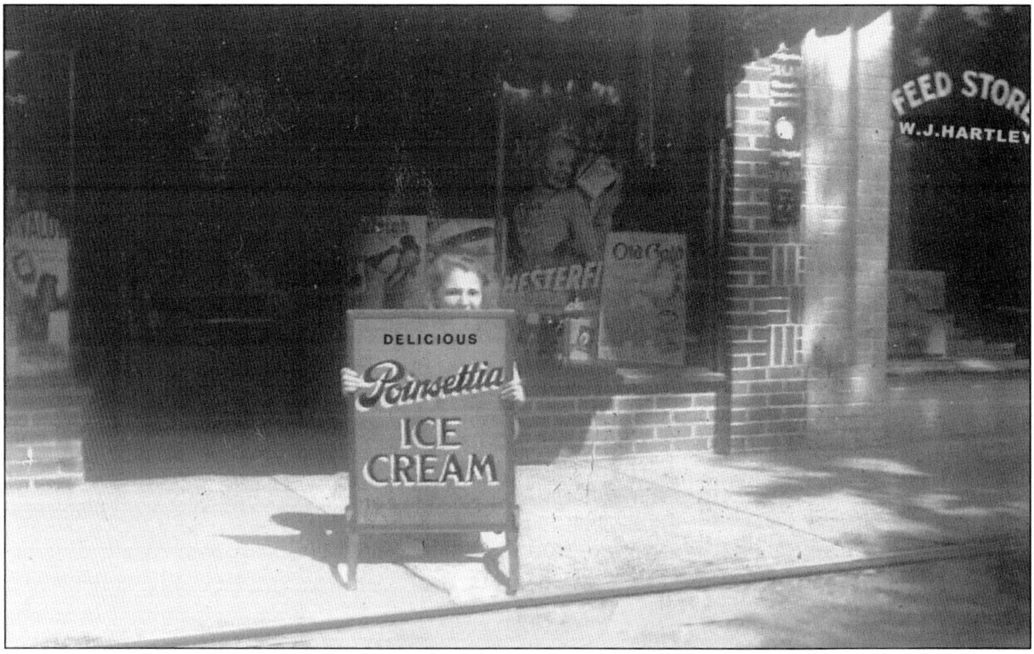

Lib Jackson hides behind the ice cream sign at her father C.C. Jackson's grocery store, next to the W.J. Hartley Feed Store, on Dixie Highway sometime in the 1940s.

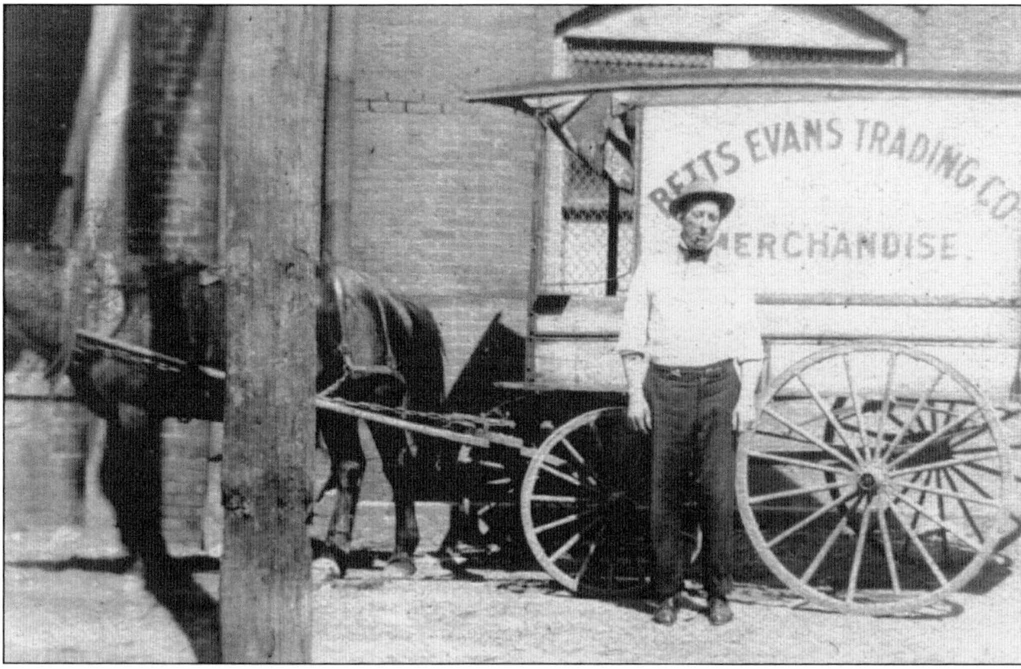

This 1914 photo shows storekeeper Lester R. Payne standing in front of a tradesman's wagon.

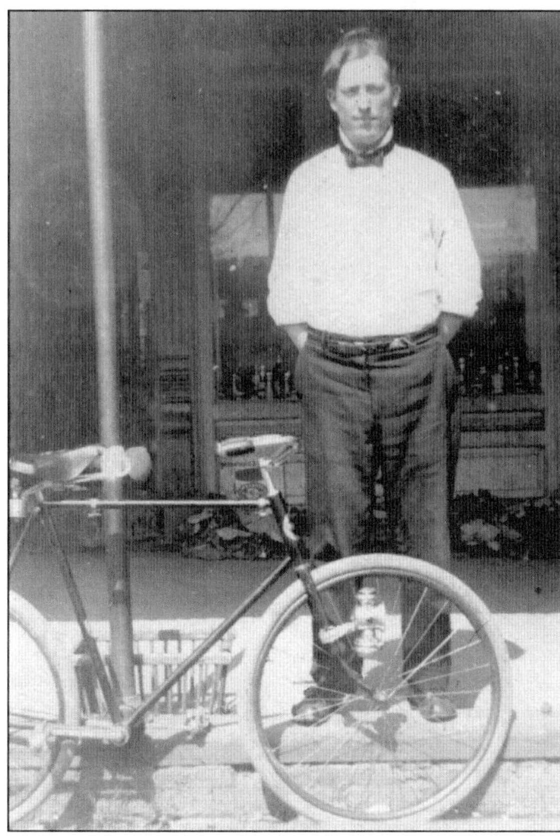

In this 1918 photo shopkeeper Lester R. Payne stands on the step of his store with a bicycle.

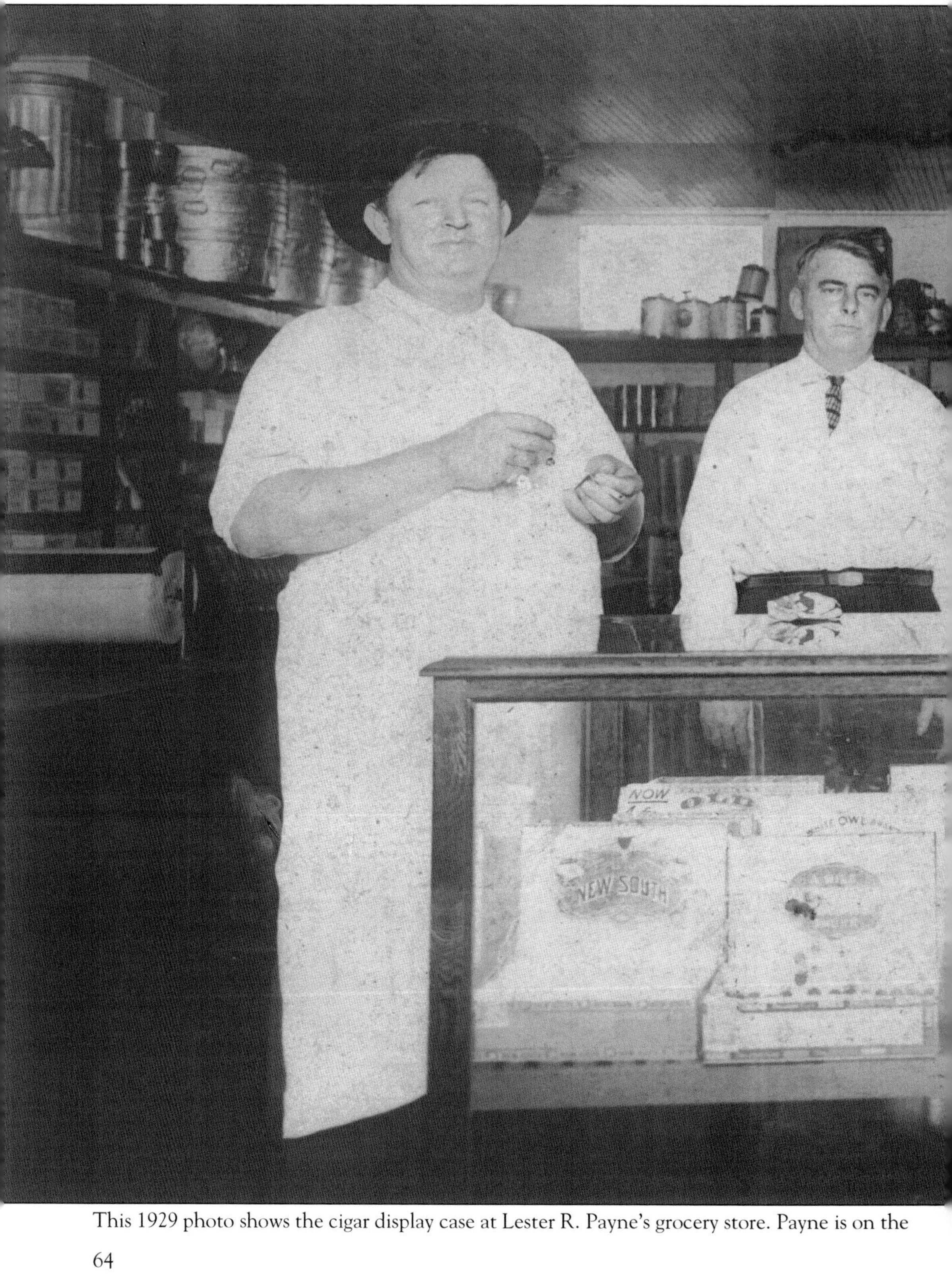

This 1929 photo shows the cigar display case at Lester R. Payne's grocery store. Payne is on the

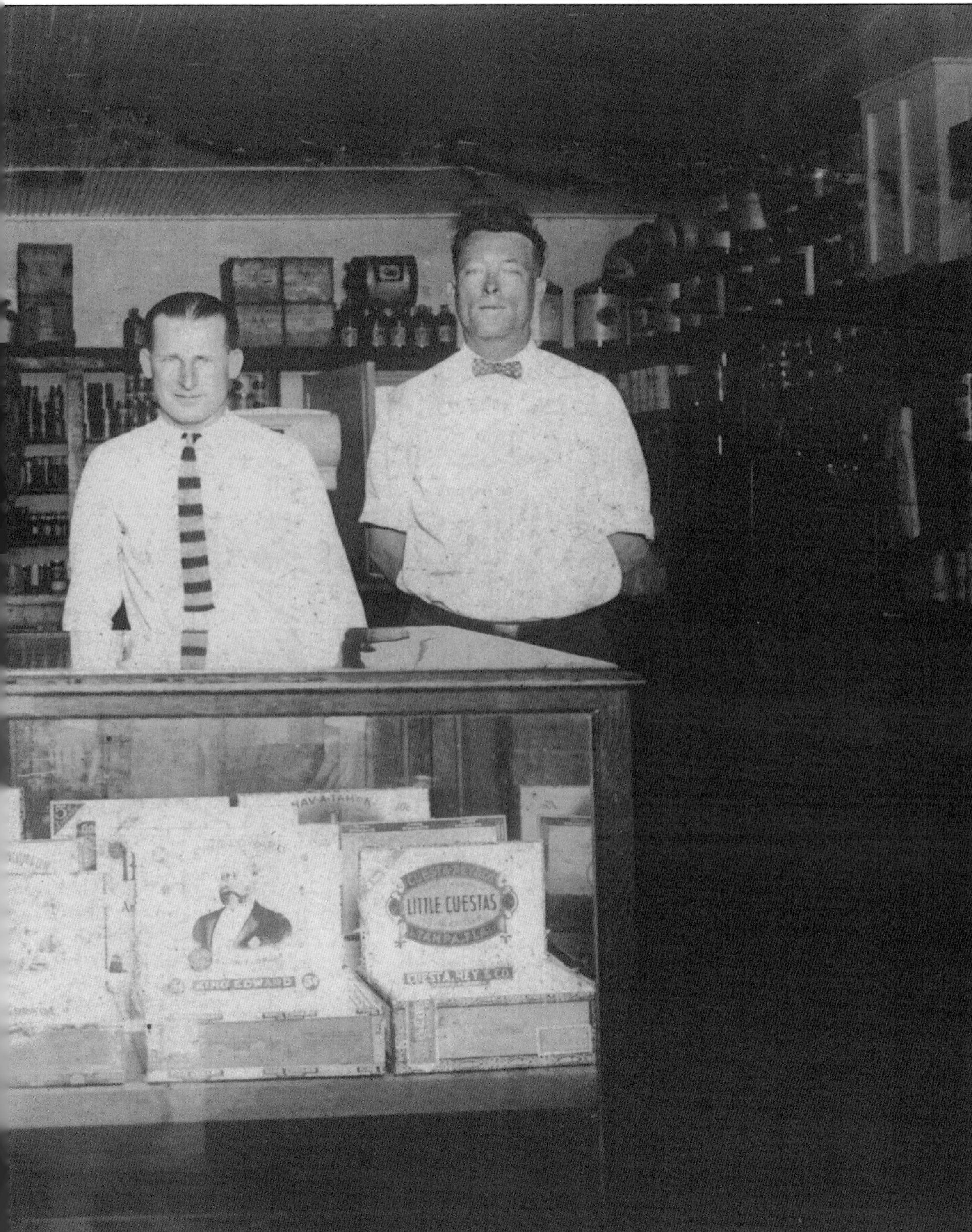

far right. Also shown is Mr. Douglas, a butcher; C.C. Jackson, a grocer; and Dan Padgett, a barber.

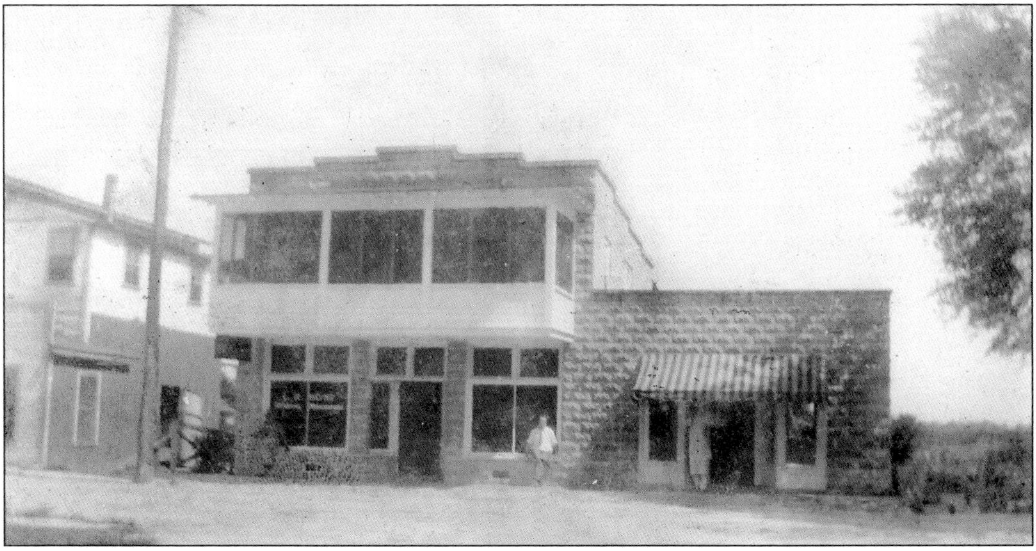

Lester R. Payne is shown here in 1929 sitting on the ledge of the family hardware store. The Payne family lived upstairs. It was there that Jim Payne was born. The Paynes also owned the post office building next door. Lester R. Payne later added another building for a hardware store.

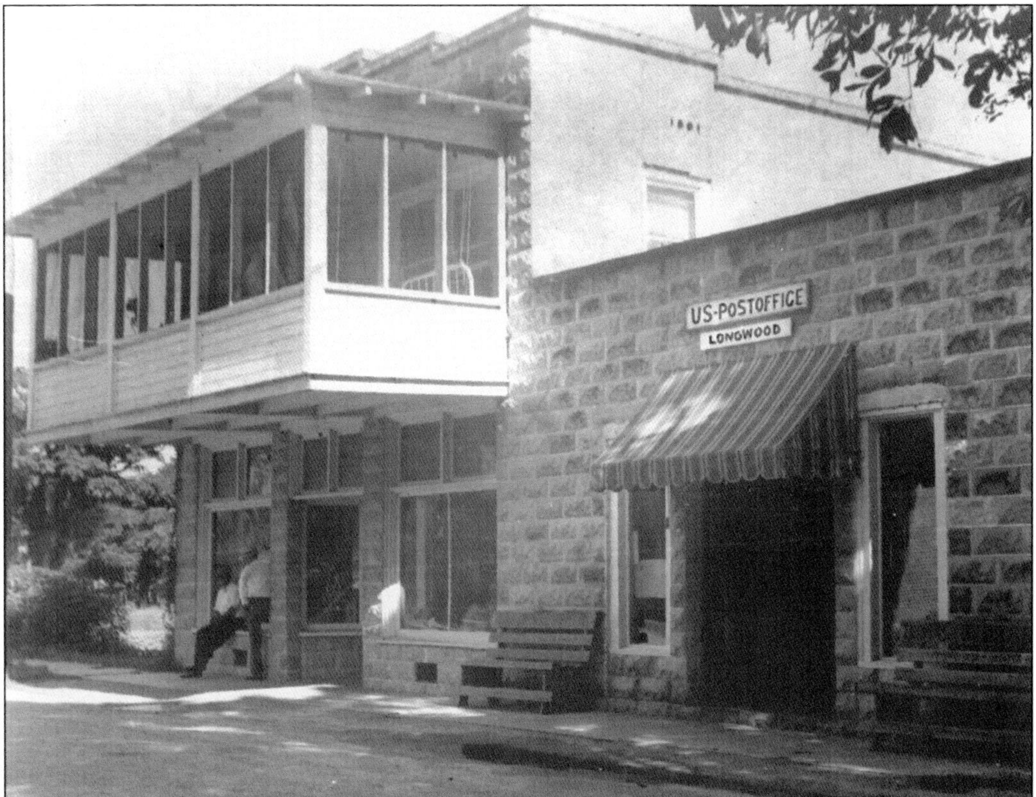

This photo taken in 1938 provides another view of the Payne hardware store and apartment next to the post office. L.R. Payne, left, sits with Bill Lewis.

Mrs. Blanche Payne, the postmistress, is shown on the left in front of the post office in 1939. The identity of the other woman is not known.

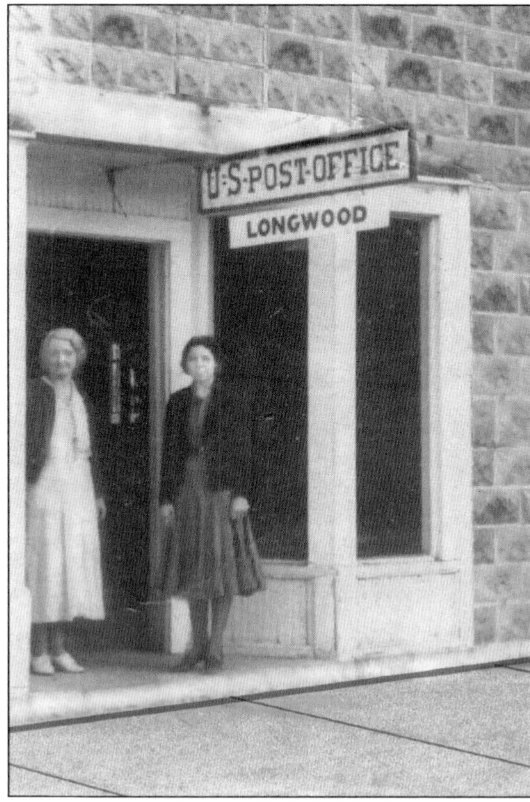

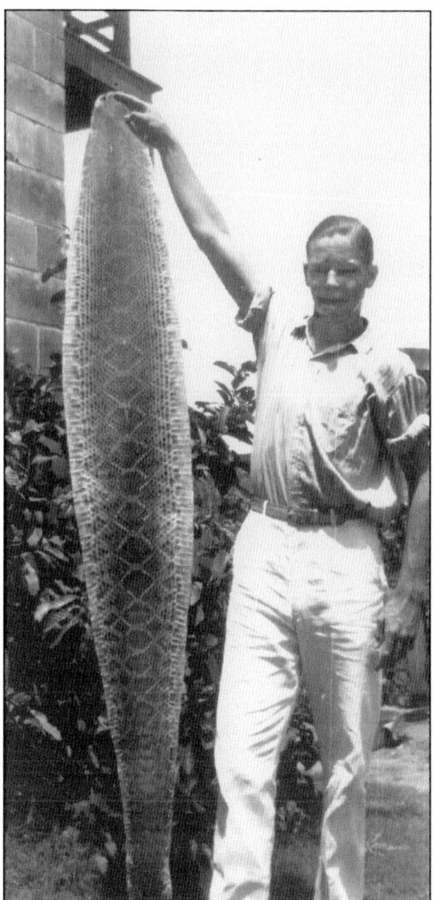

Jim Payne holds a skinned 7-foot, 8-inch rattlesnake with 19 rattles in 1936. Sal Grant killed the snake in a grove near U.S. Highway 17-92.

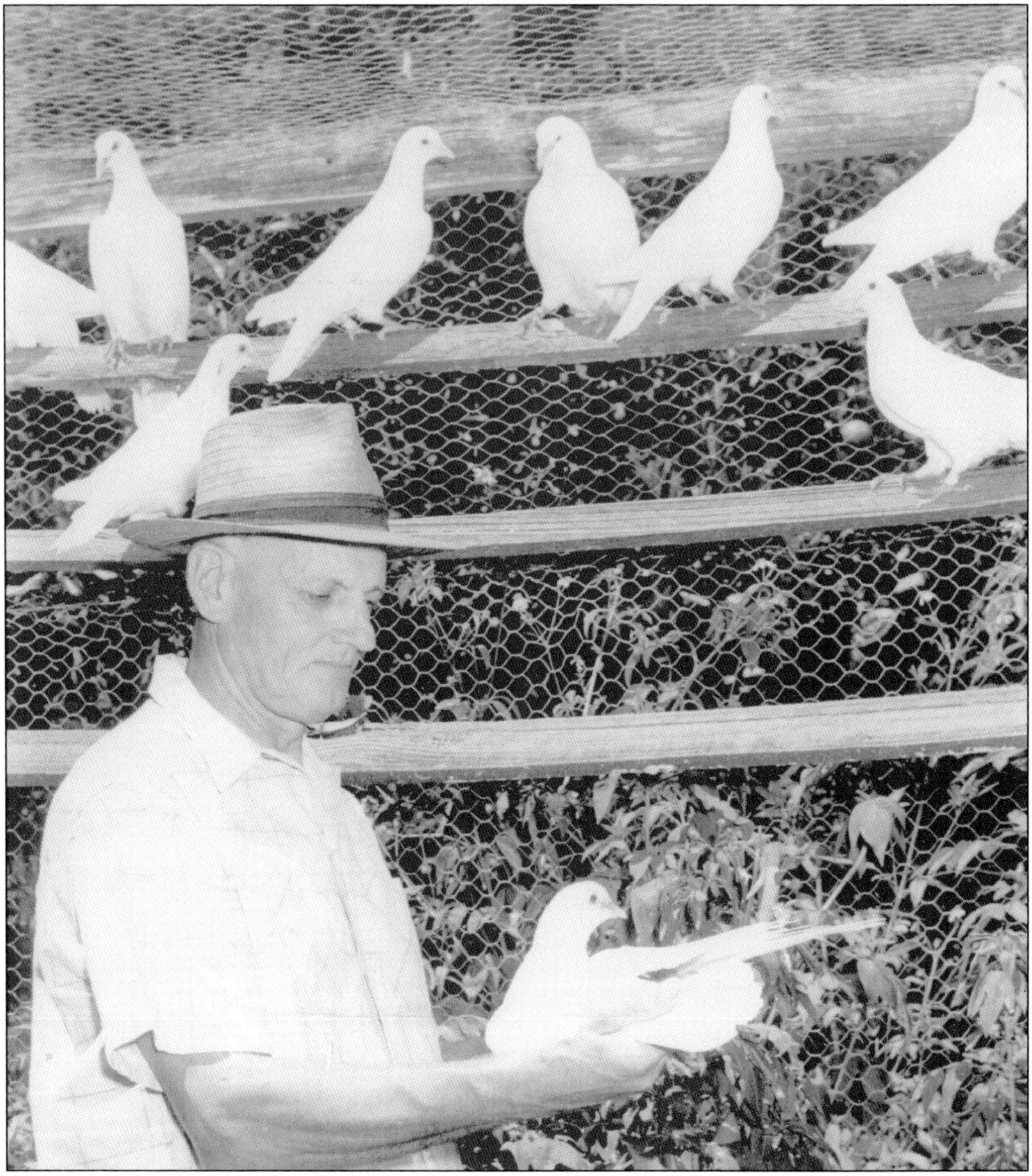

J.A. Bistline, shown here holding one of the birds from his championship farm, moved to Longwood in 1911 and worked for Josiah B. Clouser for three years. He started the Longwood Squab Farm and married Adeline Niemeyer, Clouser's granddaughter. Bistline became one of Longwood's first council members under the town government established August 28, 1917.

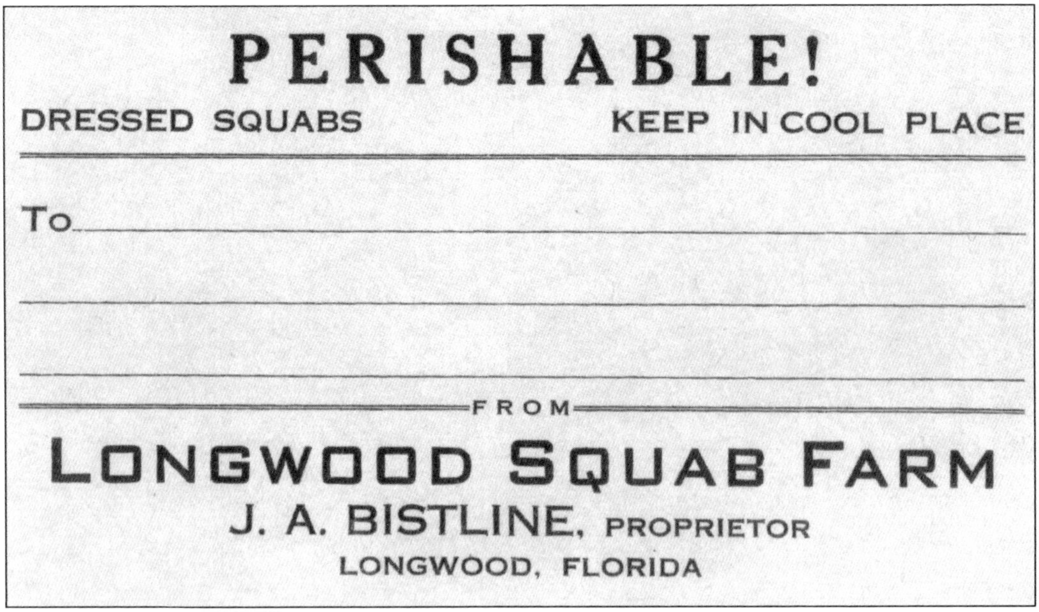
PERISHABLE!

DRESSED SQUABS KEEP IN COOL PLACE

To

FROM

LONGWOOD SQUAB FARM

J. A. BISTLINE, PROPRIETOR

LONGWOOD, FLORIDA

Shown here is a shipping label for J.A. Bistline's Longwood Squab Farm. There was a local market in the winter, and in the summer, squabs were packed on ice and shipped north via train. Squabs were shipped as far north as New York City.

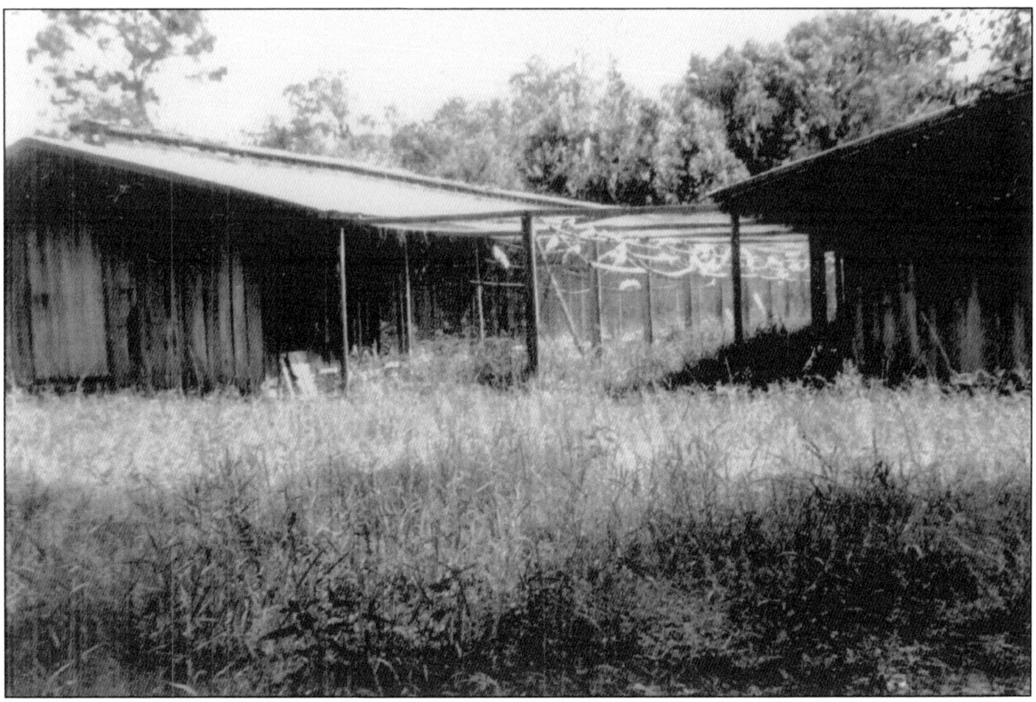

This view shows the Longwood Squab Farm, located at the corner of what is now Milwee Avenue between Church and Warren Avenues. This photo was taken prior to 1928 when the farm moved to a location on East State Road 434.

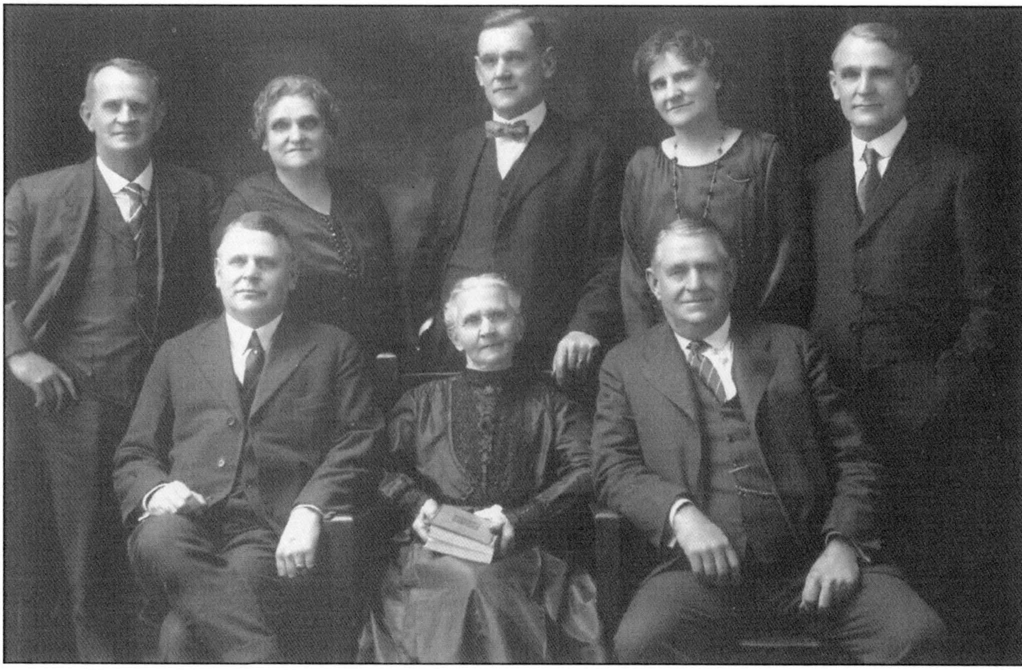

Pictured here is Elvina Miller Niemeyer surrounded by her children, who are, from left to right, (standing) Edward, Helen Niemeyer Zeller, Harry, Clara, and Charles; (seated) Walter and Frederick. Fred Niemeyer was 21 when he arrived in Longwood from Pennsylvania in 1885. In 1889, when Niemeyer married carpenter Josiah B. Clouser's daughter, Clouser helped him build a home at 192 West Warren Avenue. Niemeyer was working at Clouser's store in 1898 when he won election to the city council. The name of the store was changed to Niemeyer and Clouser General Store in the early 1900s. Later, Niemeyer became the owner. Niemeyer developed many of the homesites north and west of the Clouser property.

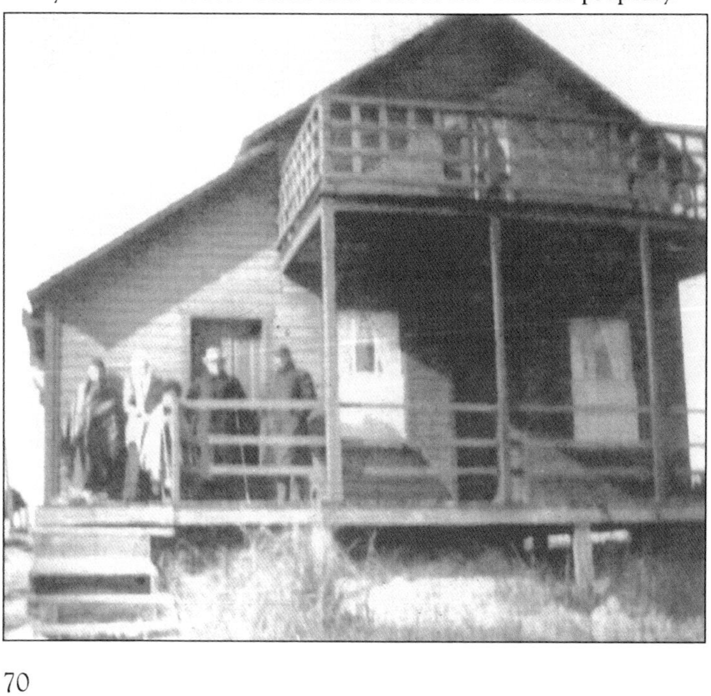

Here, Fred Niemeyer and his family, are on the porch of the family beach house. Clyde Clouser, one of Josiah B. Clouser's nephews, recalled that in the early 1900s, the family had a chicken farm near the beach. "The chicken farm was about a mile below Old Coronado and Old Coronado was about a mile below the town of New Smyrna Beach. Uncle Joe built five or seven cottages there, and there wasn't another cottage there." All beach cottages were later lost to fire.

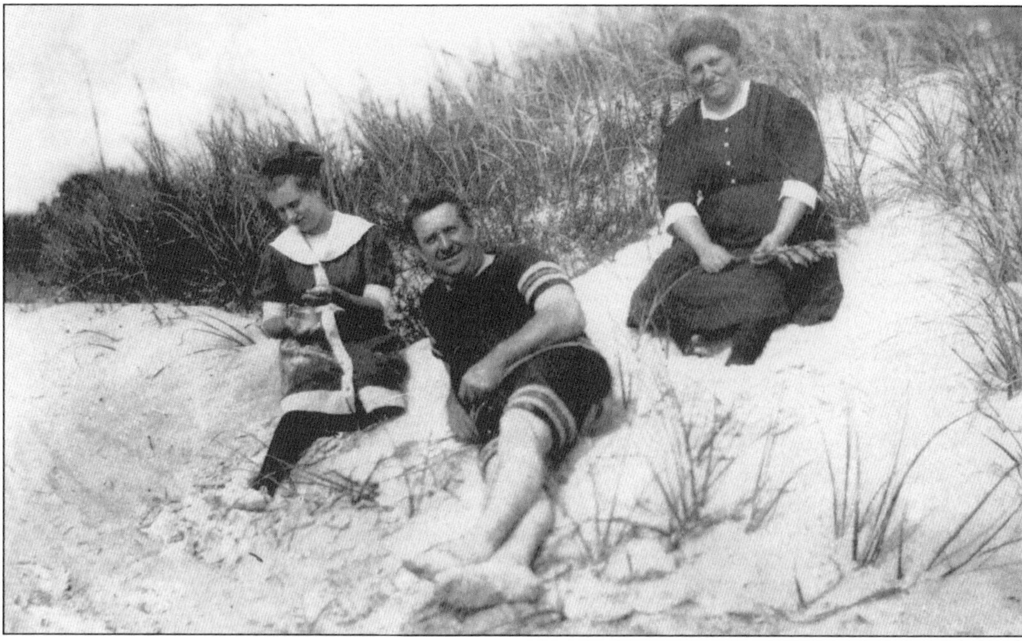

Fred Niemeyer; his wife, Frances; and daughter Addie enjoy a day at the beach near the Clouser family beach house.

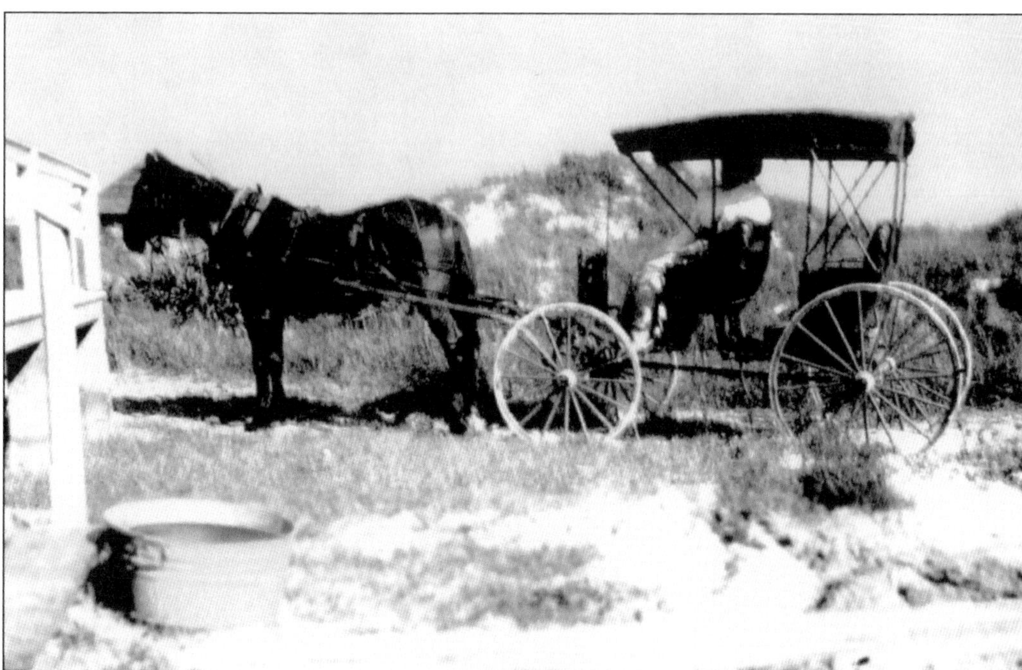

A buggy and driver wait for the family during a day at the beach.

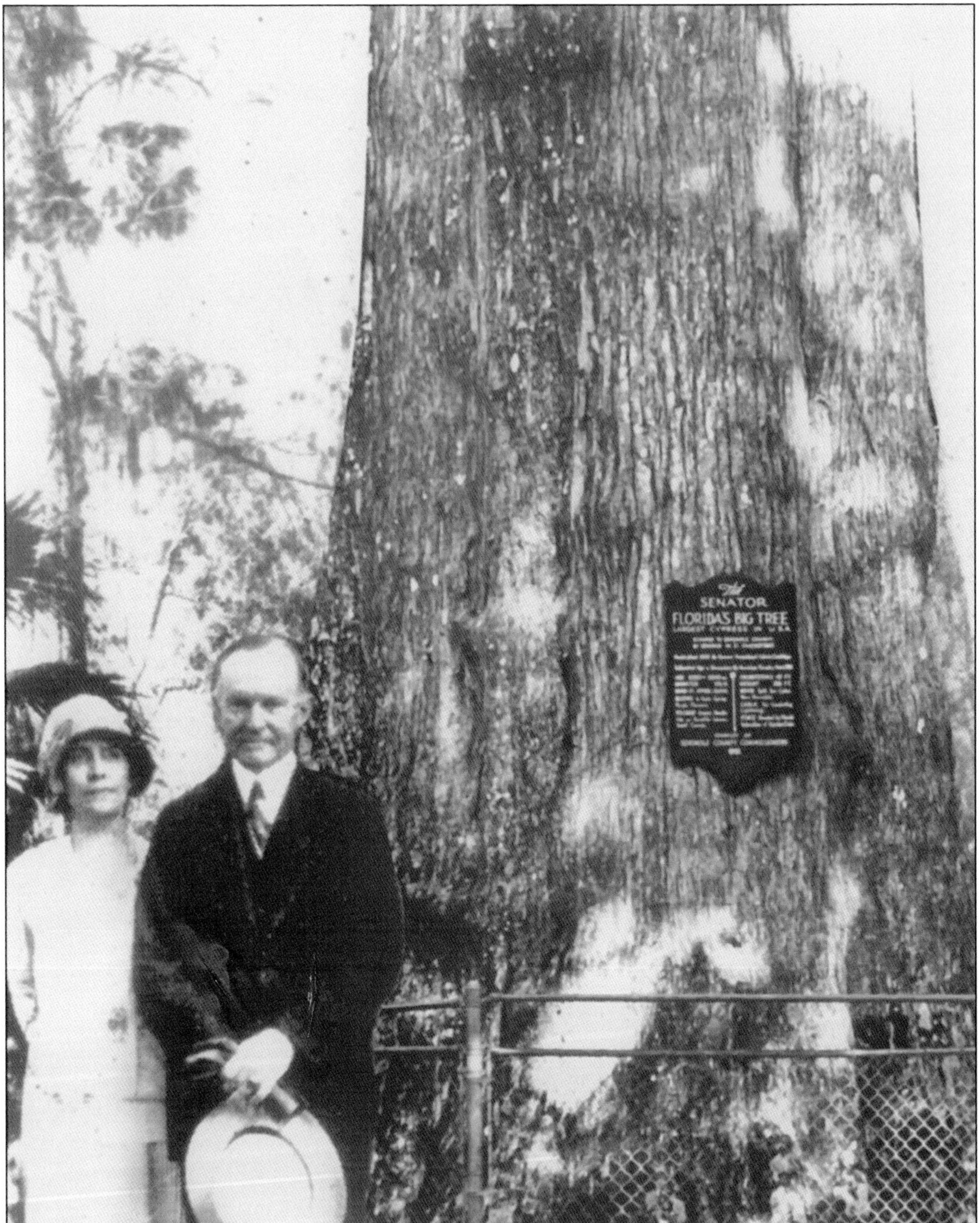

In 1934, former President Calvin Coolidge and his wife, Grace, while visiting Florida, were the guests of honor at the dedication of the Big Tree, the giant cypress tree. President Coolidge stood dwarfed under the shade of The Senator in 1929 to praise it as a national treasure, one of the nation's oldest and largest trees. The American Forestry Association in 1946 estimated that The Senator was a seedling 3,000 years before Columbus sailed to America, meaning it was towering over Florida long before the Spanish, English, or U.S. flags. Florida Senator M.O. Overstreet donated the cypress giant and the land around it to Seminole County in 1951.

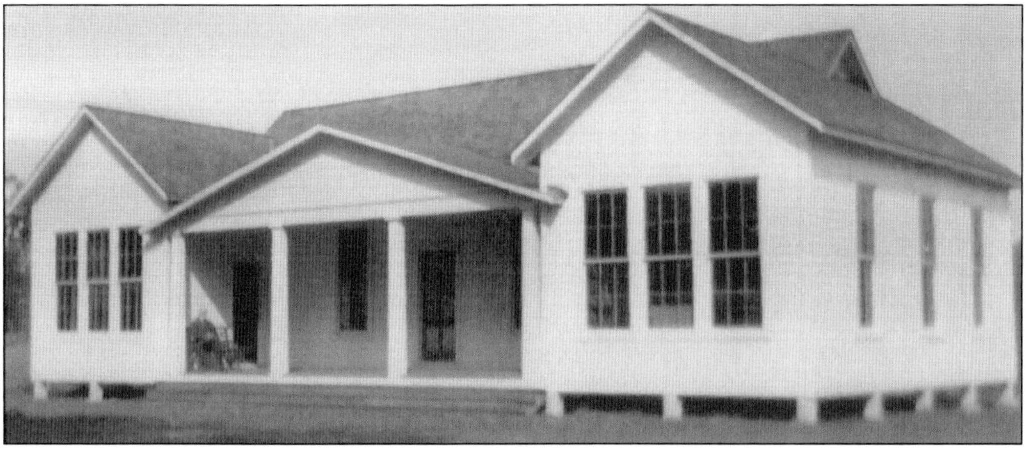

The women of Longwood in 1911 organized the Longwood Improvement Society to build up and beautify the town and improve its culture. They started by cleaning up the roadsides and placing barrels along the roads for trash. Some roads were covered with sawdust from the nearby mills. The women raised money for streetlights, established a library, and a few streets were paved. When they had extra money, they donated it to a children's home in Jacksonville. The society's name was changed to the Longwood Civic League in 1913, one month before Seminole County broke away from Orange. The Longwood Civic League's original building, once a schoolhouse and meeting place near its present location, was moved to West Longwood in the area of Stum's Corner at the old Markham Road in about 1882. Stum's Corner was located at Rangeline Road at Church Avenue. The Longwood Civic League's building was originally called the Self Union Chapel and West Longwood Chapel, headquarters of the West Longwood Pioneers. The building was abandoned after the Great Freeze. The Longwood Civic League bought the building in 1914 and moved it to its present location on Church Avenue. Later, the front porch was closed in to make more room, as it became a center for social life. The Central Florida Society for Historical Preservation, which now owns the building called the Woman's Club, is planning to renovate it as an archive museum.

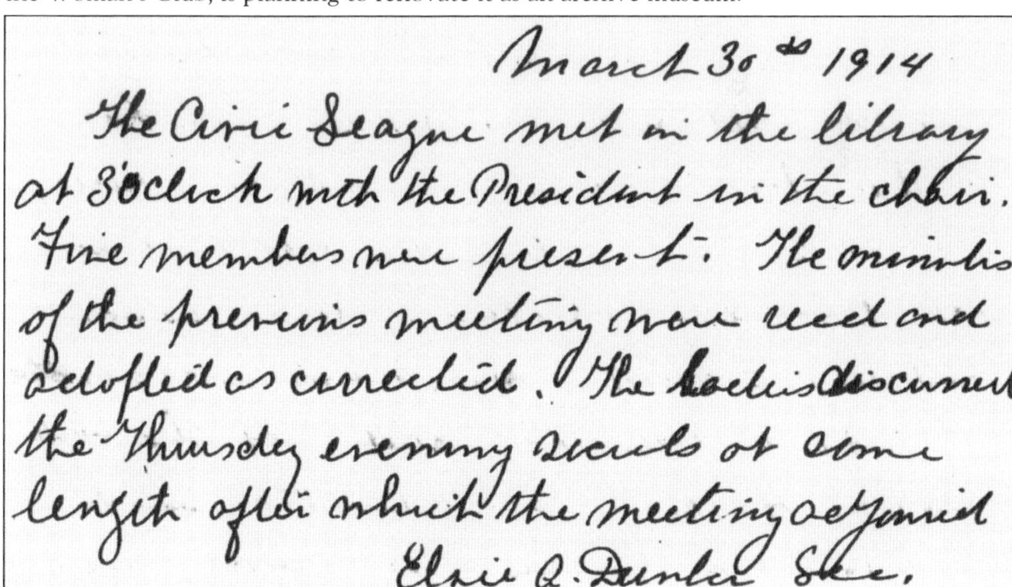

March 30th 1914

The Civic League met in the library at 3 o'clock with the President in the chair. Five members were present. The minutes of the previous meeting were read and adopted as corrected. The ladies discussed the Thursday evening socials at some length after which the meeting adjourned.

Elsie A. Dunbar Sec.

Sample minutes from 1914 are shown above.

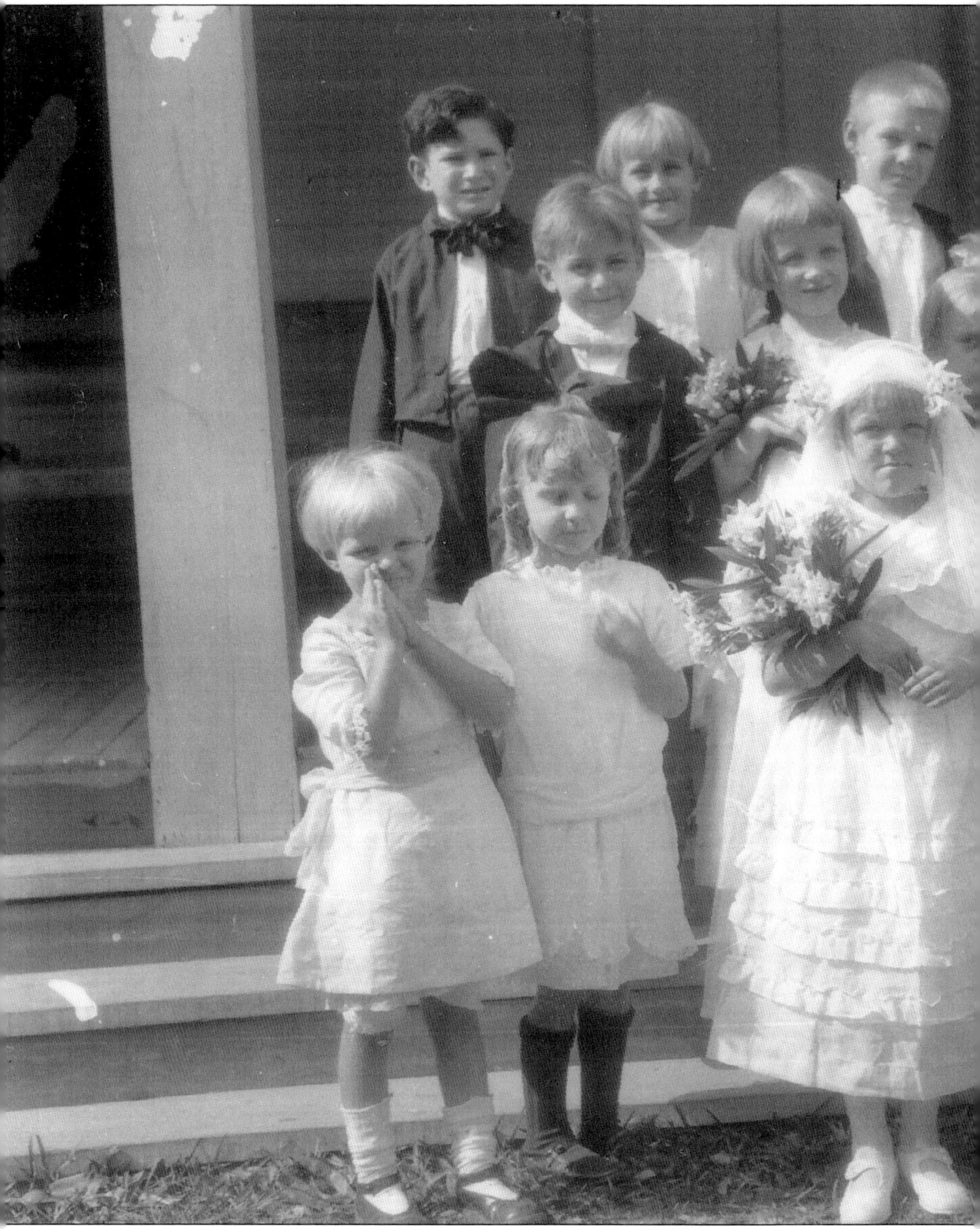

This "Tom Thumb" wedding was staged about 1923 at the Longwood Civic League's building. During that time, mock weddings for children became popular when P.T. Barnum promoted

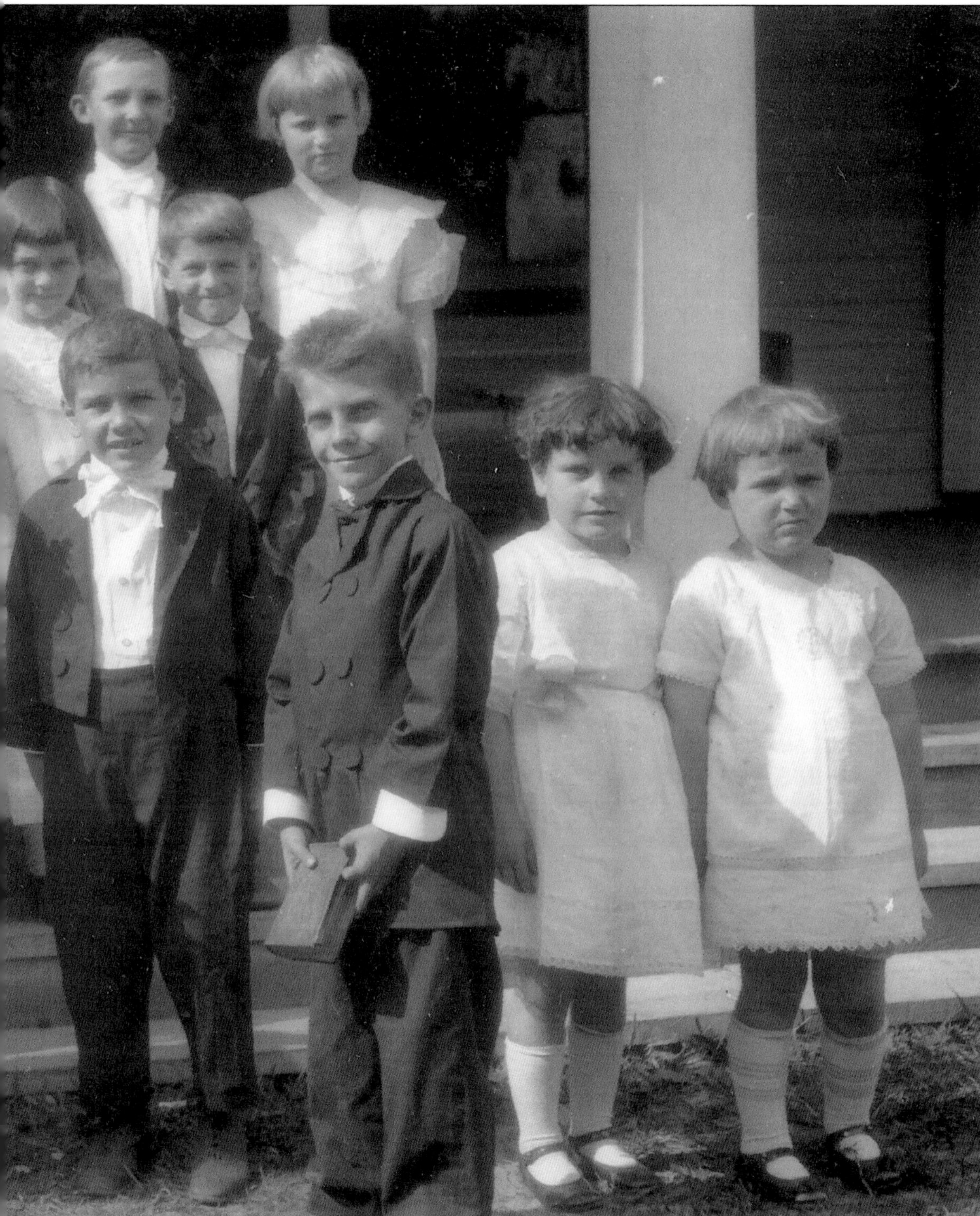

the wedding of circus performer Tom Thumb.

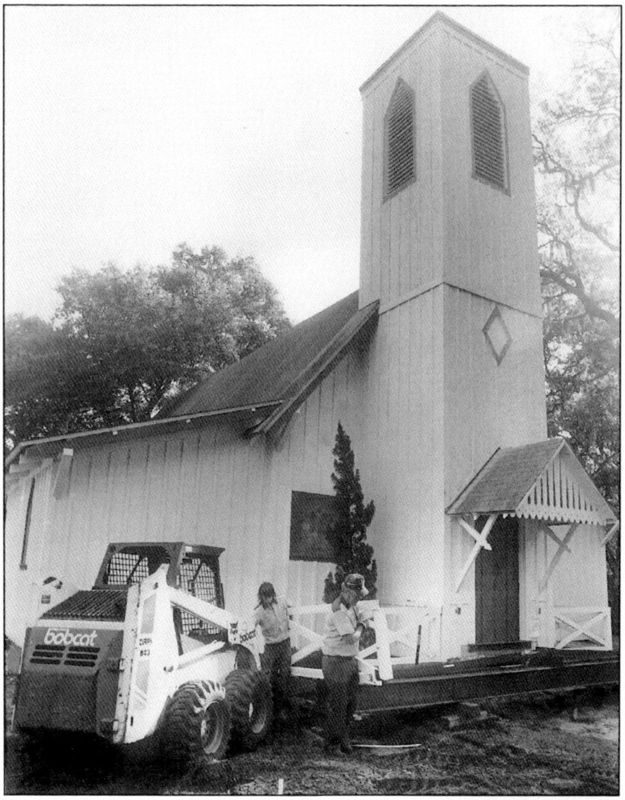

The Christ Episcopal Church, a structure in the Longwood Historic District, is on the National Register of Historic Places. The church was built on land donated by E.W. Henck. Frederic H. Rand's parents in Boston raised the construction money. Rand, treasurer for 30 years for the Episcopal diocese, also was a generous supporter of Sanford's Holy Cross Episcopal Church. In 1988, the church was moved approximately 100 feet to make room for an addition. Pictured at left are preparations being made to move the church.

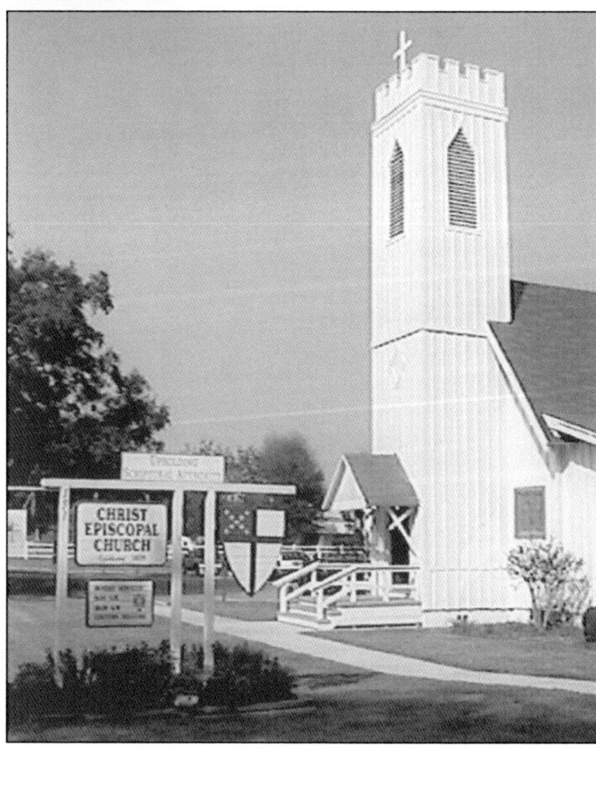

Steven Provost, a partner in Yeilding & Provost, the architects, engineers, and planners who surveyed the homes and businesses in Longwood to document the city's historic district, identifies Christ Episcopal on West Church Avenue as the oldest existing church in Seminole County. Frederic Rand helped organize the first Episcopal mission in Longwood in 1877, and the mission built its first church on West Church Avenue in 1880. It was dedicated on Easter Sunday 1882 and is still in use. The community's first school building (the Civic League Building) was on this site before the church.

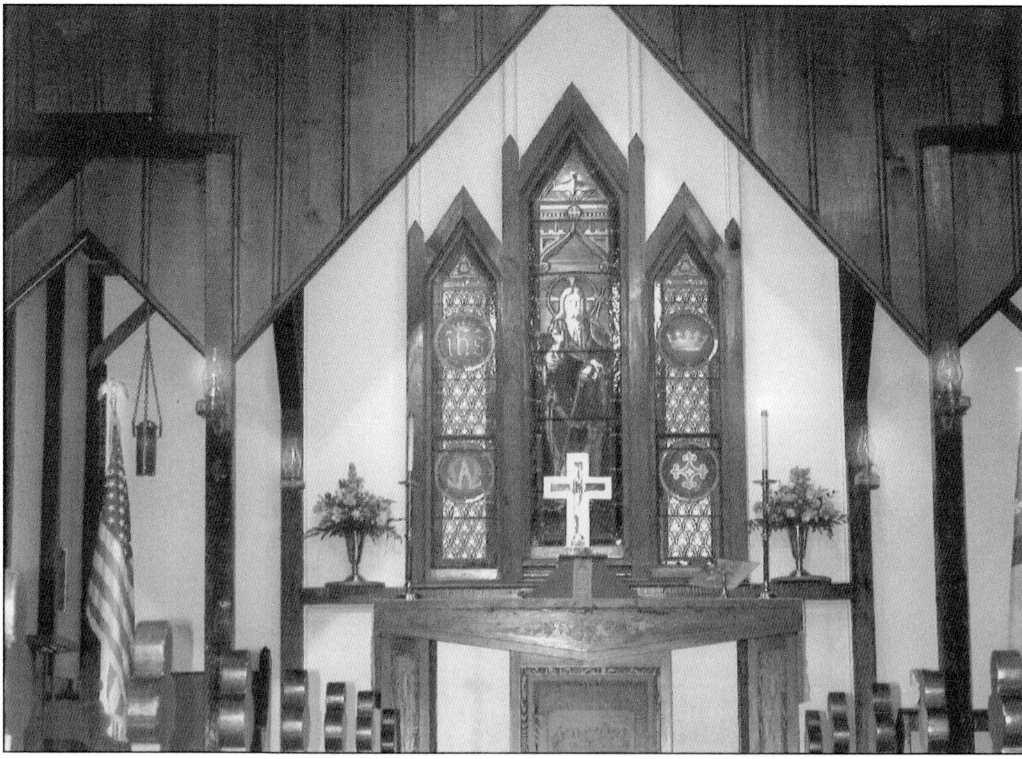

The money to buy the stained-glass windows for Christ Episcopal came from the family of Frederic Rand, a Bostonian and war veteran who took part in early Longwood's development. Rand, arrived in Longwood in 1876, buying land in West Longwood and planting citrus. By the 1890s he owned one of the largest groves in the area. He later owned a home in Sanford. Rand was general manager for Henry Sanford's land company, which provided some of the land for Henck's railroad. Rand was also general freight and passenger agent for the railroad's Sanford office after Henck and investors organized the South Florida Railroad. Rand was one of Sanford's first mayors and vice president of the First National Bank of Sanford.

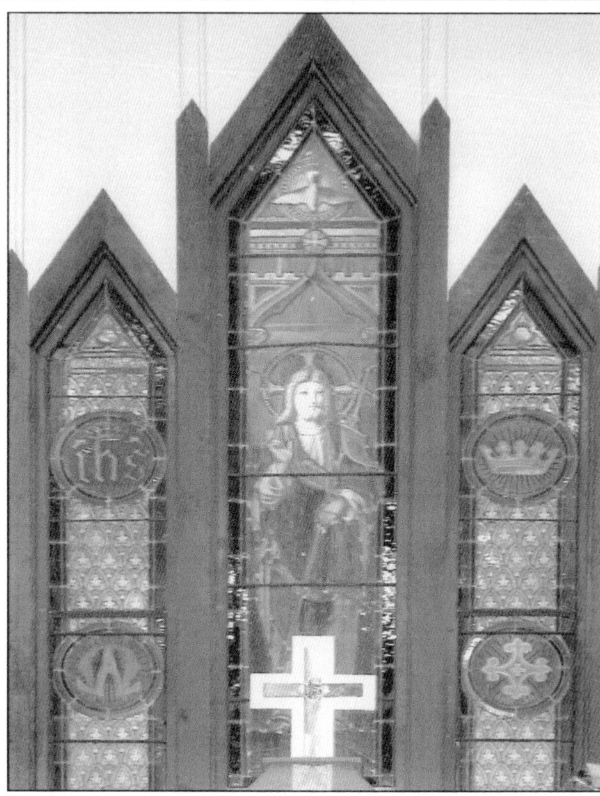

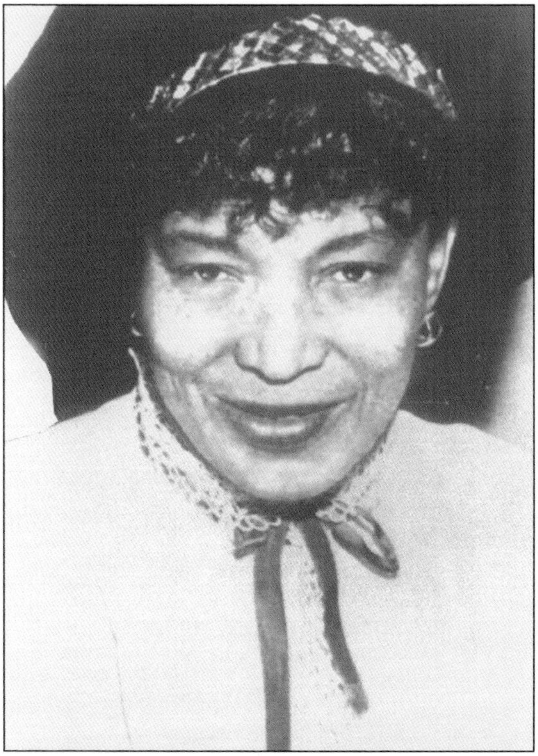

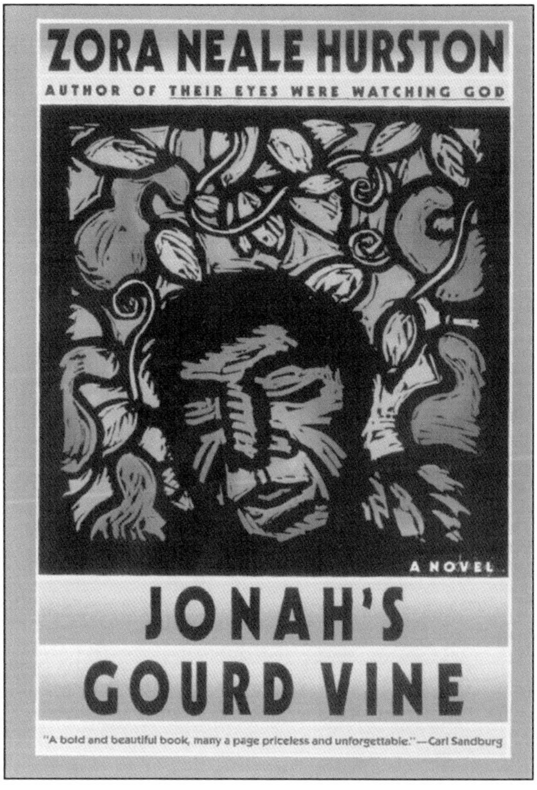

Zora Neale Hurston, a writer who became a legend among readers of Florida folklore, wrote many of her works from stories she heard in the 1920s while wandering around Florida. The novel, *Jonah's Gourd Vine*, loosely based on her father, Baptist minister John Hurston, whose preaching took him to many Florida towns, including Longwood, was written while she lived in Sanford and published in 1934. By the time the novel came to public attention, Hurston was living in Longwood. She signed one of the copies with this note, "To My Godmother [Mrs. Osgood Mason]—Who is one of the low-flying angels, and her harp sings silver in the wind breezes. She puts music into mud-sills, and wings onto clods. She is a battle-ax in the time of trouble and a shelter in the time of storm. With Devotion, Zora / Longwood, Fla. May 18, 1934, when Godmother is 80 years old."

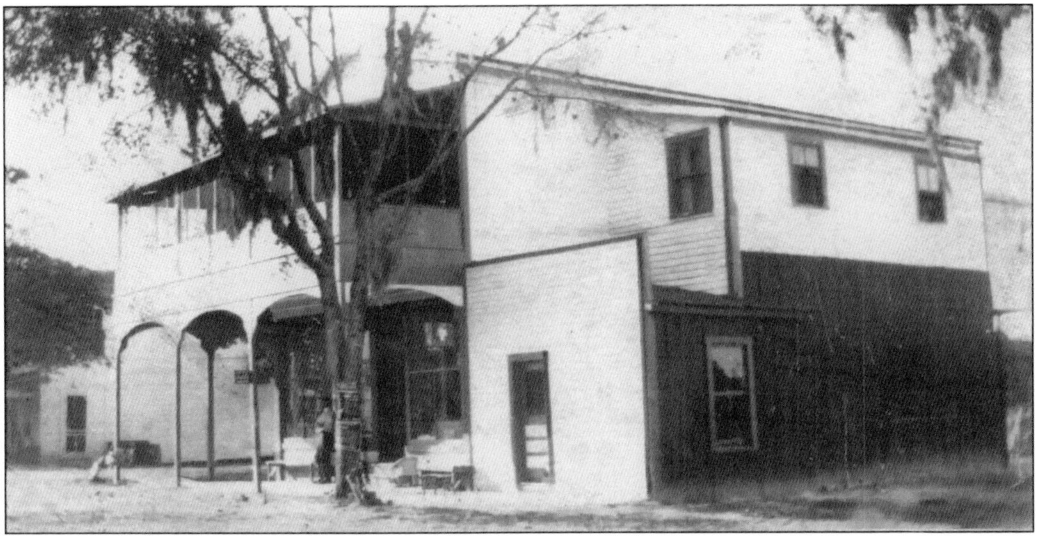

This is Allen's Store and the adjacent buildings at Church Avenue and Country Road 427 in the commercial area of Longwood Road in 1920.

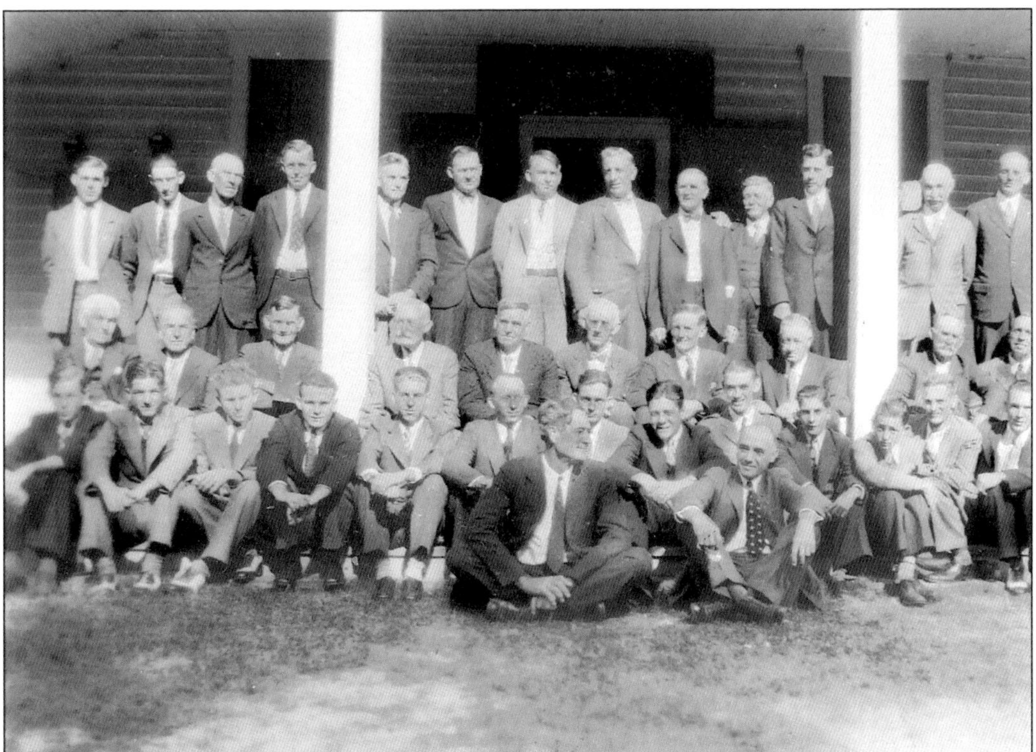

The men of Longwood pose for this picture taken on the steps of the Woman's Club Building in the early 1930s.

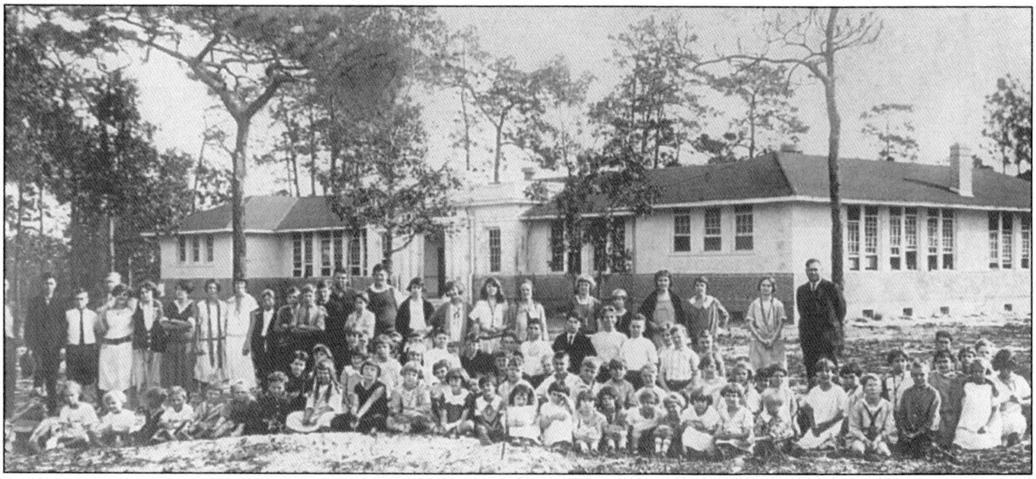

The first Lyman School campus replaced the Longwood School on Wilma Avenue, which was in use until 1924 when busing became possible. The Lyman School, shown here on the first day of school in 1926, consolidated the schools of Longwood, Altamonte Springs, Fern Park, Forest City, and the Bear Lake area. It contained grades one through seven. By 1932, it became an accredited high school with all 12 grades. There were about 200 students. The site is now the campus of Milwee Middle School, named for R.T. Milwee, who in 1953 took over as superintendent. The county had about 5,000 students.

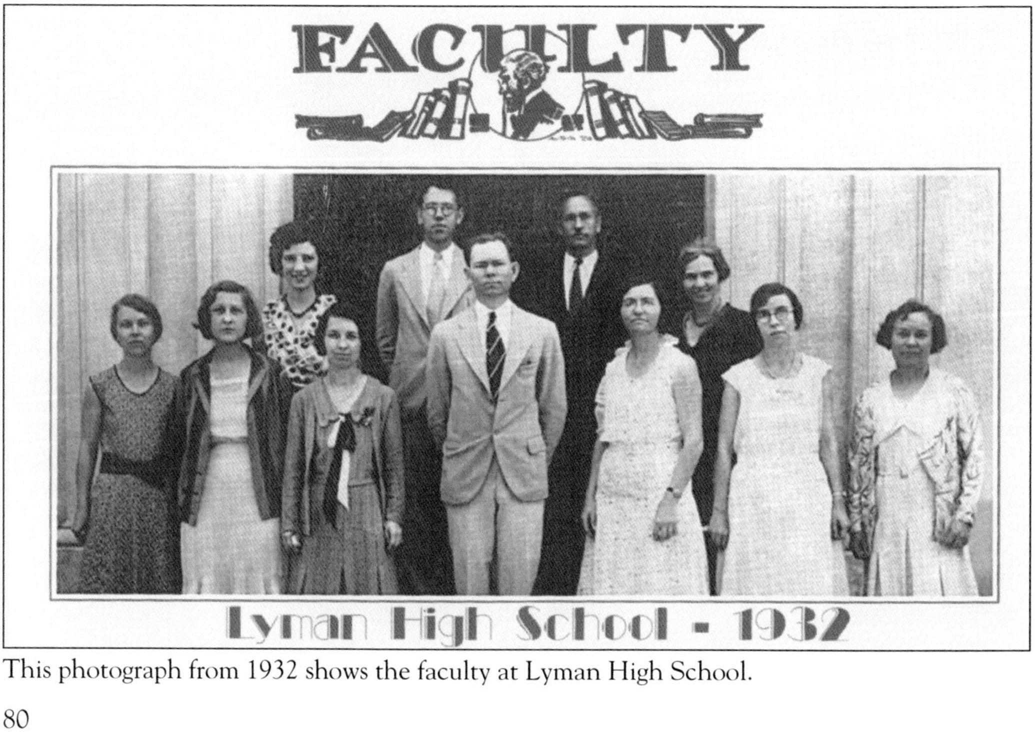

This photograph from 1932 shows the faculty at Lyman High School.

This Lyman Leaflet is the cover of the annual yearbook in 1932.

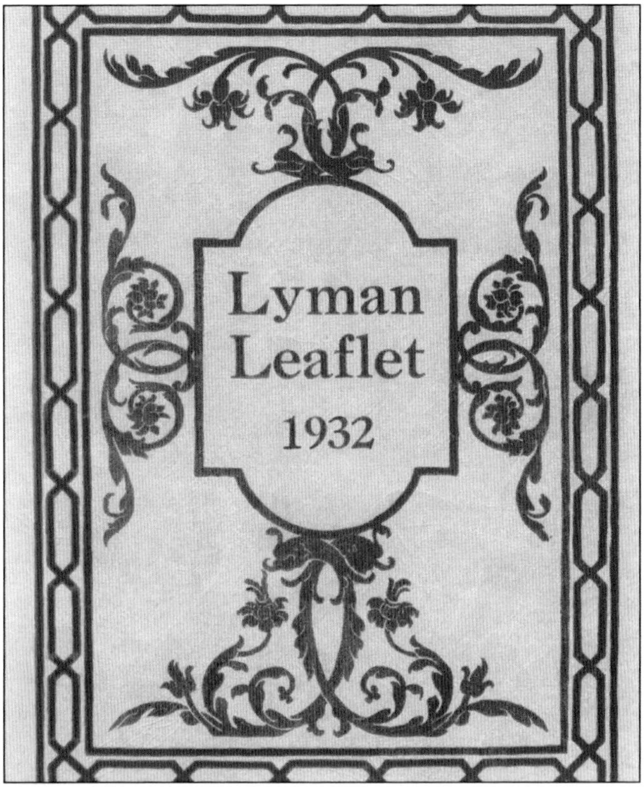

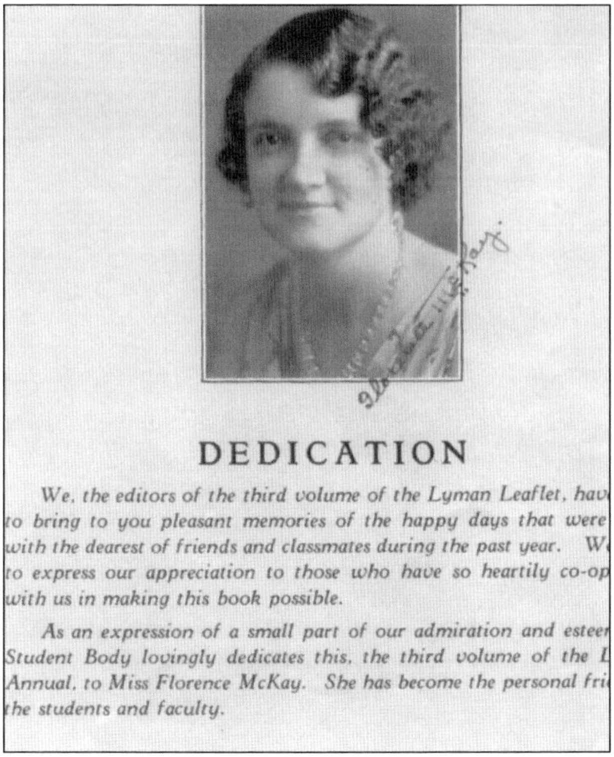

DEDICATION

We, the editors of the third volume of the Lyman Leaflet, hav[illegible] to bring to you pleasant memories of the happy days that were with the dearest of friends and classmates during the past year. W[illegible] to express our appreciation to those who have so heartily co-op[illegible] with us in making this book possible.

As an expression of a small part of our admiration and estee[illegible] Student Body lovingly dedicates this, the third volume of the L[illegible] Annual, to Miss Florence McKay. She has become the personal fri[illegible] the students and faculty.

This is a dedication for Miss Florence McKay who taught Spanish and English at Lyman High School.

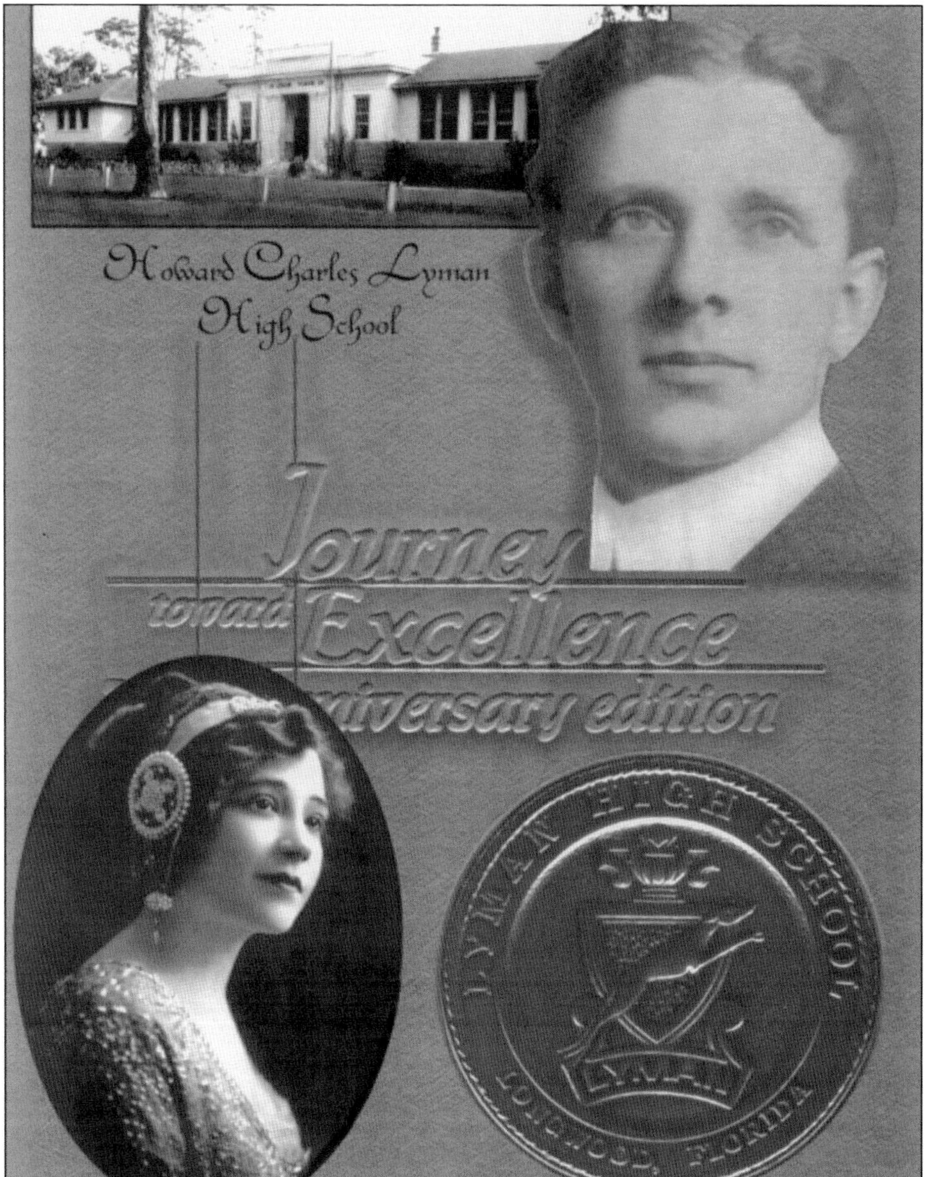

This photo of Lyman's 75th anniversary edition/yearbook shows Howard Charles Lyman, the early school board member who is the high school's namesake, and his wife, Emma. Both were New York entertainers who first came to Florida to perform for winter guests at the Altamonte Hotel and Sanlando Country Club. Howard Lyman won election to the school board when Seminole County was created in 1913. Emma Lyman was among the 28 Altamonte voters who called for a town referendum. She and her husband voted to create the town. The vote passed on November 11, 1920, by 38 votes to 7. Emma was chairman of the town's board of aldermen in 1925 and also taught music at the Lyman School twice a week. During the Great Depression years, she supervised a garden of cowpeas and sweet potatoes at Lyman and Rosenwald schools. She also distributed surplus government flour to needy families. To keep civic organizations active during those lean years, Emma put on community picnics and political rallies. She remained active with the Lyman School through the 1930s.

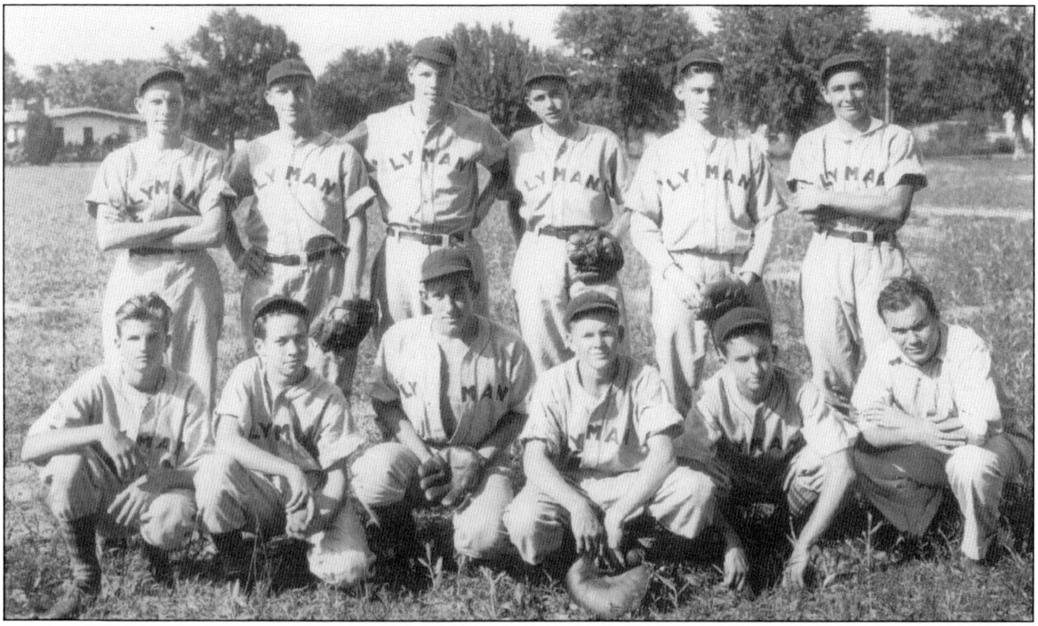

Jim Payne (back row, fourth from the left) is shown with Lyman High School's 1938 baseball team. Payne was a science and biology teacher and coach at Lyman.

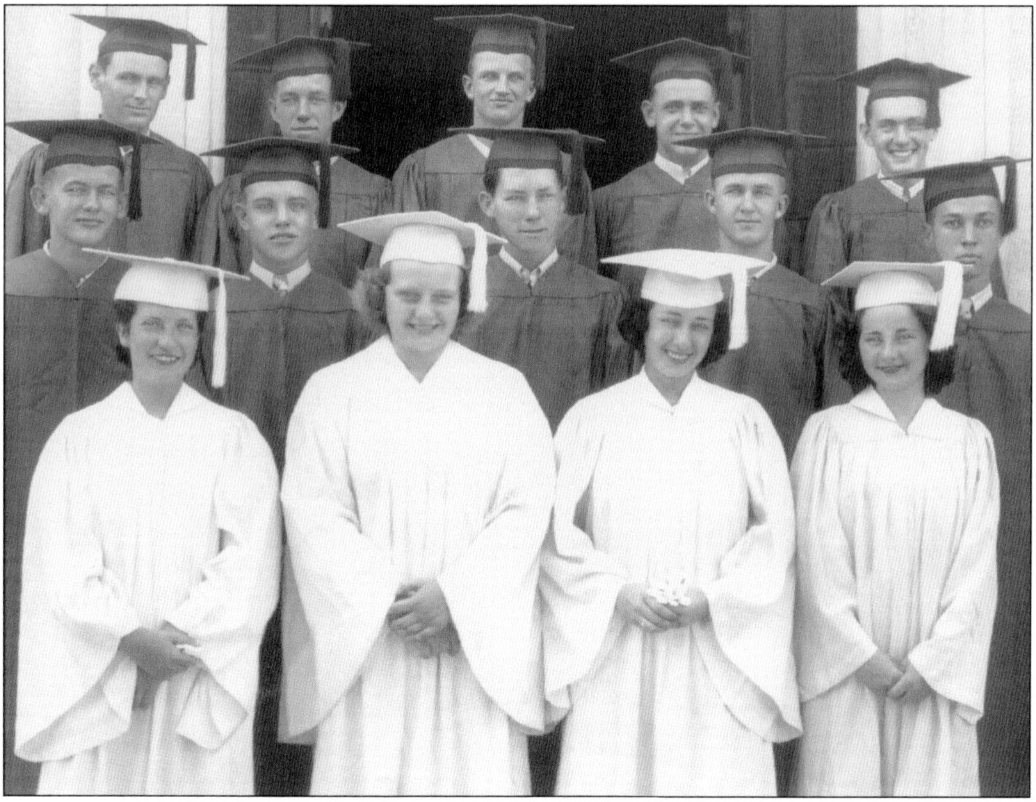

This photo showcases the Class of 1940 at Lyman High, which includes class president John Bistline in the middle row, second from the left.

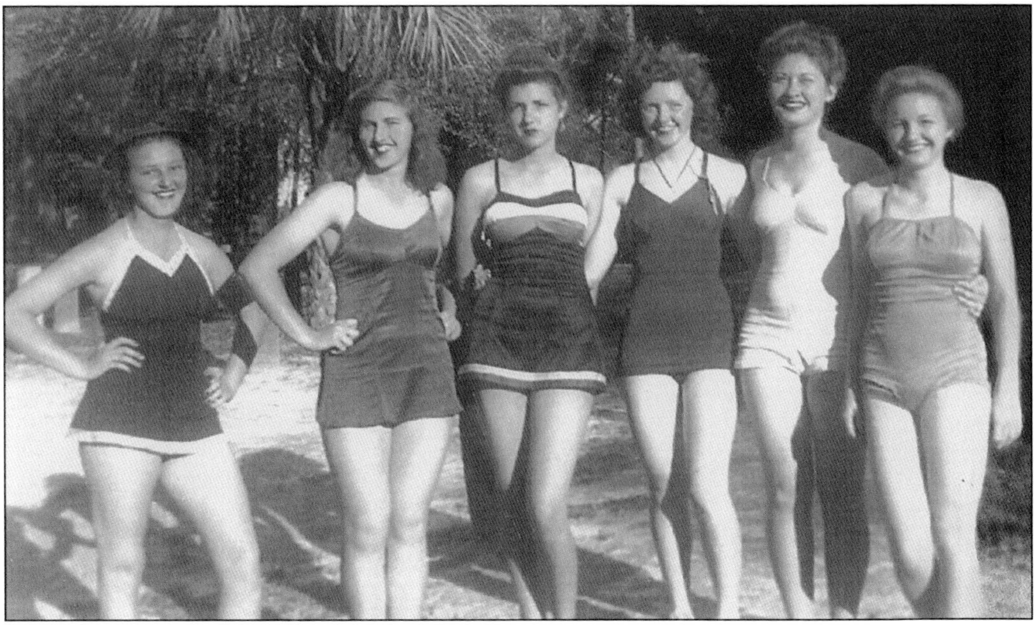

In 1943, the Lyman High girls basketball team celebrated the year at Sanlando Springs. From left to right are Lib Jackson, Muriel Prescott, Frances Farina, Eddie Meetze, Lois Walker, and June North.

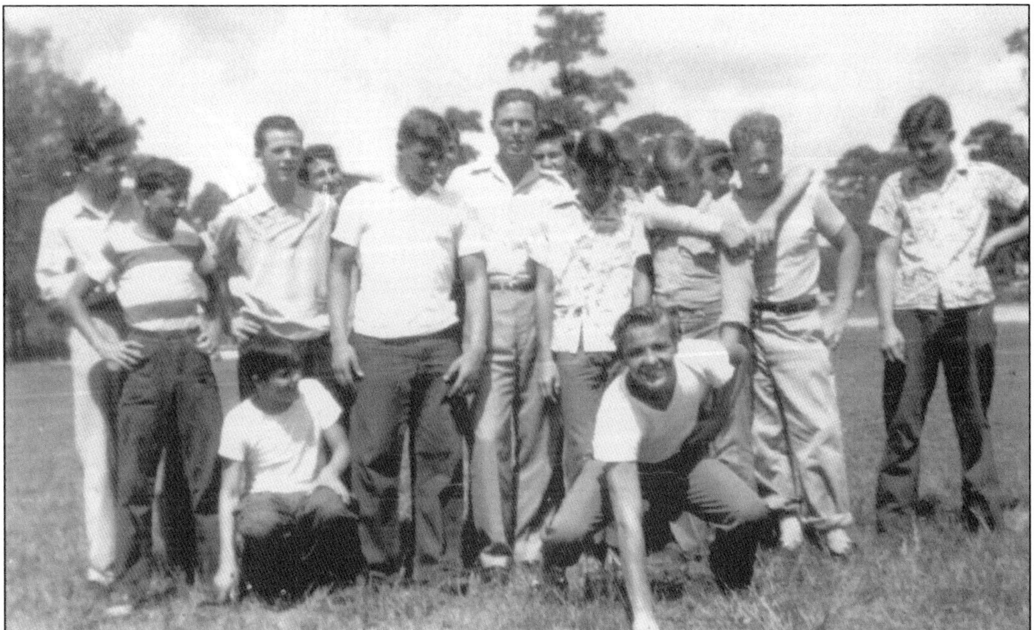

Coach Jim Payne is shown with his 1947–1948 Lyman High football team.

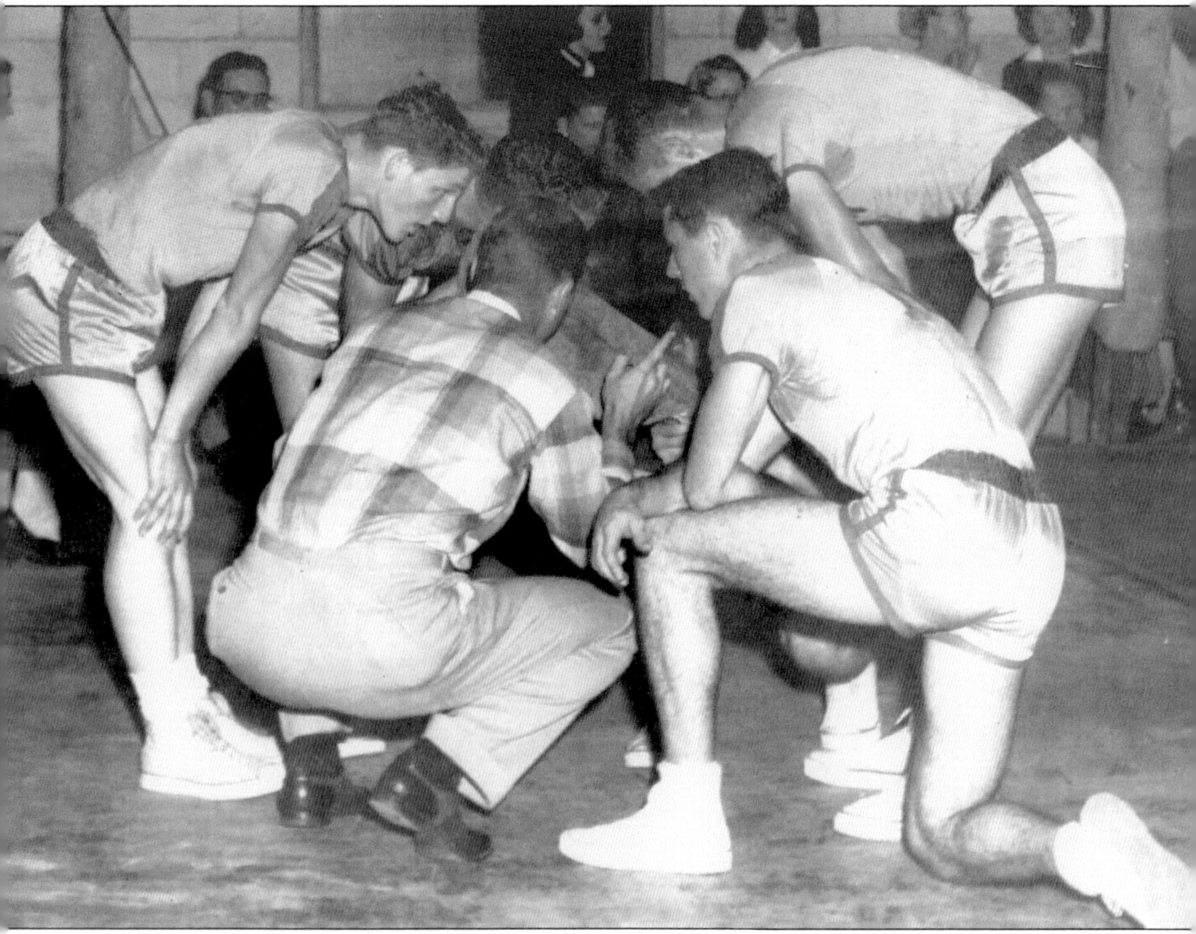

Coach Jim Payne huddles with the 1957 Lyman boys basketball team during a game against Oviedo. Jim's mother, Blanche Payne, ran the Longwood Post Office that adjoined his father's grocery store on Church Avenue between the railroad depot and what is today County Road 427. The family lived in an apartment above the store. Lester R. Payne, Jim's father, later added a hardware store. Jim Payne, a Lyman graduate, was 22 in 1942 when he graduated from Stetson University in DeLand. He would spend that summer waiting for orders from the U.S. Army. He had enlisted as an aviation cadet. After the war, he returned to Longwood and taught science and biology at Lyman. He also coached baseball, football, and basketball teams until he retired.

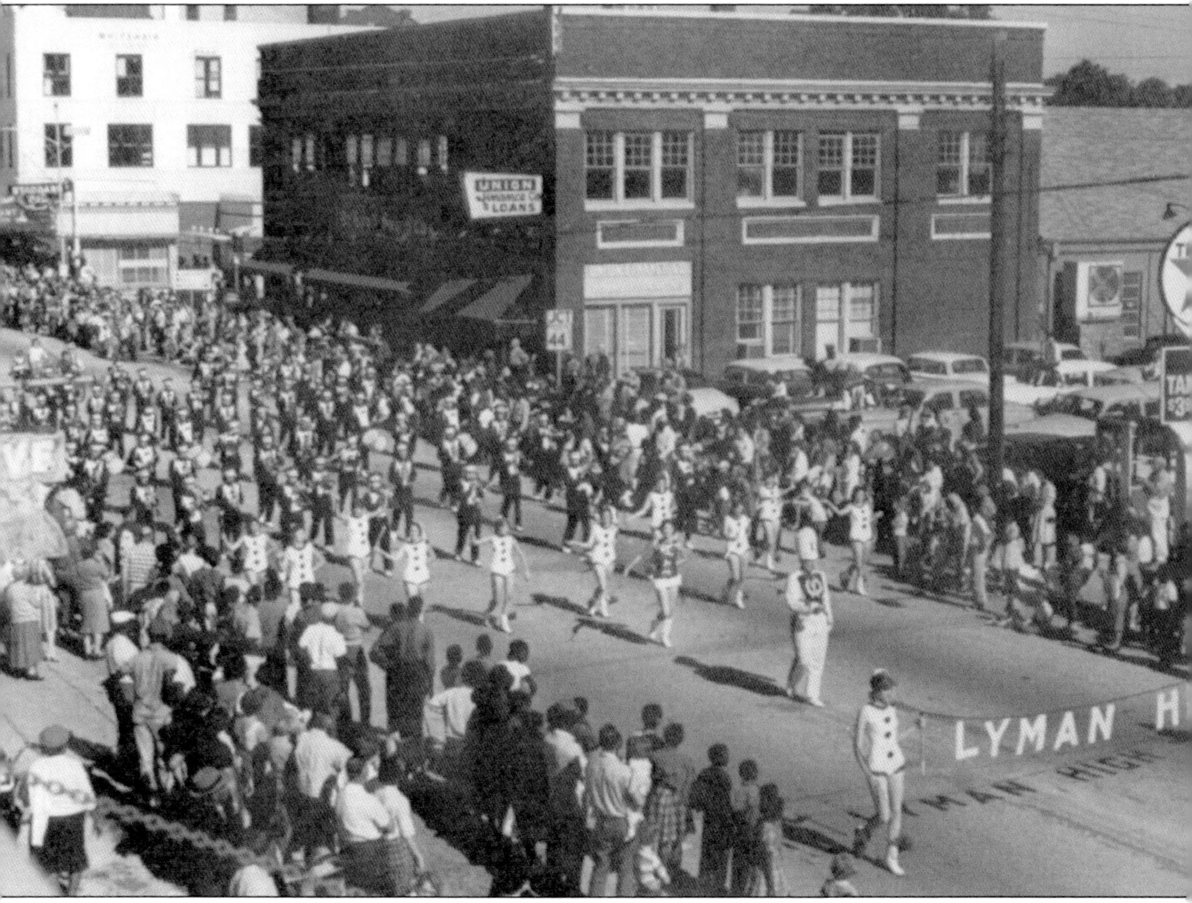

The Lyman High marching band is shown here in a 1962 parade along Sanford's First Street.

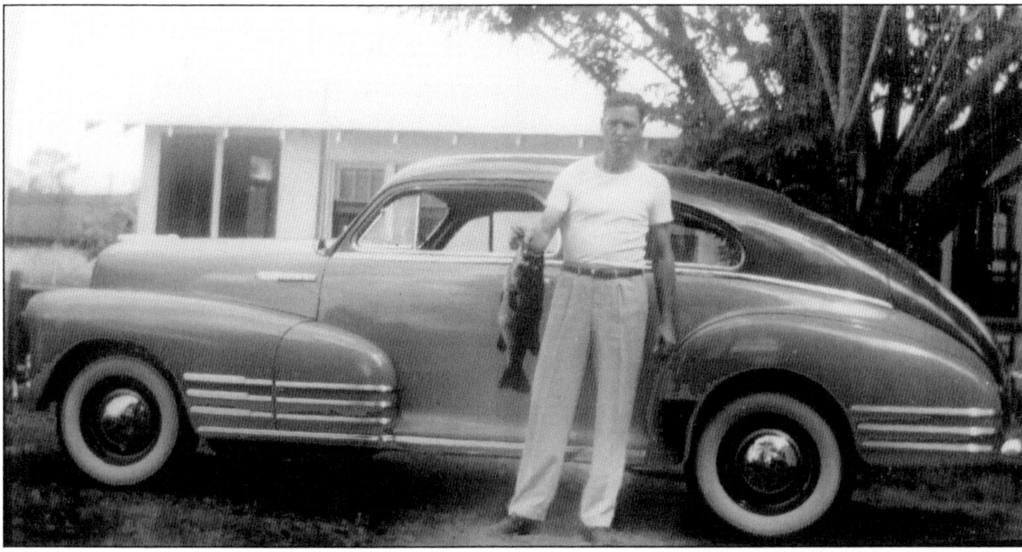

Jim Payne stands with his 1948 Chevy. An avid fisherman, Jim frequently fished in the many lakes in the region as well as in the Wekiva River.

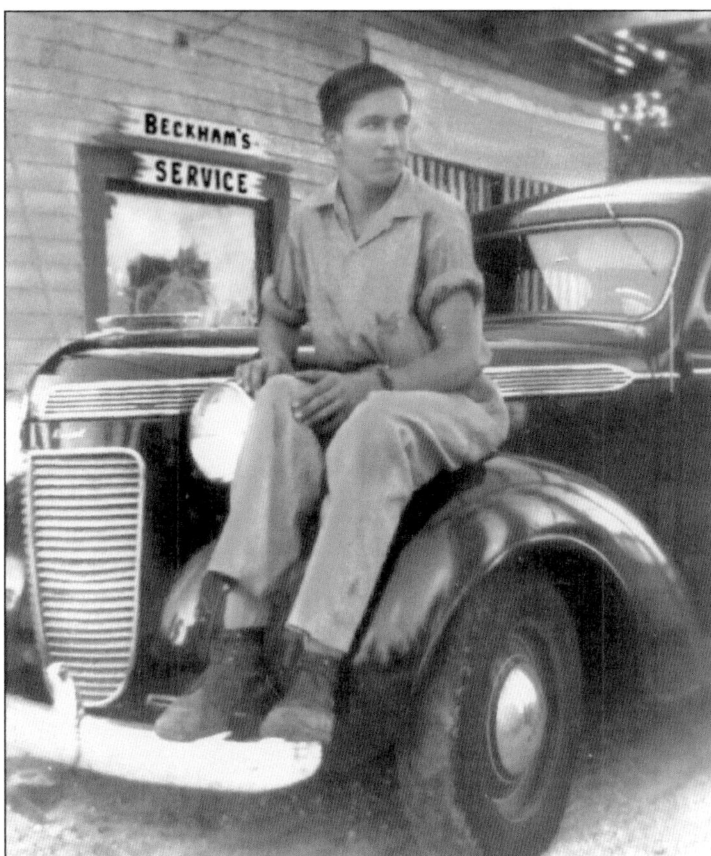

Frank Beckham, shown in this May 10, 1944 photograph, sits on his family's car at Beckham's Service Station.

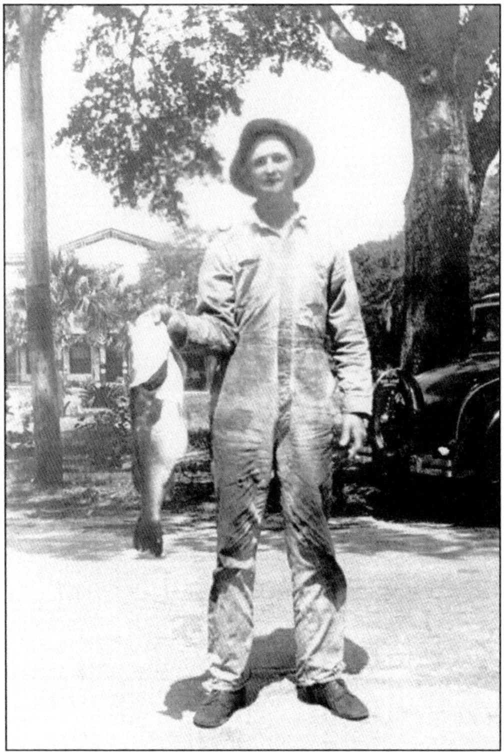

Frank Beckham Sr. with his catch of the day stands near his garage on County Road 427. Behind him is the Longwood hotel.

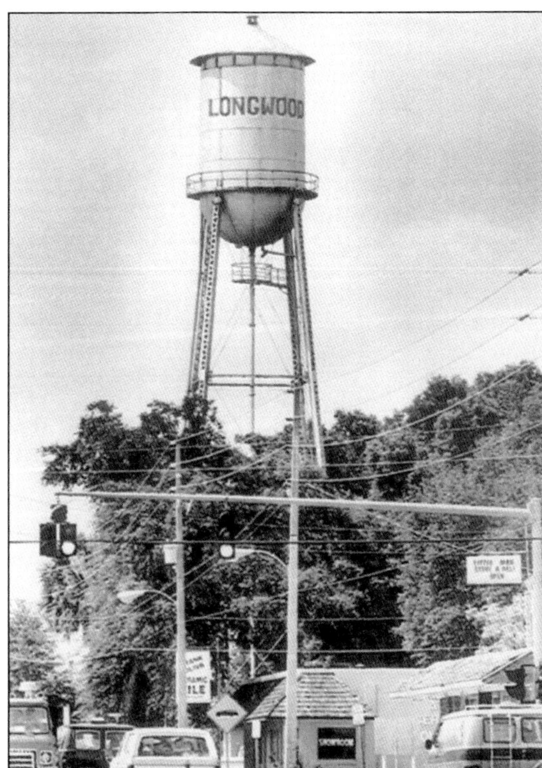

Long a landmark of the city, the Longwood water tower could be seen from miles away until it was taken down in the early 1980s.

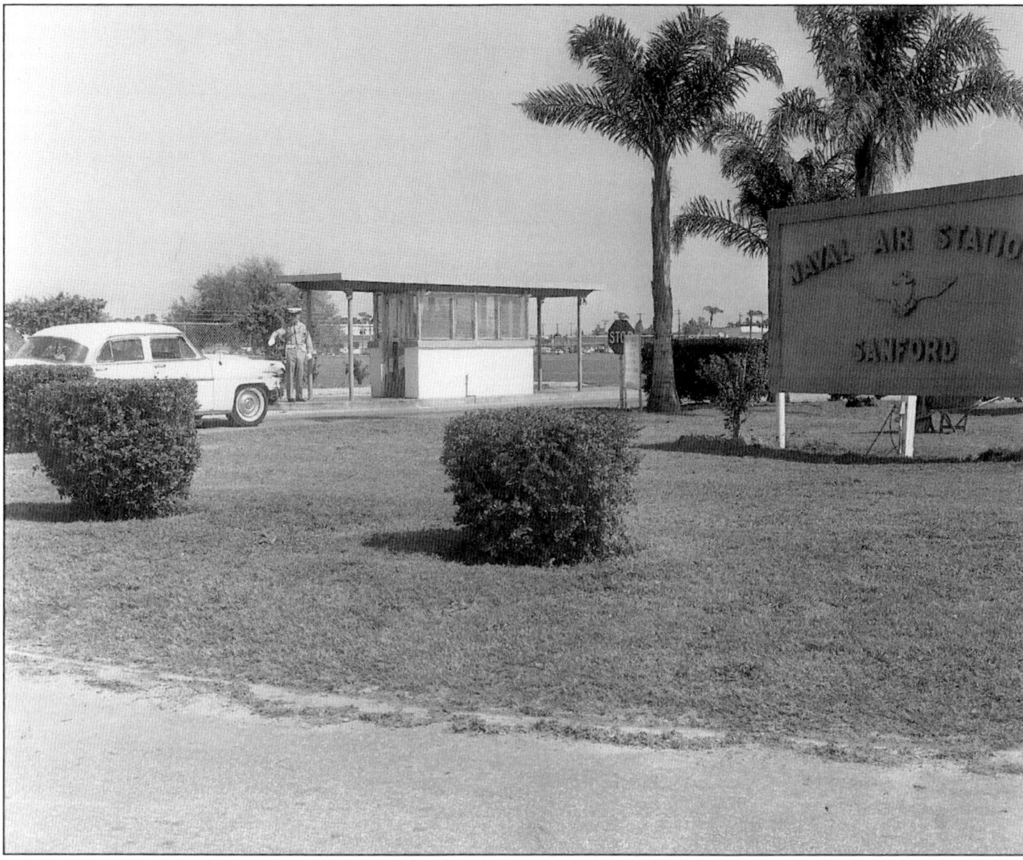

Many of the World War II Navy pilots who landed on aircraft carriers trained at the Sanford Naval Air Station near Longwood. Many of their families would return to Longwood after the war to buy homes. The navy base, now an international airport, remained an important part of the community during the 1950s and 1960s. During the Korean War, the airport became a jet base. Anyone who lived in Sanford and Longwood in the 1960s remembers the noisy Vigilante, shown below.

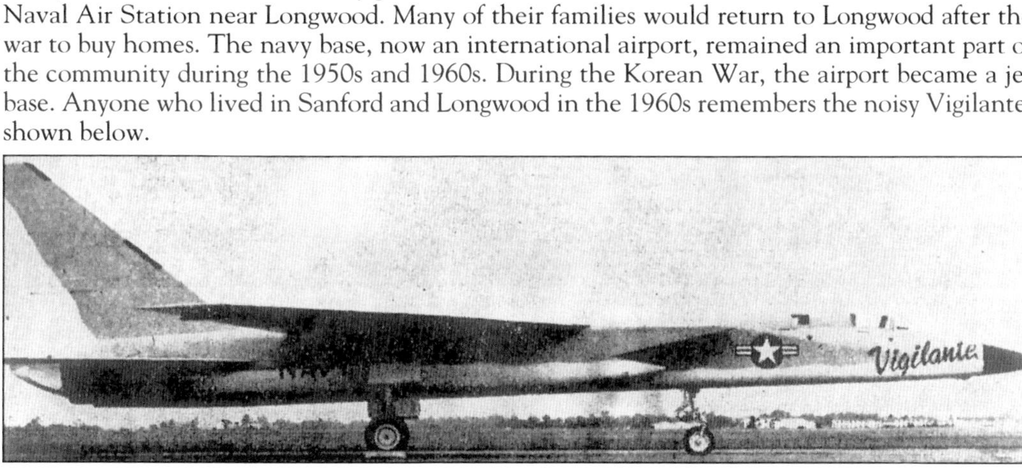

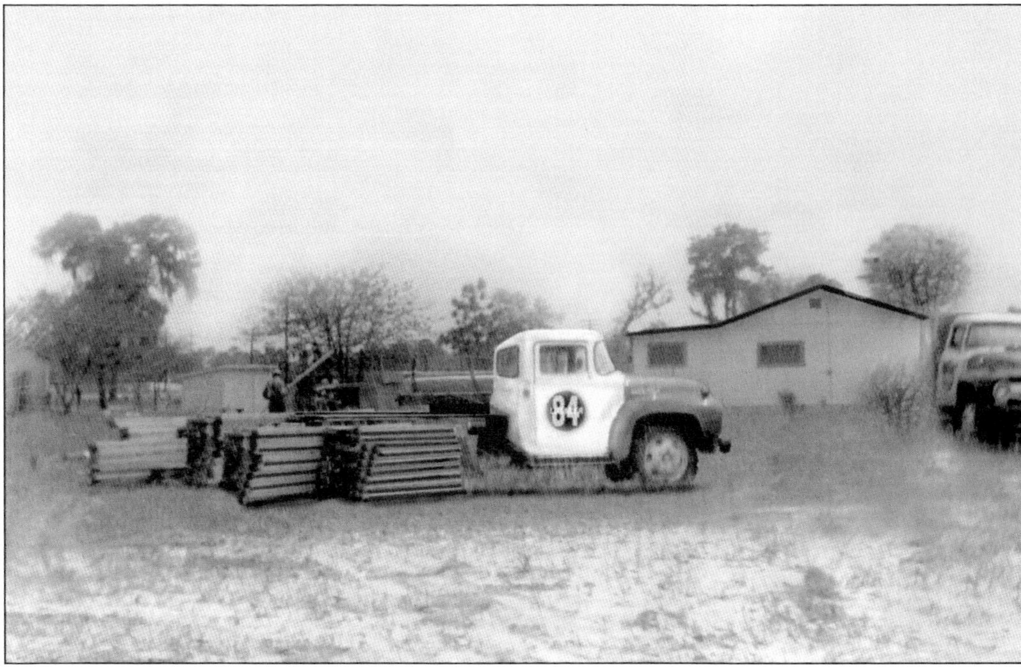

Crews from Jim Walters Homes deliver building supplies for the home of Forest "Barney" Barnes at 825 Second Place. The house, shown below, was built in 1957 and is one of many Jim Walters Homes constructed in Longwood's residential areas that grew up after World War II.

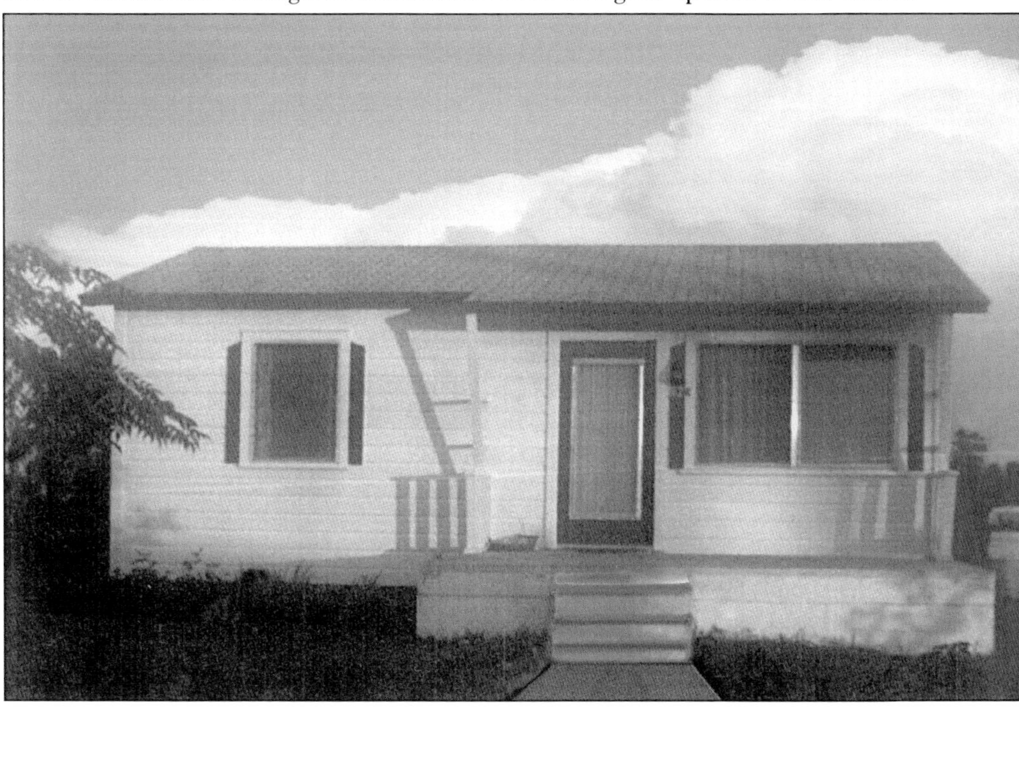

Dr. and Mrs. Burmaster, who lived on Lake Wildmere, opened their hearts and home to those in need in the Central Florida area.

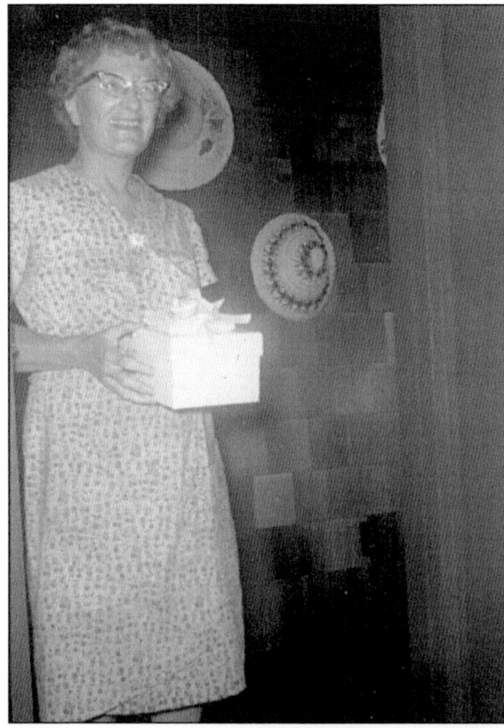

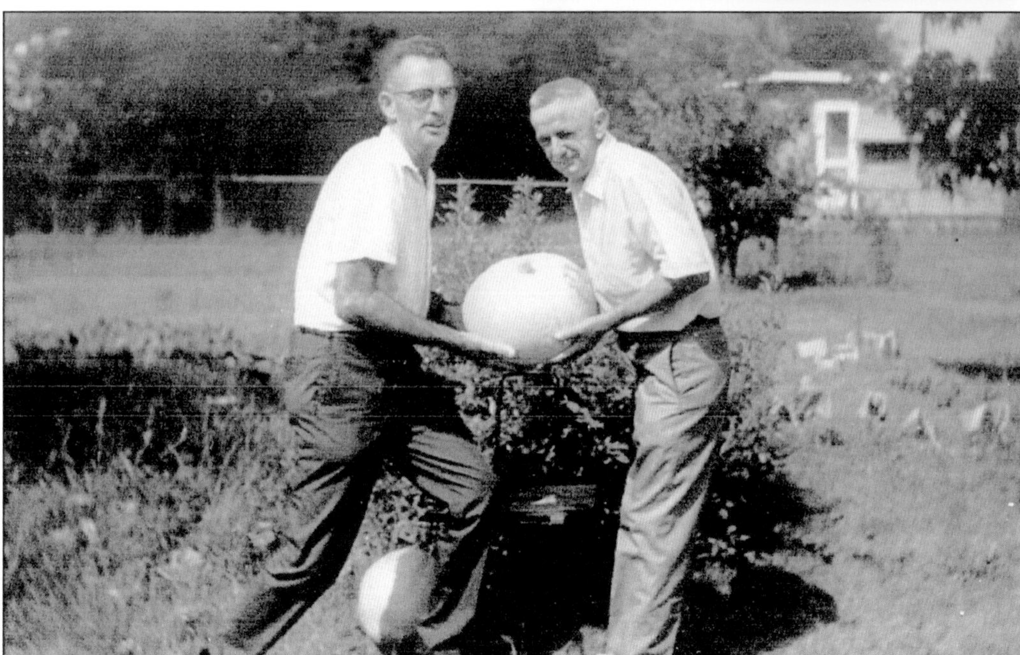

Ben Carson of New Hampshire with neighbor Barney Barnes show off a huge pumpkin that grew from a seed scattered from a bird and squirrel feeder at the Carson's winter home on Second Place. Carson brought the seeds from their Penacook, New Hampshire garden when they made their winter visits to Florida. Their home was among many built in the 1940s in the Entzmingers addition to Longwood.

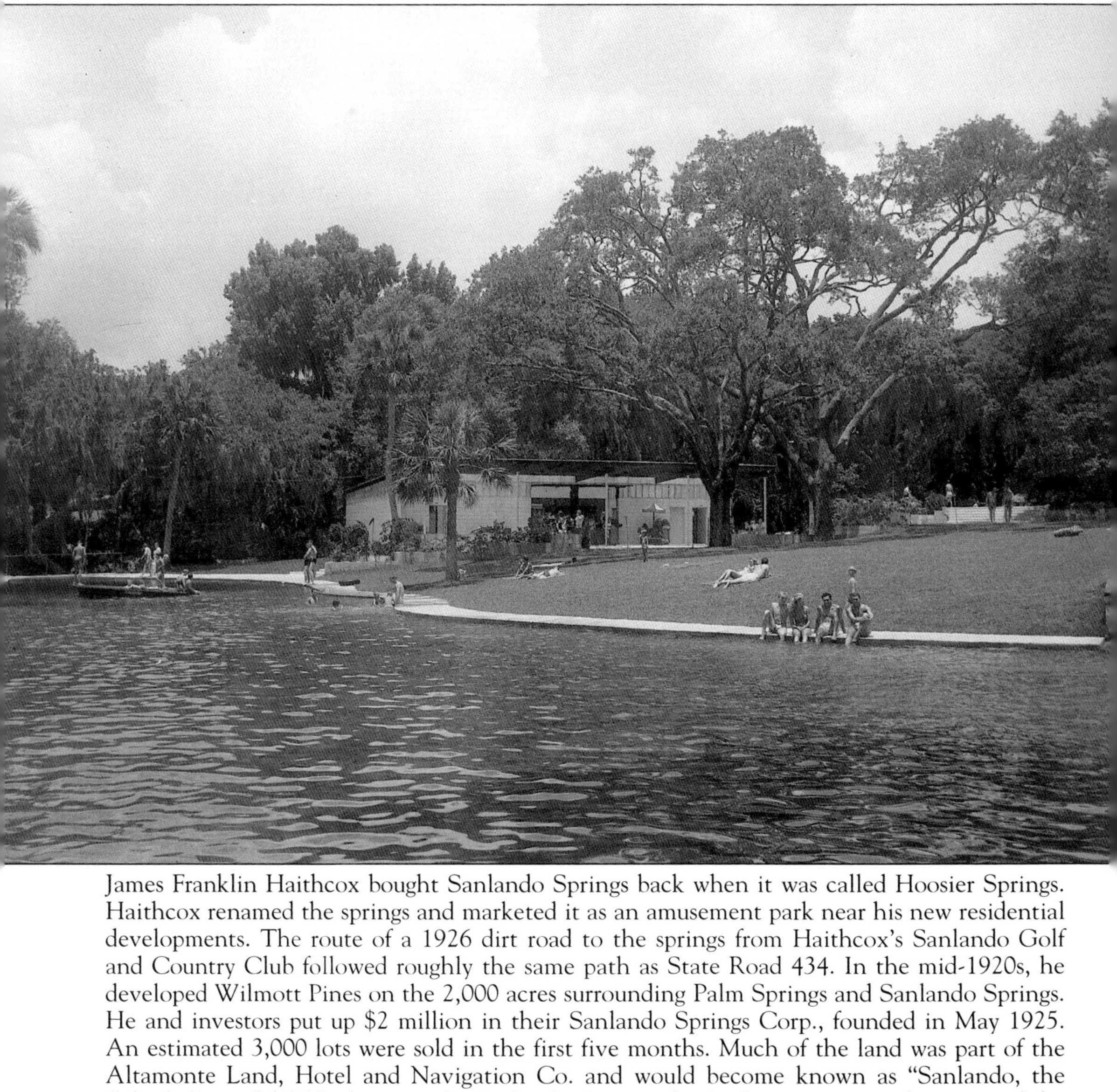

James Franklin Haithcox bought Sanlando Springs back when it was called Hoosier Springs. Haithcox renamed the springs and marketed it as an amusement park near his new residential developments. The route of a 1926 dirt road to the springs from Haithcox's Sanlando Golf and Country Club followed roughly the same path as State Road 434. In the mid-1920s, he developed Wilmott Pines on the 2,000 acres surrounding Palm Springs and Sanlando Springs. He and investors put up $2 million in their Sanlando Springs Corp., founded in May 1925. An estimated 3,000 lots were sold in the first five months. Much of the land was part of the Altamonte Land, Hotel and Navigation Co. and would become known as "Sanlando, the Suburb Beautiful." Haithcox made Sanlando Springs the leading attraction for some of the best communities in Central Florida. During these boom times, Haithcox bought more tracts from the springs southeast to his Altamonte development. Much of the land came from the Overstreet Investment Co., which mortgaged it to him in April 1925 for $120,000, then considered a pricey sum. Haithcox gave Calvin O. Black of Cleveland 400 lots to build an 18-hole golf course and clubhouse. Rollins College president Hamilton Holt joined the club, and Rollins students played on the golf course. Moses Overstreet was forced to repossess Sanlando Springs Tropical Park after the boom busted, and Haithcox lost interest in his developments. The park reopened, and visitors came to see the park's addition of more than 10,000 azalea plants in 1935. The park also offered swimming lessons and weekly aquatic shows. The Marchand family put on professional log rolling contests and demonstrations in 1941. After dark, the pavilion at Sanlando Springs opened for dances that drew many young people in the 1940s.

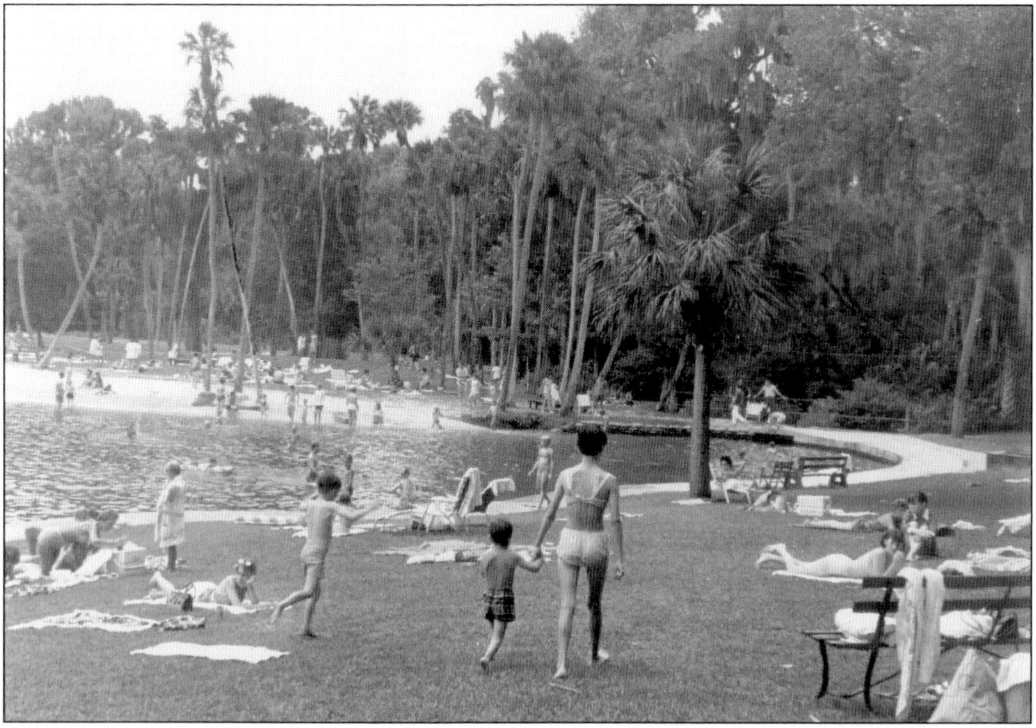

Once a private recreation park, Sanlando Springs drew crowds from the early 1900s through the end of the 1960s. This 1968 scene shows the popularity of the springs.

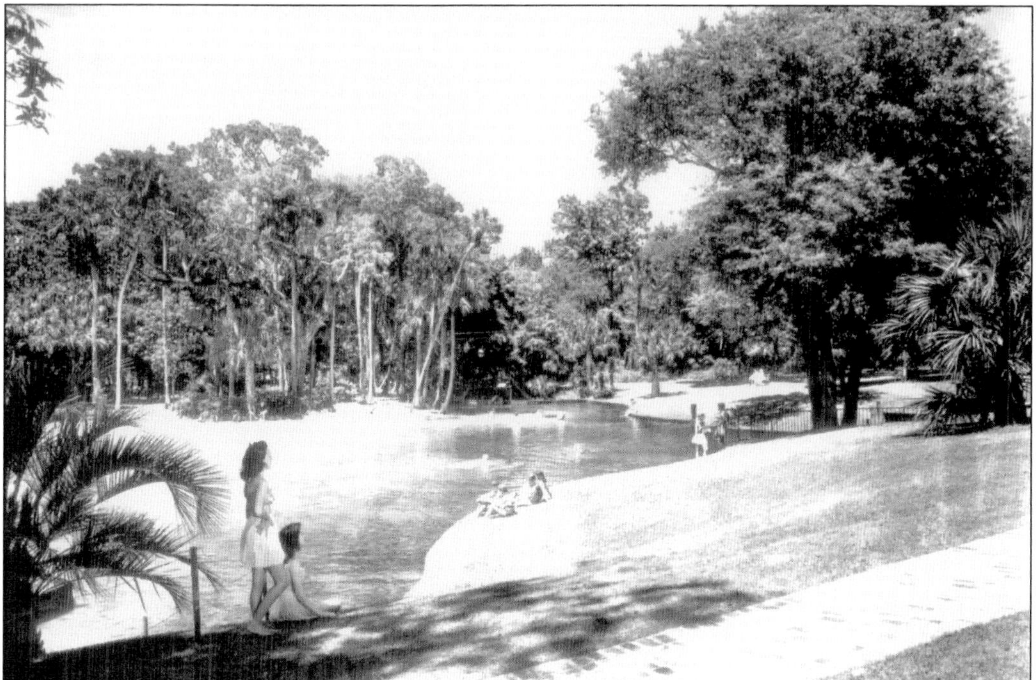

This picture-perfect scene of Sanlando Springs was taken in the mid- to late 1940s and has been used in many advertisements and postcards.

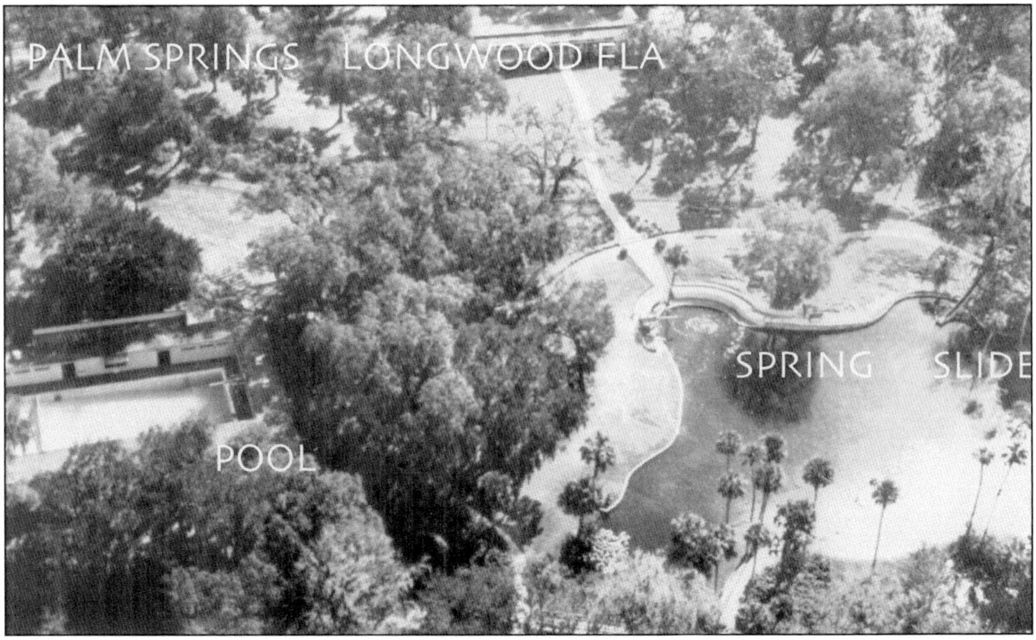

This overview shows the main attractions at Sanlando Springs. James Franklin Haithcox built a dam to raise the water level, landscaped the shoreline with tropical plants, and added a swimming pool and bathhouse. This property would become Sanlando Springs Tropical Park. The Sanlando swimming pool, the first in the area, opened in April 1926.

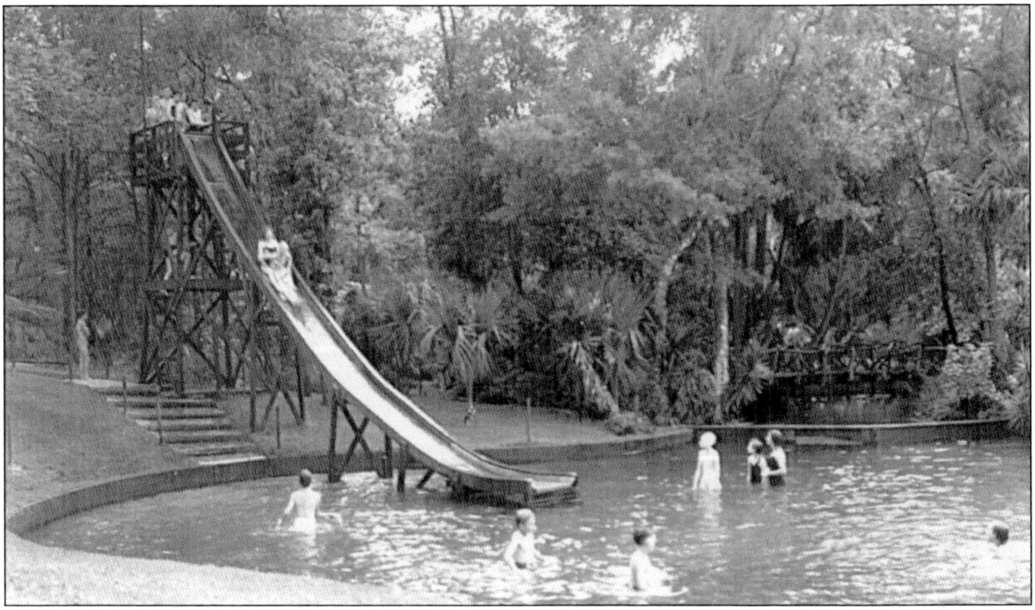

For at least three generations, young people and families enjoyed Sanlando Springs and its slide into cool, clear water. In the 1930s, when Sanlando Springs drew large crowds on the weekends as families searched for relief closer than Daytona Beach's shores, a newspaper advertised, "It's fun to be cooled swimming in fresh, clear spring water." Sanlando Springs had the best waterslide in Central Florida. Hour after hour, kids could climb the steps of a giant slide and scream their heads off before splashing into the spring waters.

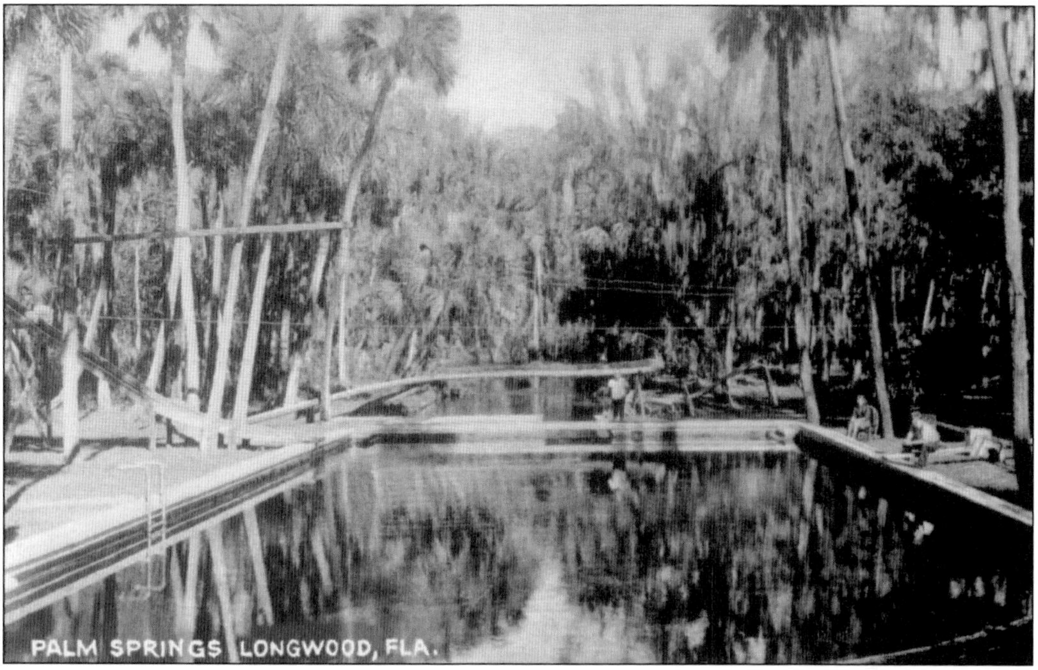

Palm Springs, the pool at Sanlando Springs, is shown here. One dollar was all it cost to get into Sanlando Springs on a hot Saturday in the 1960s. That dollar stretched a long way. There was shade under the trees and the pavilion and tables for picnics. A youngster with a few extra coins could eat at the snack bar or play the pinball games in the clubhouse. The large pool had three diving boards.

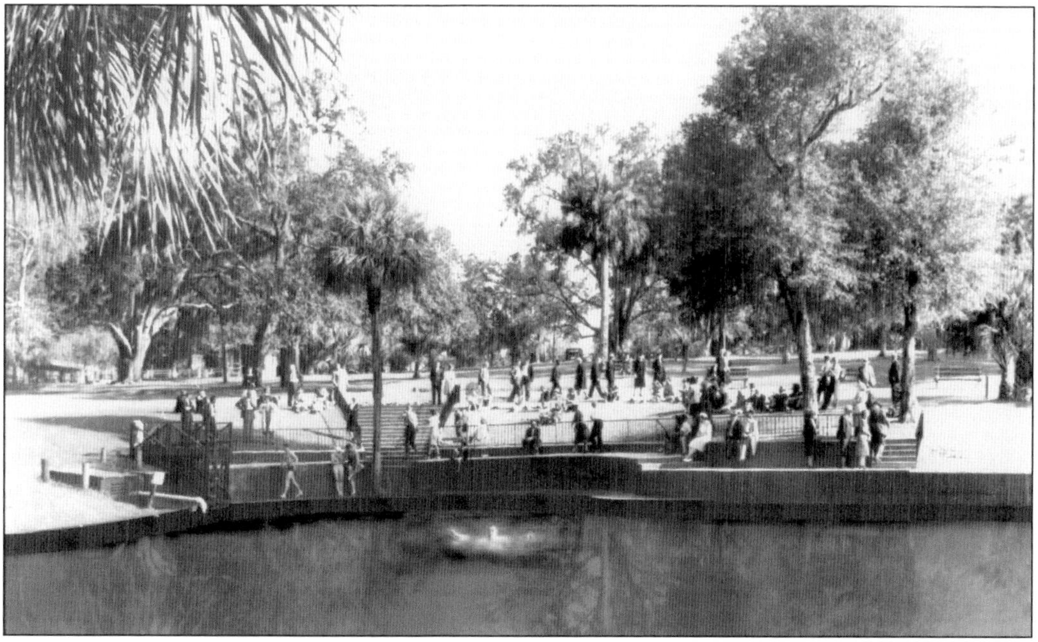

This scene shows the wall built around the south side of the deepest part of the springs. Teenagers and families gathered by day at the springs and young adults showed up for dances at the pavilion at night. J.E. Robinson owned and ran the park from about 1950 until 1970 when it was one of Central Florida's most popular water parks.

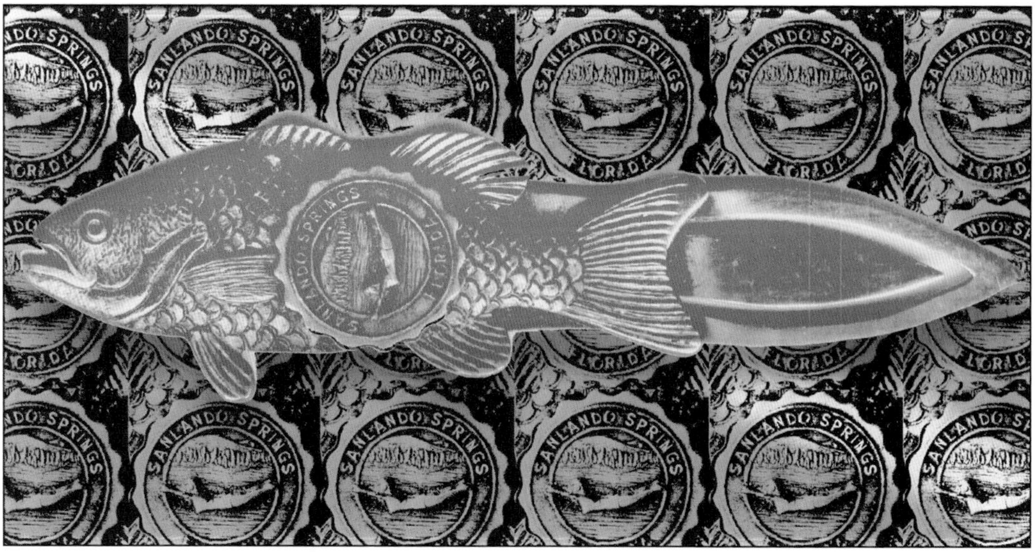

This souvenir bookmark was given away to promote Sanlando Springs and real estate development in the area. Sanlando Springs closed to the public in 1970 when it became a gated community. Developers in the early 1970s turned the 350 acres of rolling forest and crystal-clear waters that feed into the Little Wekiva River into home sites known as The Springs.

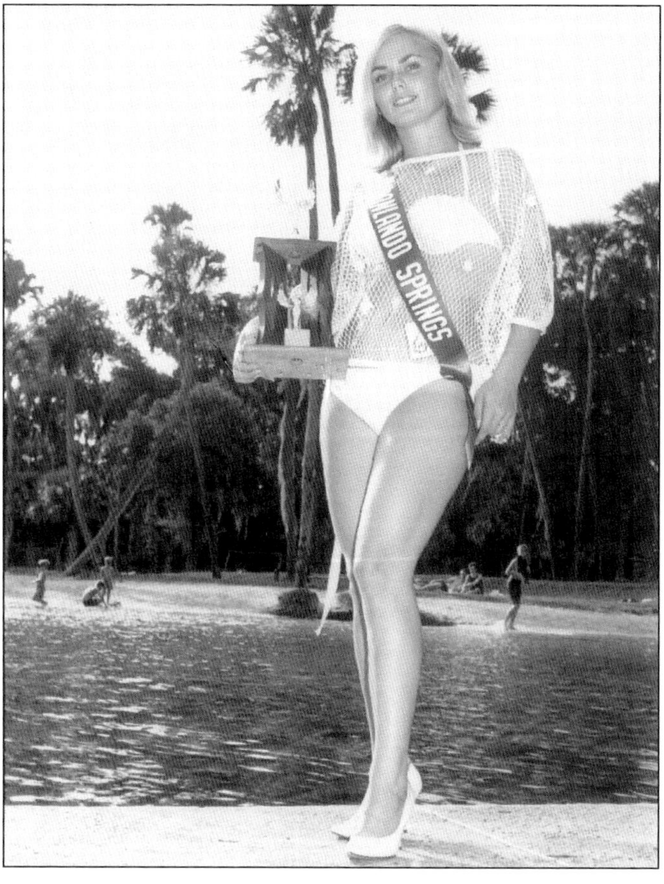

Sanlando Springs was the site of many beauty pageants. This is Jackie LeTellier of Holly Hill, Miss Sanlando Springs in 1965.

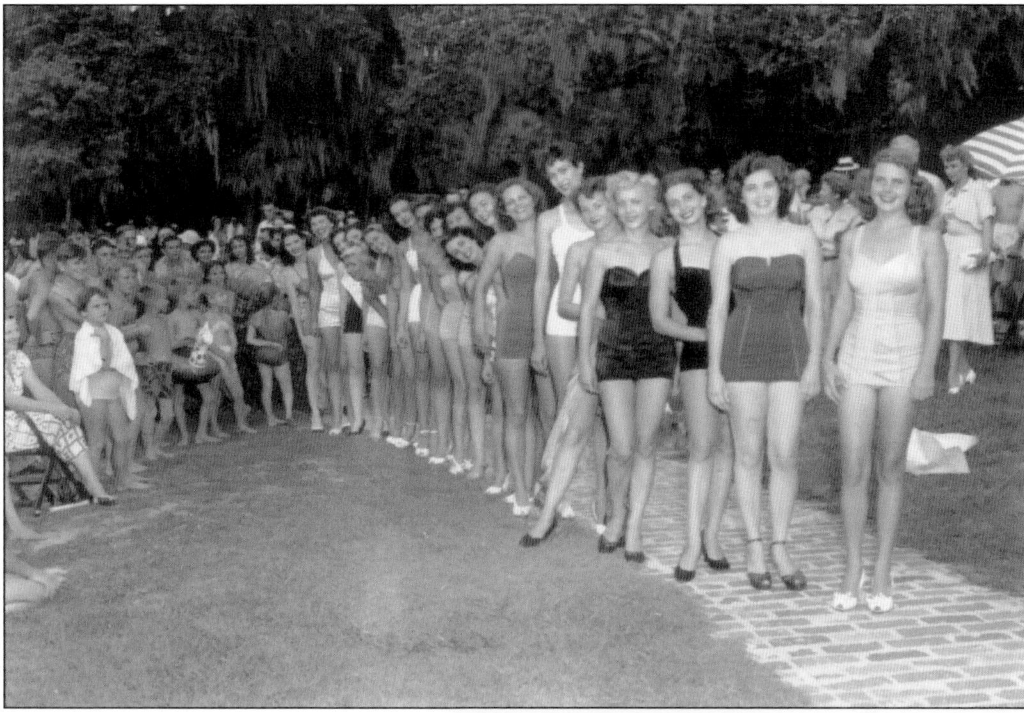

The 1951 contestants for Mrs. Sanlando Springs are pictured above. The winner, Peggy Creel, is third from the front.

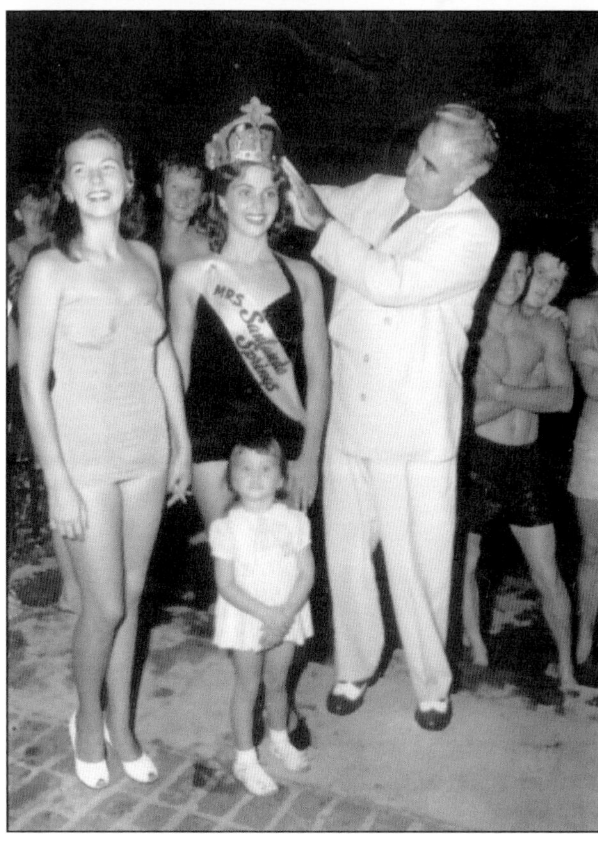

Peggy Creel was crowned Mrs. Sanlando Springs of 1951. Shown with her are her daughter Vicky and the runner-up, Carol Lee.

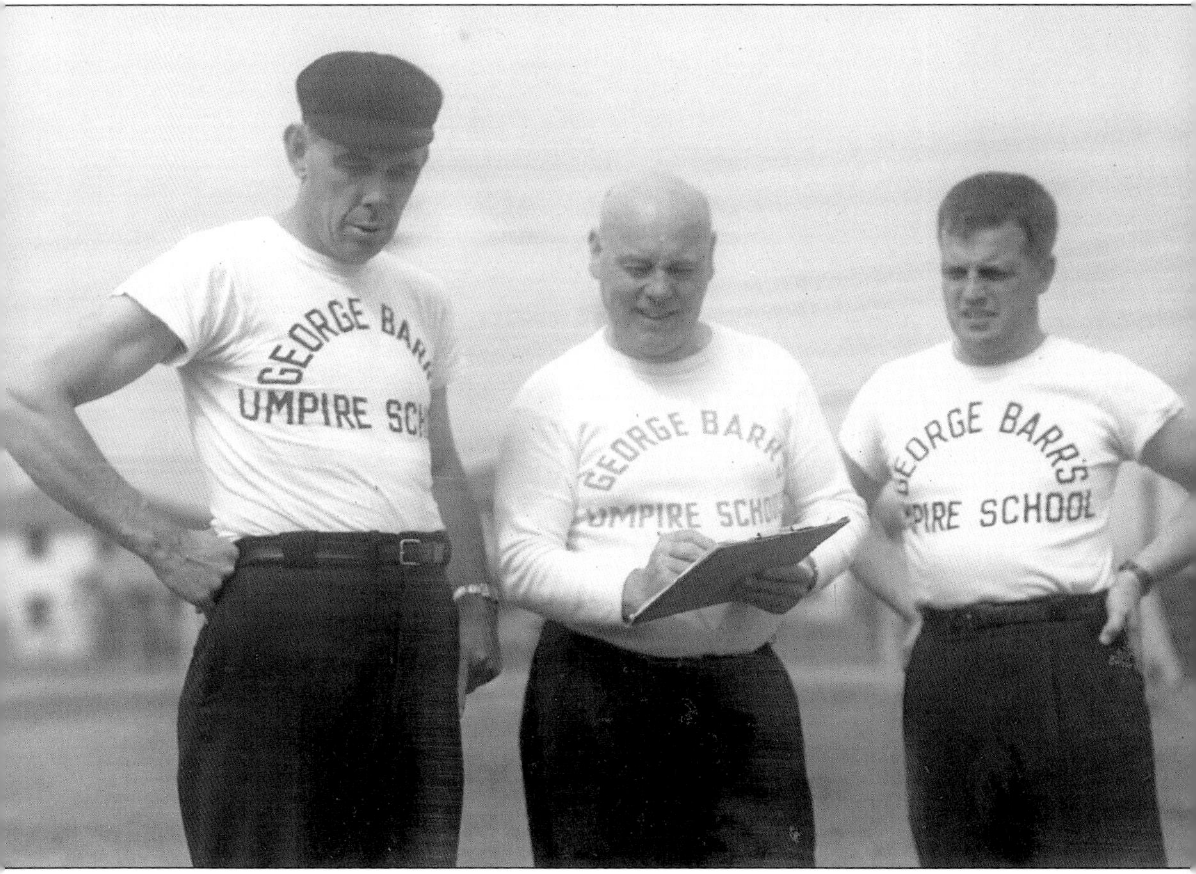

During the 1950s, baseball umpire George Barr (center) ran an umpire school in Longwood. Gene Bothell (right) and Ward Mohs (left) are pictured here with Barr on the grounds of the Longwood Hotel.

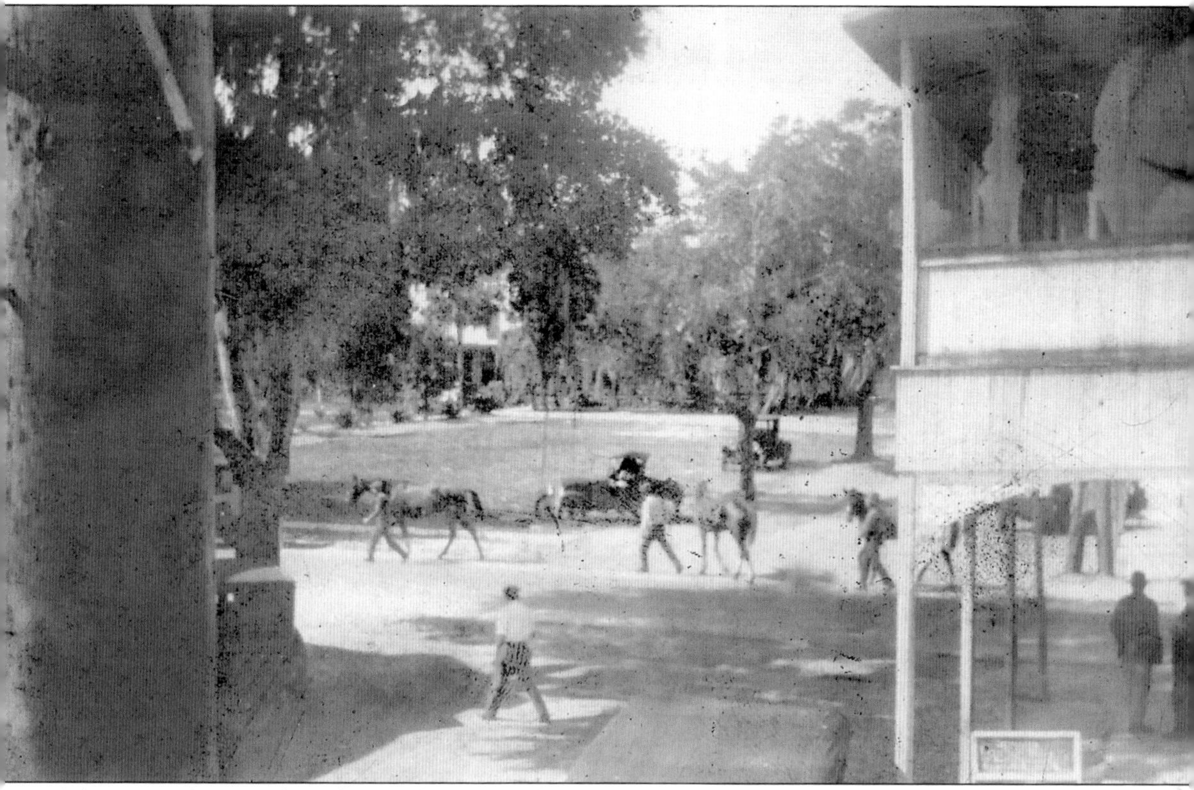

A horse track opened southeast of Longwood, in what is now part of Casselberry, as a flat track offering betting in the 1920s. Racehorses were brought to Longwood by rail during the winter and kept at the grounds on the track. This photo shows horses being lead through Longwood in 1926. The track later was used for harness racing and is now a dog track.

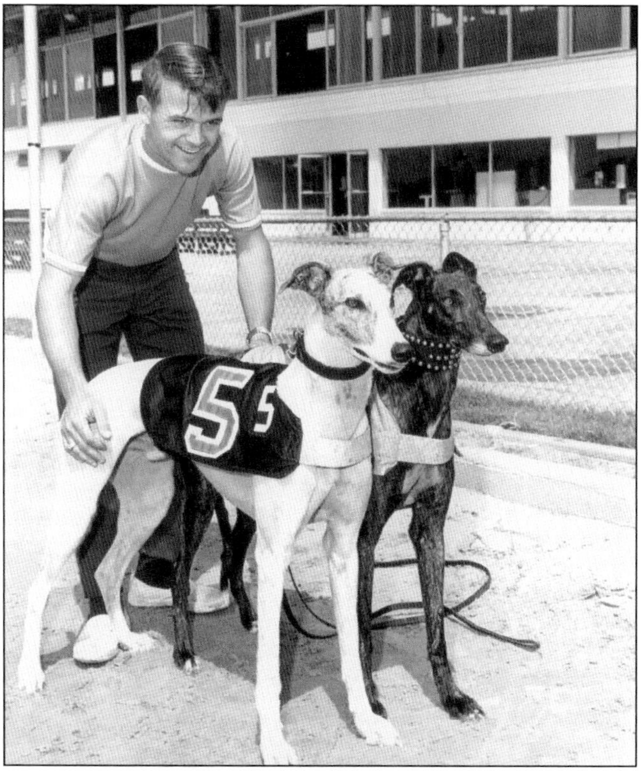

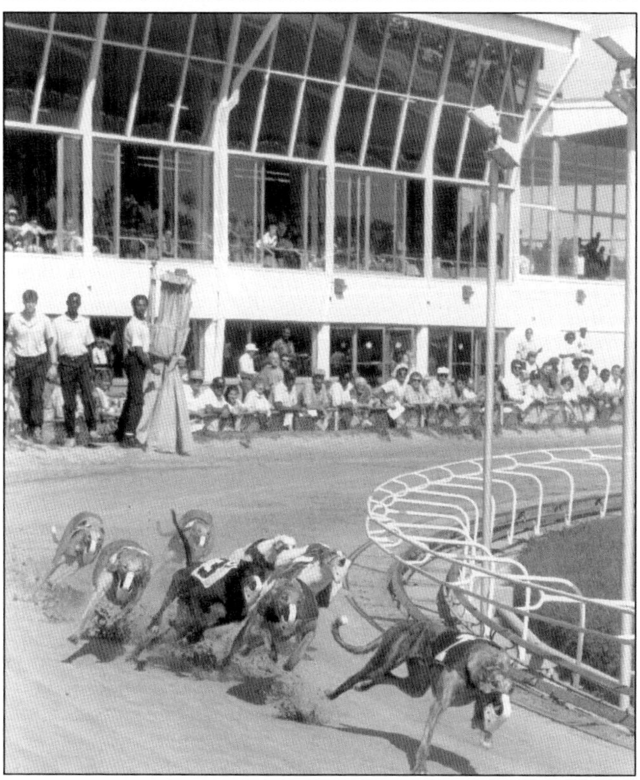

Greyhound racing has been a tourist attraction in Longwood since the 1930s. Shown above are two racing dogs and their trainer, Danny Williams, in 1972. Below is a 1992 scene of greyhounds making the turn in front of the grandstands.

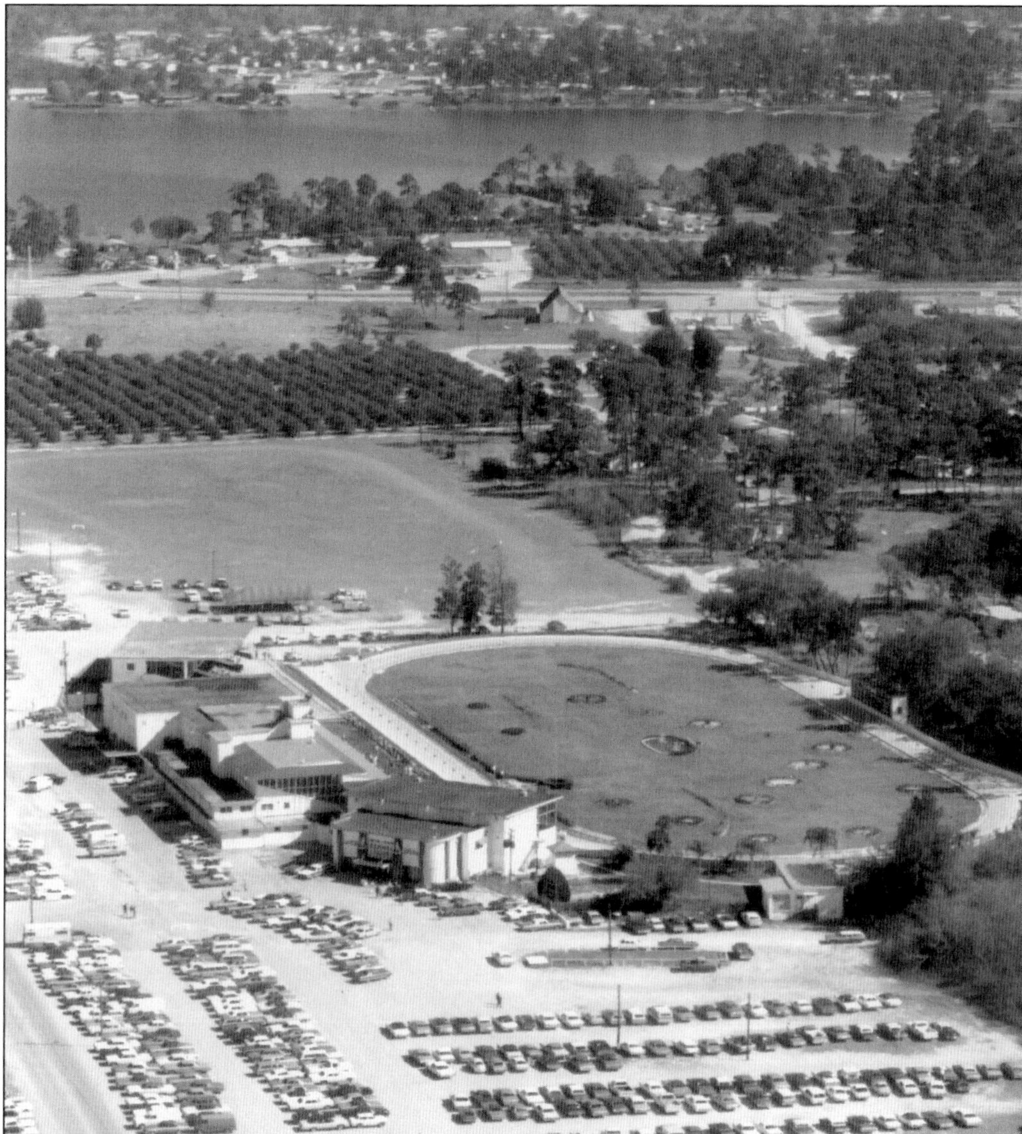

The Sanford Orlando Kennel Club opened in 1935, and the track has been owned by the Collins family since 1954. The family has owned and managed other tracks in Florida since the late 1920s. Jerry Collins, a former policeman, state legislator, and motorcycle stunt man, started the family business. U.S. Highway 17-92 is visible in the background.

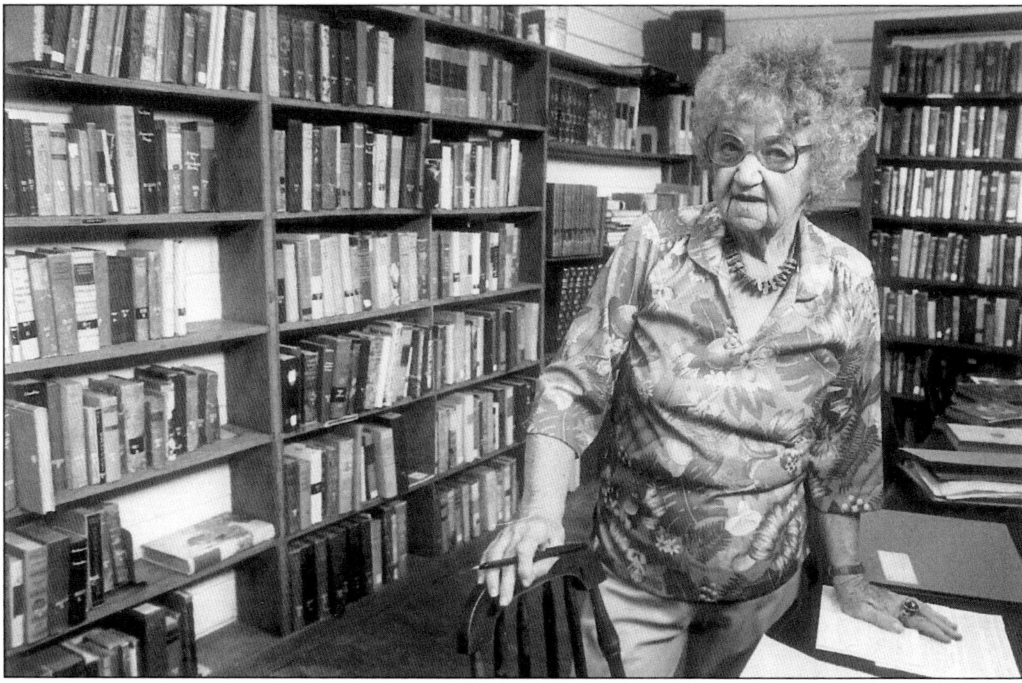

Maxine McGrath's father purchased the Longwood Hotel in 1922, when cattle still roamed the streets of Longwood, and Maxine lived at the hotel from 1922 until 1947. She loved Longwood and the library at the Woman's Civic League building, pictured here.

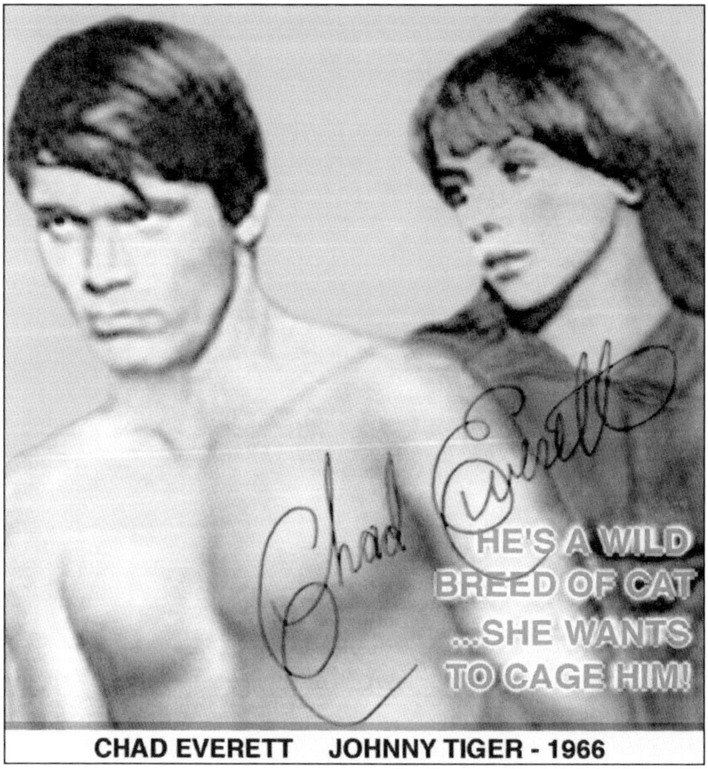

Chad Everett, who signed his autograph for Areva Barnes of Longwood, played an alligator wrestler in the movie, *Johnny Tiger*, but a stunt actor, a Seminole from Okeechobee, performed the wrestling stunts. In the movie, Robert Taylor, a teacher, befriends Everett, cast as a "promising half-breed Seminole in Florida." The storyline involves Taylor joining the Seminoles' struggles on an Everglades reservation.

Four

PRESERVING ARCHITECTURAL TREASURES

In the early 1970s, the Central Florida Society for Historical Preservation (CFSHP) saved two of Seminole County's best-known historic homes, the Bradlee-McIntyre House and the Inside-Outside House, from booming nearby Altamonte Springs. The structures were moved to land in the newly established Longwood Historic District. Betty Jo McLeod took charge of getting the two homes moved to new sites in Longwood in May 1973 on land donated by Robert and Grace Bradford. The CFSHP pulled together city officials, bankers, developers, real estate companies, and the community in a massive fund-raising effort. When that didn't generate enough money, society members assumed the debt themselves. Pearson and McLeod were also partners in restoring the Clouser Home at 211 West Warren Avenue for an antiques store. "A lot of people helped and contributed," Dottie Pearson says. "So many people have been a part of the Central Florida Society for Historical Preservation that . . . credit should simply be given to the CFSHP."

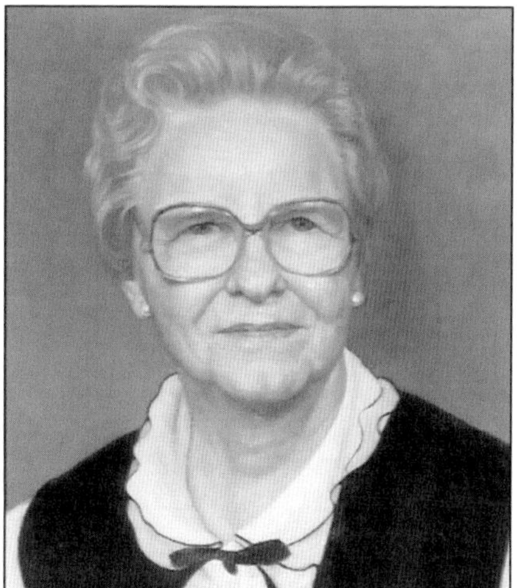

Historic preservationist Grace Bradford saved the dilapidated Longwood Hotel from being razed in 1972 and gave it its present name, the Longwood Village Inn. Since its million-dollar restoration in 1986, the building is used for professional offices.

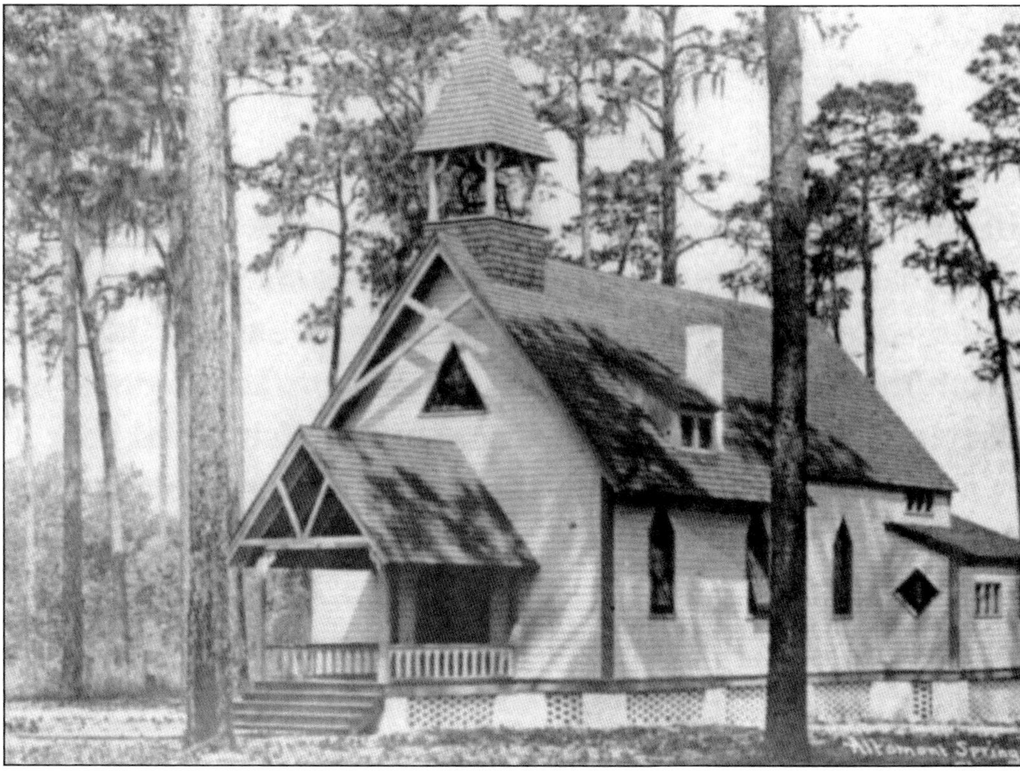

Above is the Lake Brantley Union Chapel in the late 1800s when it was on Lake Brantley, and below is a sketch of the chapel's interior drawn by J.B. Simonsen in 1884. Today the chapel is set back from State Road 436 just east of Maitland Avenue in Altamonte Springs. Josiah B. Clouser built it between 1882 and 1885 as a gift to the community from Bostonian Carlos Cushing. The chapel was abandoned after the Great Freezes of 1894 and 1895. A decade later citrus grower Arthur Fuller and wealthy Bostonian Maxwell McIntyre stumbled on the church in the woods while hunting. They moved it to its present site near Hermit's Trail Park.

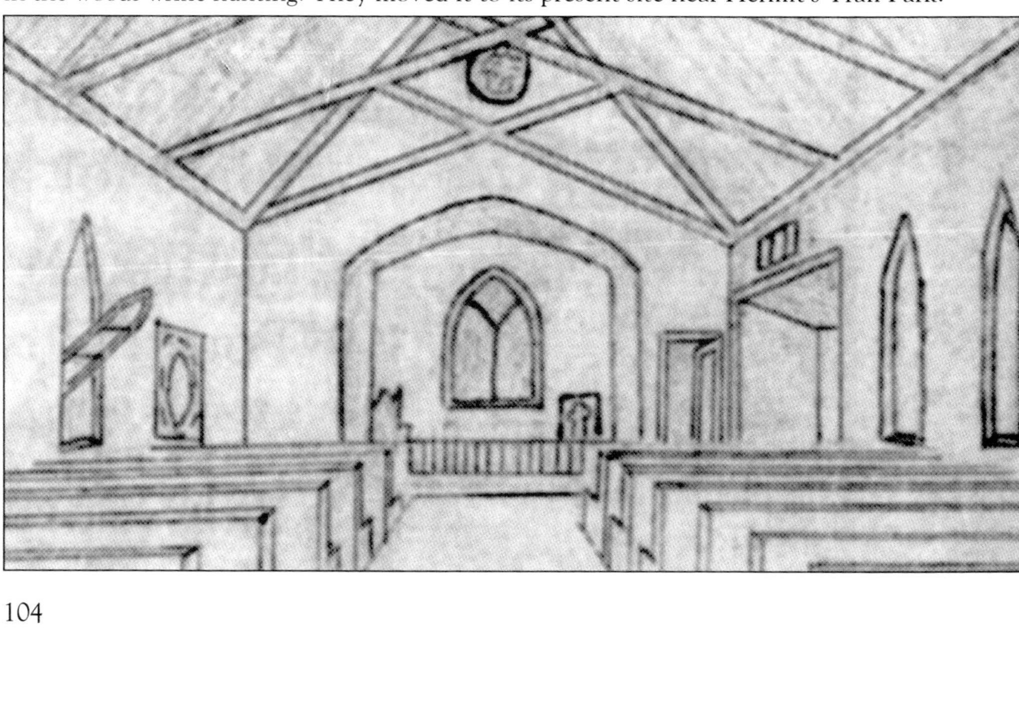

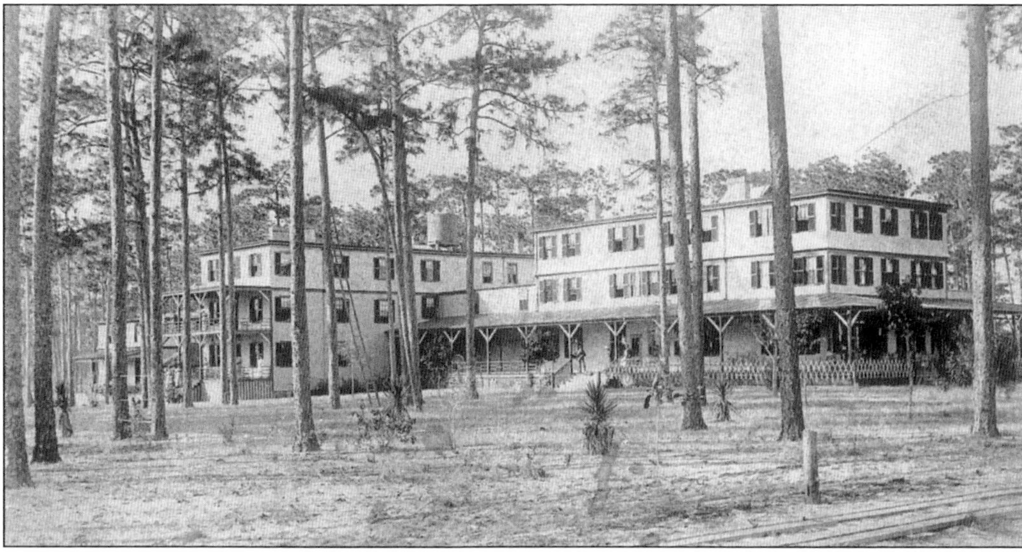

At the same time E.W. Henck was promoting Longwood, his South Florida Railroad brought winter tourists to a resort and winter homes near Lake Orienta and Lake Adelaide. Then known as Snow Station, Altamonte Springs was a popular resort village near the train depot. Boston millionaires bought 1,200 acres along the shore of the spring-fed lakes and built the grand Altamonte Hotel with 130 rooms, 49 fireplaces, and 500 feet of verandas. Winter visitors, including George Westinghouse, came to the sprawling hotel to enjoy the relaxing surroundings and cool water from the nearby springs.

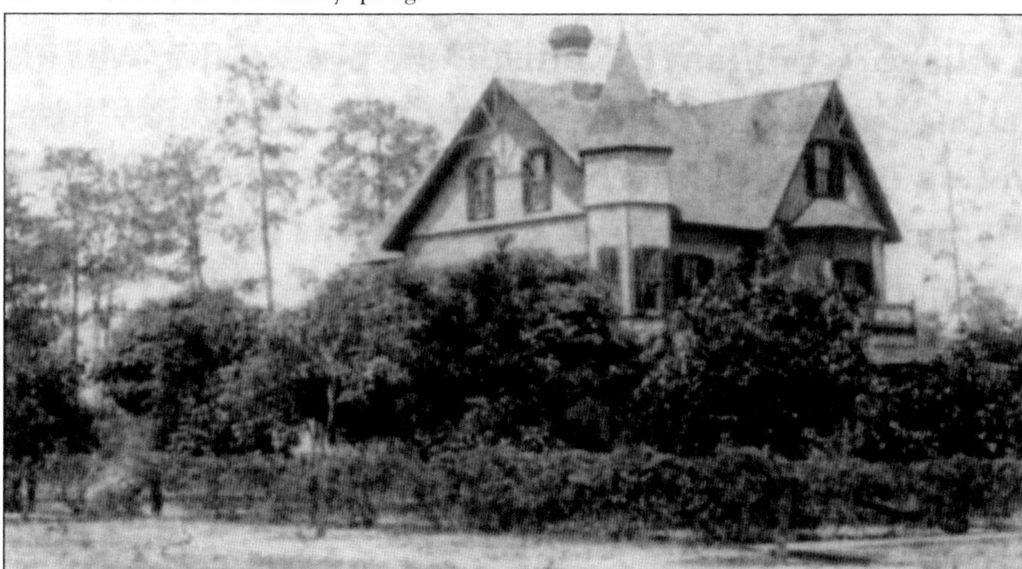

This is the Bradlee-McIntyre House in the late 1800s when many similar winter "cottages" were built for Northerners escaping the cold season back home. Gone is its 14-room Victorian twin, Henry Herman Westinghouse's winter home on Lake Orienta. The Westinghouse home, destroyed by fire in 1930, was a mirror image of the Bradlee-McIntyre House, and they were situated diagonally across from each other at the corner of what today is the intersection of Maitland Avenue and State Road 436. Westinghouse, the youngest brother of noted inventor George Westinghouse, enjoyed the winter climate with other wealthy Northerners.

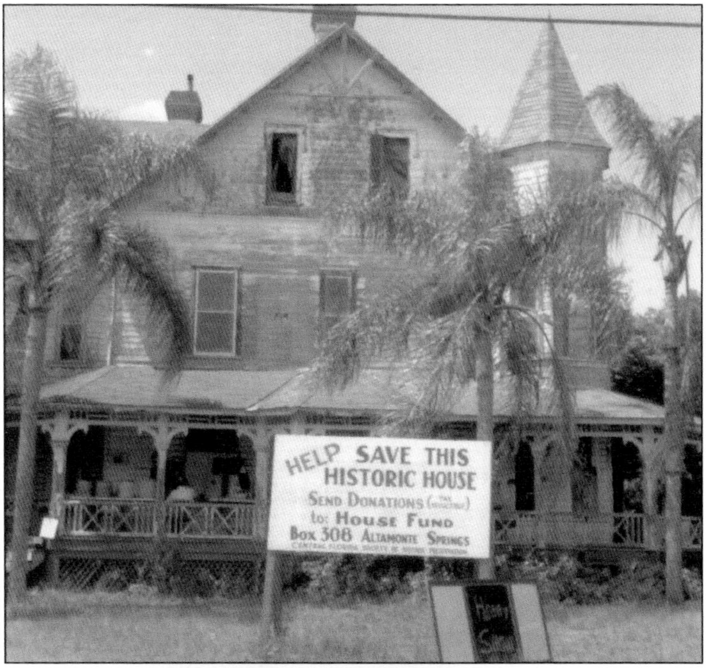

The Bradlee-McIntyre House, shown here in 1972, and the Inside-Outside House are two historic structures saved from Altamonte's suburban sprawl. Many of the city's oldest winter cottages were burned as city-sanctioned practice for firefighters. That same fate was planned for the captain's old home and the 1883 Bradlee-McIntyre House, both now listed as architectural treasures.

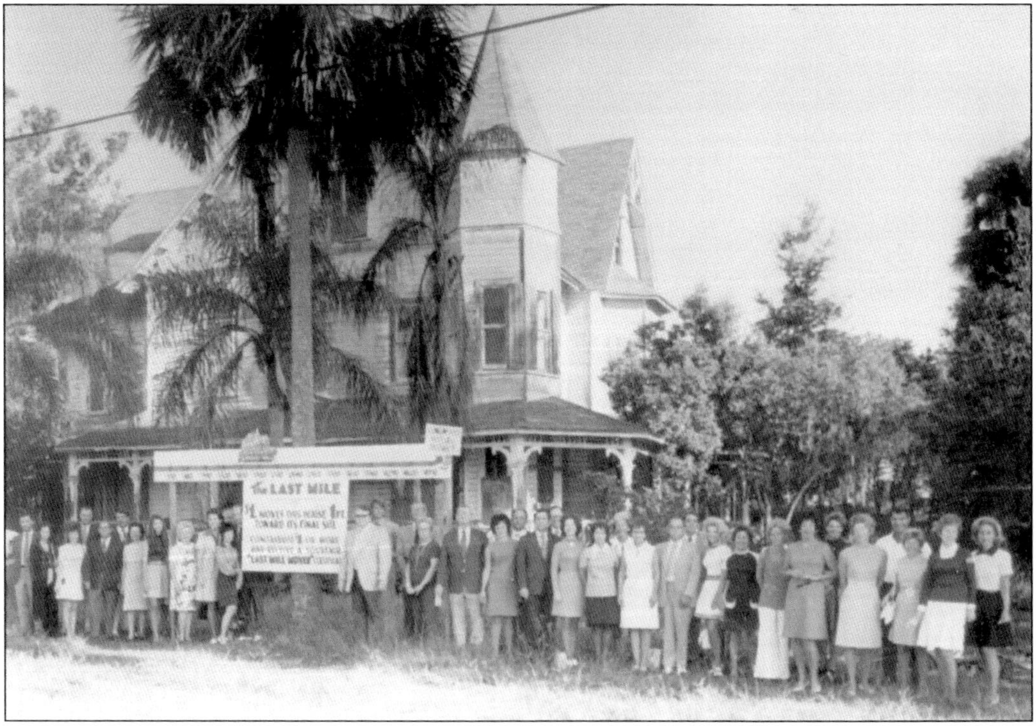

The Central Florida Society for Historical Preservation rallied community support to move the old homes to Longwood's historic district in 1973. The society started The Last Mile Club to raise money for the move. Once standing in the path of progress, the Bradlee-McIntyre House serves today as the only remaining winter cottage of its size built in the 1880s when Florida was first being discovered as a vacation mecca.

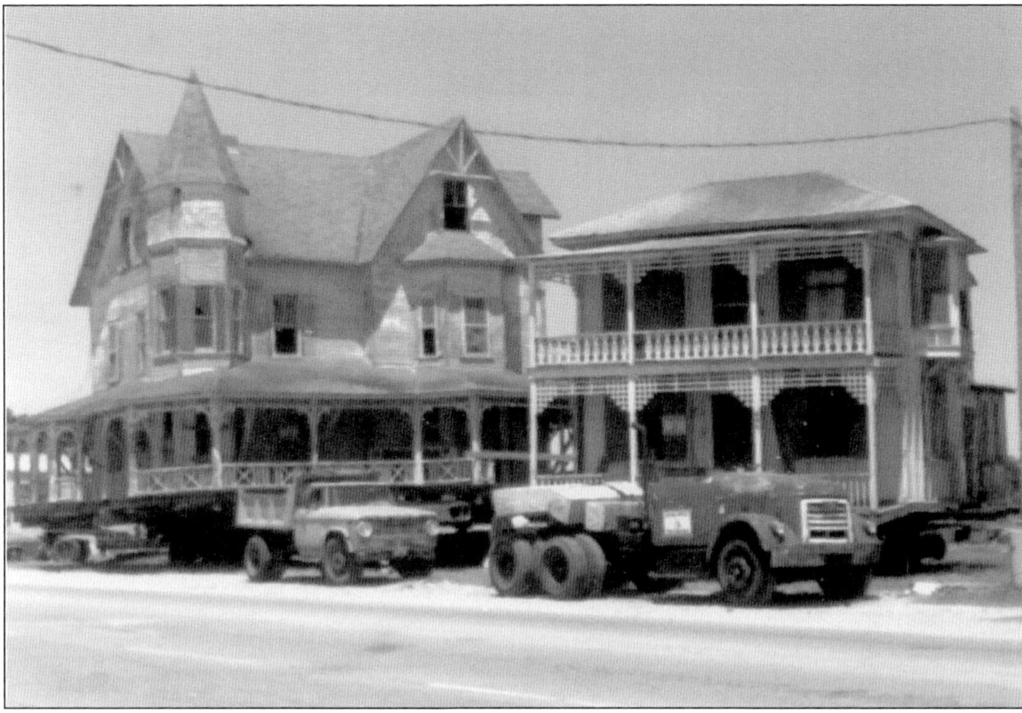

Shown here are two scenes of the 1973 move of the Bradlee-McIntyre House and the Inside-Outside House, both built during Altamonte's resort days of the late 1800s. Roughly a hundred years later, Altamonte Springs was booming. The Central Florida Society for Historical Preservation saved both houses from destruction by moving them to the Longwood Historic District.

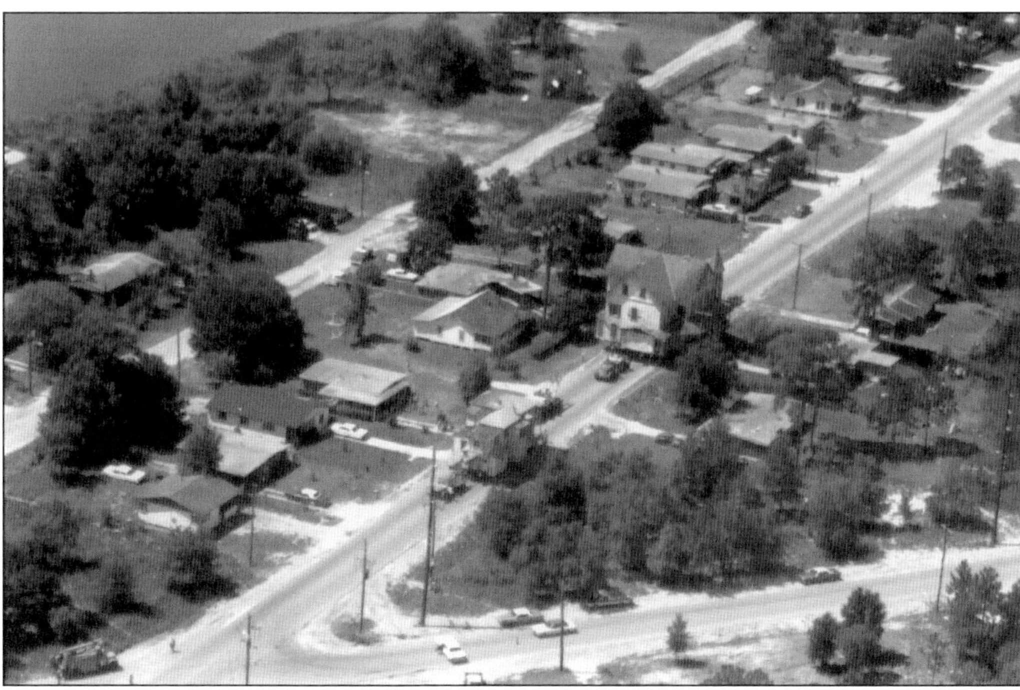

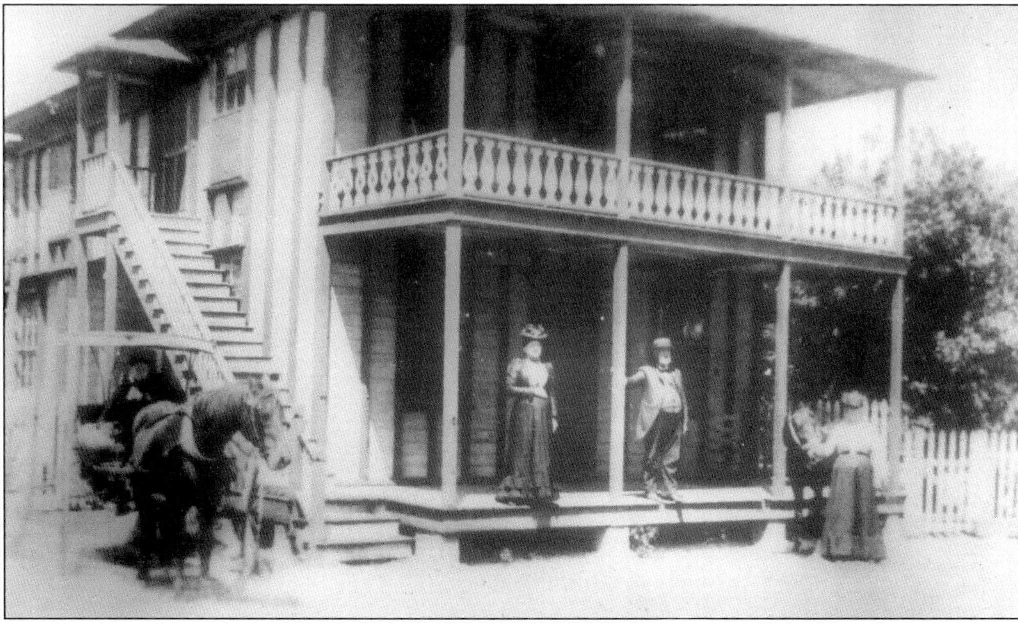

The Inside-Outside House gets its name from its odd construction that features support studs on the outside and panels bolted together in ship-lap fashion. It was once part of a cluster of winter cottages at Snow Station in the 1880s. The Inside-Outside House was built in Boston for a ship captain who had it disassembled and shipped by steamer in 1873 to Sanford and by mule team to Altamonte Springs, where soldiers used it for a way station. The captain moved into the house in 1878.

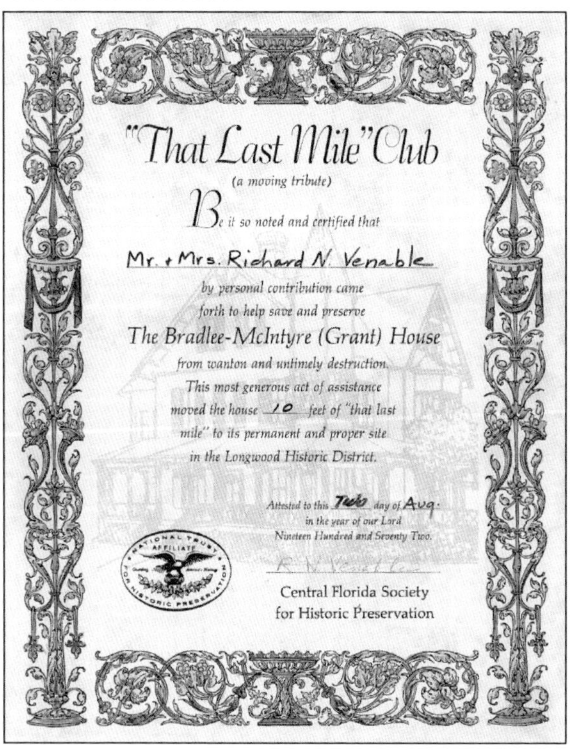

"That Last Mile" Club

(a moving tribute)

Be it so noted and certified that

Mr. + Mrs. Richard N. Venable

by personal contribution came forth to help save and preserve

The Bradlee-McIntyre (Grant) House

from wanton and untimely destruction. This most generous act of assistance moved the house 10 feet of "that last mile" to its permanent and proper site in the Longwood Historic District.

Attested to this Two day of Aug. in the year of our Lord Nineteen Hundred and Seventy Two.

R. N. Venable

National Trust Affiliate for Historic Preservation

Central Florida Society for Historic Preservation

"The Last Mile Club" certificates, like this one issued to Mr. and Mrs. Richard N. Venable, were awarded to people who helped raise the money needed to move the Bradlee-McIntyre House and the Inside-Outside House to Longwood.

Five

Walking Tour of Historic Longwood

A walking tour of Longwood begins at the Bradlee-McIntyre House, the last of Central Florida's sprawling "cottages" built by wealthy Northerners as winter homes when Florida first became a vacation mecca. Boston architect Nathaniel Bradlee built the house in the resort village of Snow Station (now Altamonte Springs) on a narrow, sandy wagon trail near the South Florida Railroad depot. S. Maxwell McIntyre, who acquired much of Altamonte Springs, bought the house in 1904. The Bradlee-McIntyre House is now restored as a Victorian home with furnishings selected to represent that time and style. Besides the dining room and the grand salon, the first floor includes a ladies parlor and library. The second floor consists of four bedrooms, a large central hall, and an unusually large room that may have served as a family gathering place or as the master bedroom. Once standing in the path of progress, the Bradlee-McIntyre House, added to the National Register of Historic Places on October 30, 1973, stands today as the centerpiece of the Longwood Historic District.

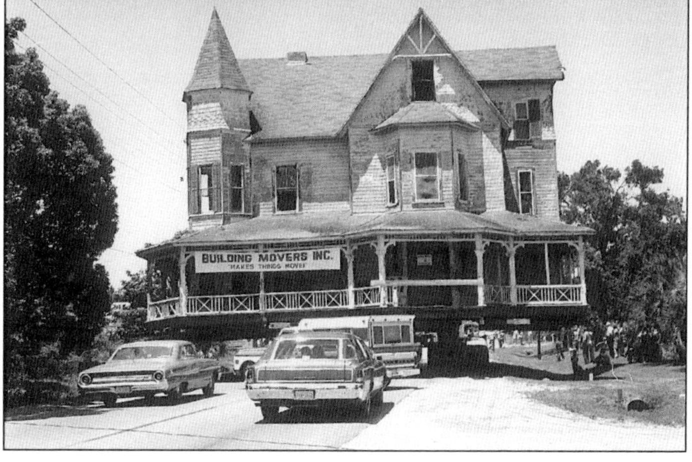

This is the Bradlee-McIntyre House during the last few miles of its move along County Road 427 just before reaching the Longwood city limits.

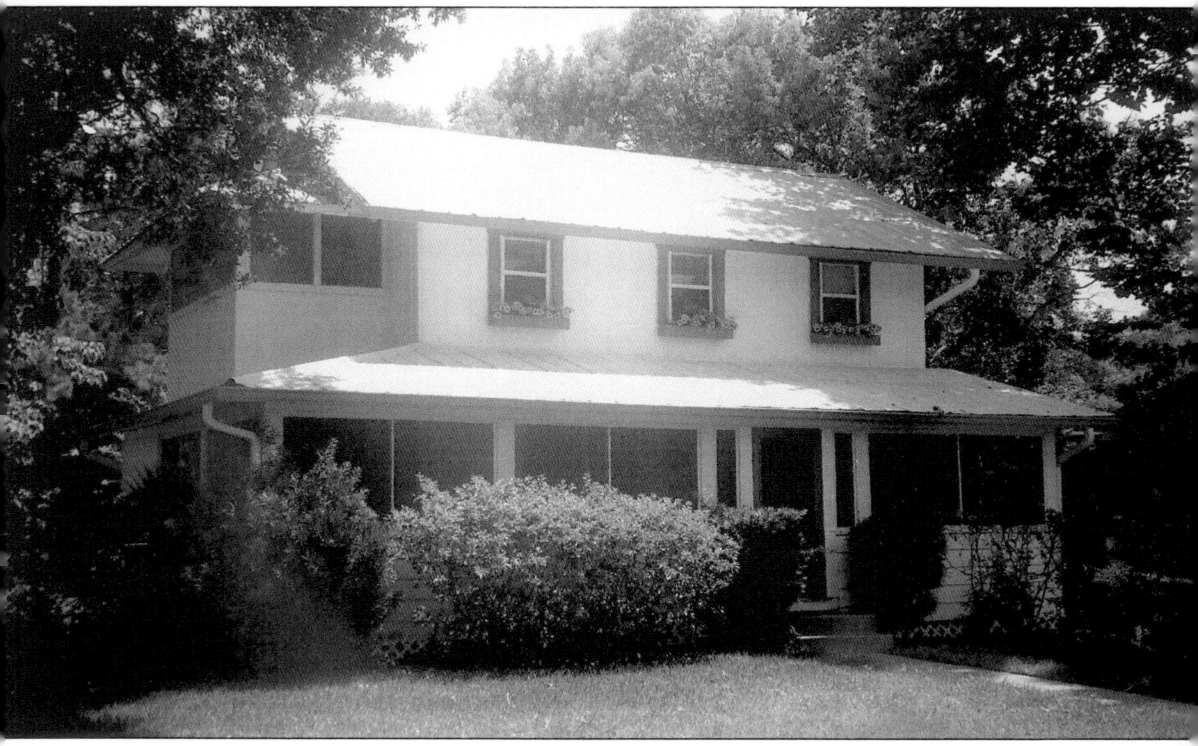

Charles Entzminger built this house at 110 West Magnolia in 1926, and it was originally used as a garage apartment. The two-story portion and the second-floor sleeping porch are original. The front and side porches were probably added when the ground floor garage was converted to living space.

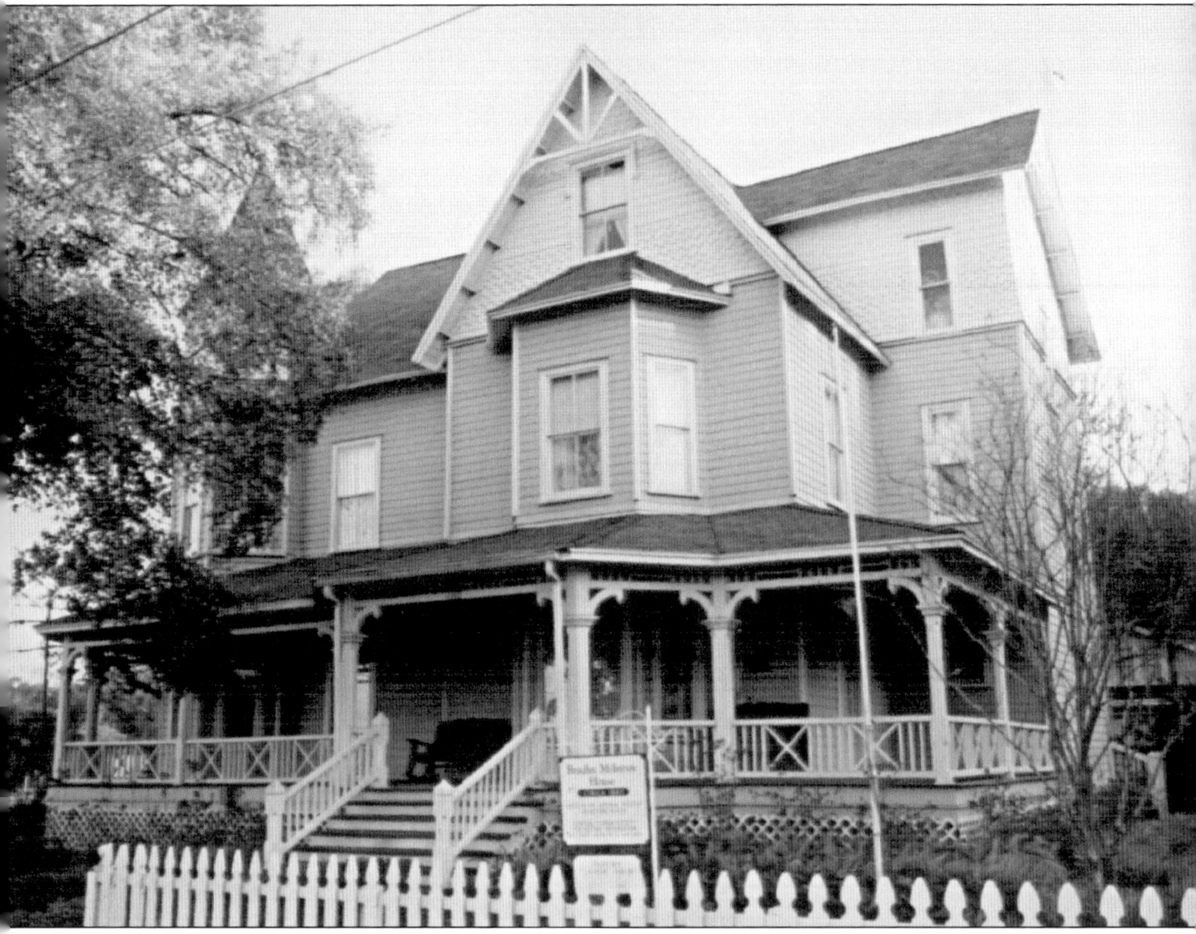

The Bradlee-McIntyre House, shown here, is a Victorian Queen Anne–style winter home built in 1885 in Altamonte Springs. It is now a museum in Longwood's downtown historic district at 130 West Warren Avenue. The builder is believed to have been Joseph Lewis, who also built other homes in the area. Josiah Clouser provided the interior stairs and other finish carpentry. The home's Queen Anne detail includes asymmetrical tower placement, steep pitched roofs, decorative shingle patterns, and elaborate porch detailing.

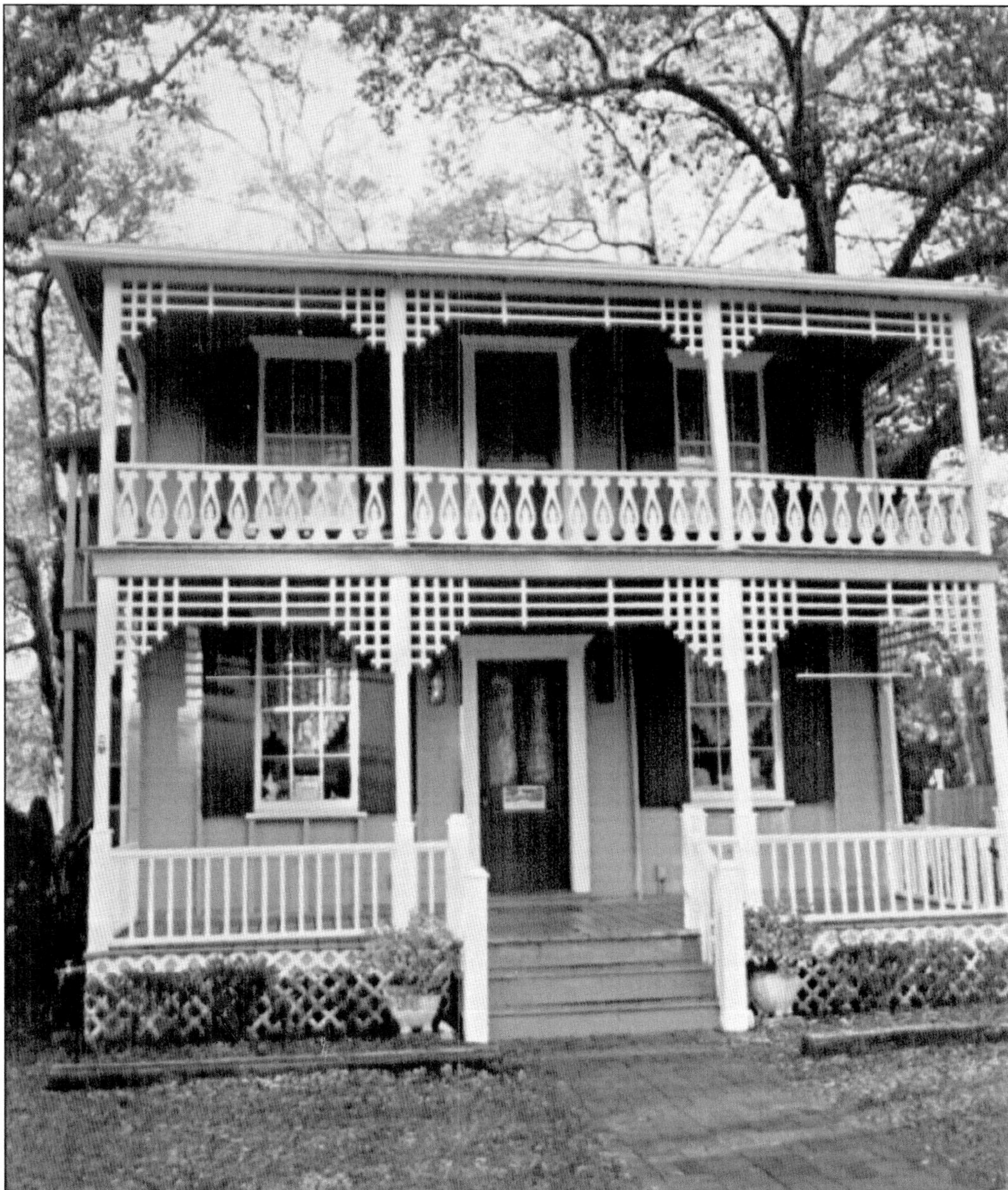

One of the highlights of Longwood's walking tour is a stop at the elaborate wood porch of the Inside-Outside House at 141 West Church Avenue. Capt. W. Pierce had the prefabricated house, possibly one of the nation's first, built in Boston in the early 1870s, taken apart, and shipped by barge and mule cart to Sanford. The house was then reassembled on Boston Avenue in 1873, joining a cluster of cottages at what was then called Snow Station. By error or by design, its walls were put together with its studs exposed on the outside. Federal troops used it as a way station between Jacksonville and Tampa. When it was used as a cabinet shop, the family lived upstairs, which they reached using an outside stairway. Later, an interior spiral staircase like a ship's ladder was added. The Inside-Outside House was moved to the Longwood Historic District along with the Bradlee-McIntyre House in April 1973. The Inside-Outside House is owned by the Central Florida Society for Historical Preservation.

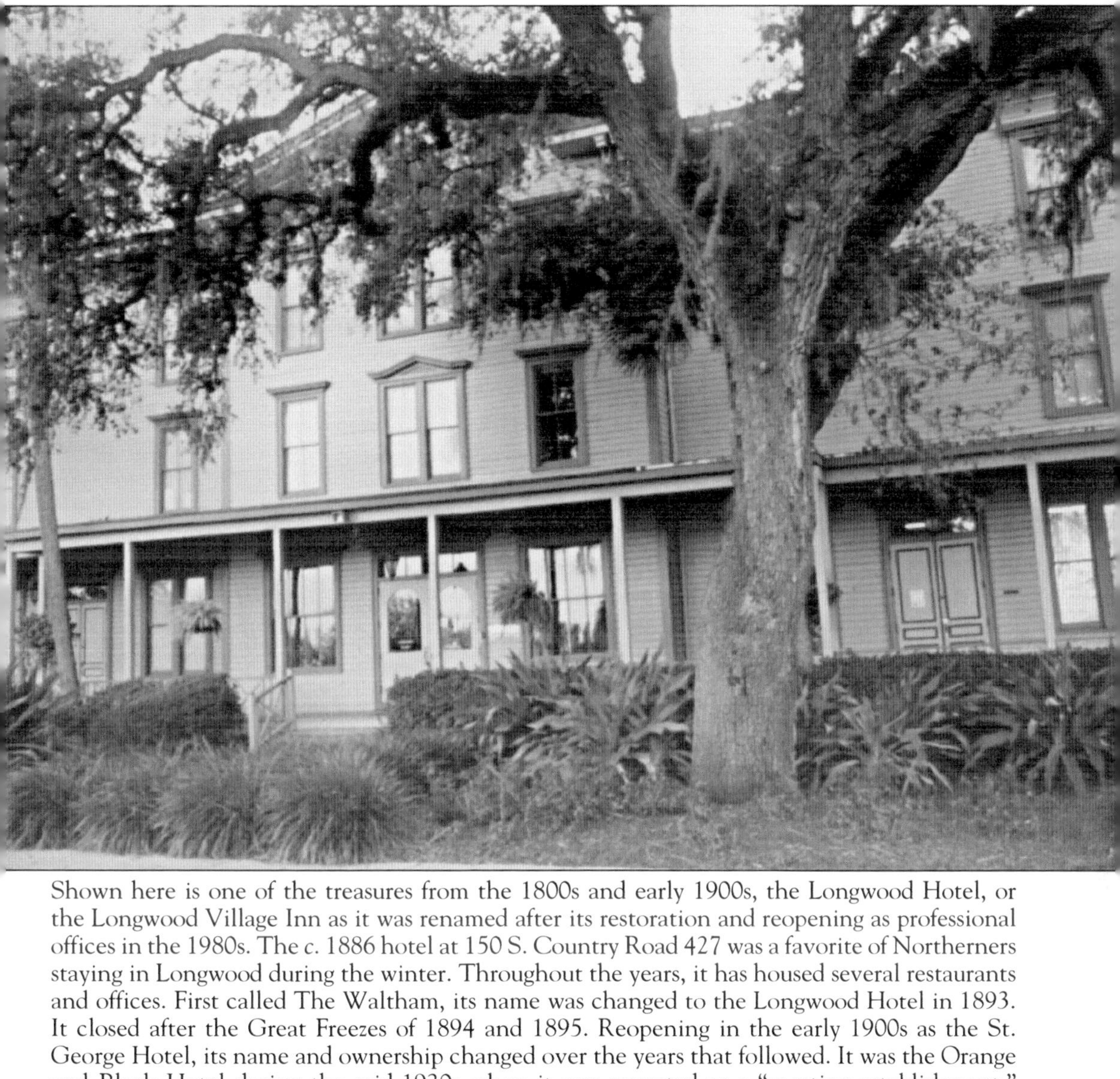

Shown here is one of the treasures from the 1800s and early 1900s, the Longwood Hotel, or the Longwood Village Inn as it was renamed after its restoration and reopening as professional offices in the 1980s. The *c.* 1886 hotel at 150 S. Country Road 427 was a favorite of Northerners staying in Longwood during the winter. Throughout the years, it has housed several restaurants and offices. First called The Waltham, its name was changed to the Longwood Hotel in 1893. It closed after the Great Freezes of 1894 and 1895. Reopening in the early 1900s as the St. George Hotel, its name and ownership changed over the years that followed. It was the Orange and Black Hotel during the mid-1920s when it was operated as a "sporting establishment." Cornell University owned it during the early 1970s when it was used as a hotel operation school. Renovated in the 1980s for office use, the hotel is now listed on the National Register of Historic Places.

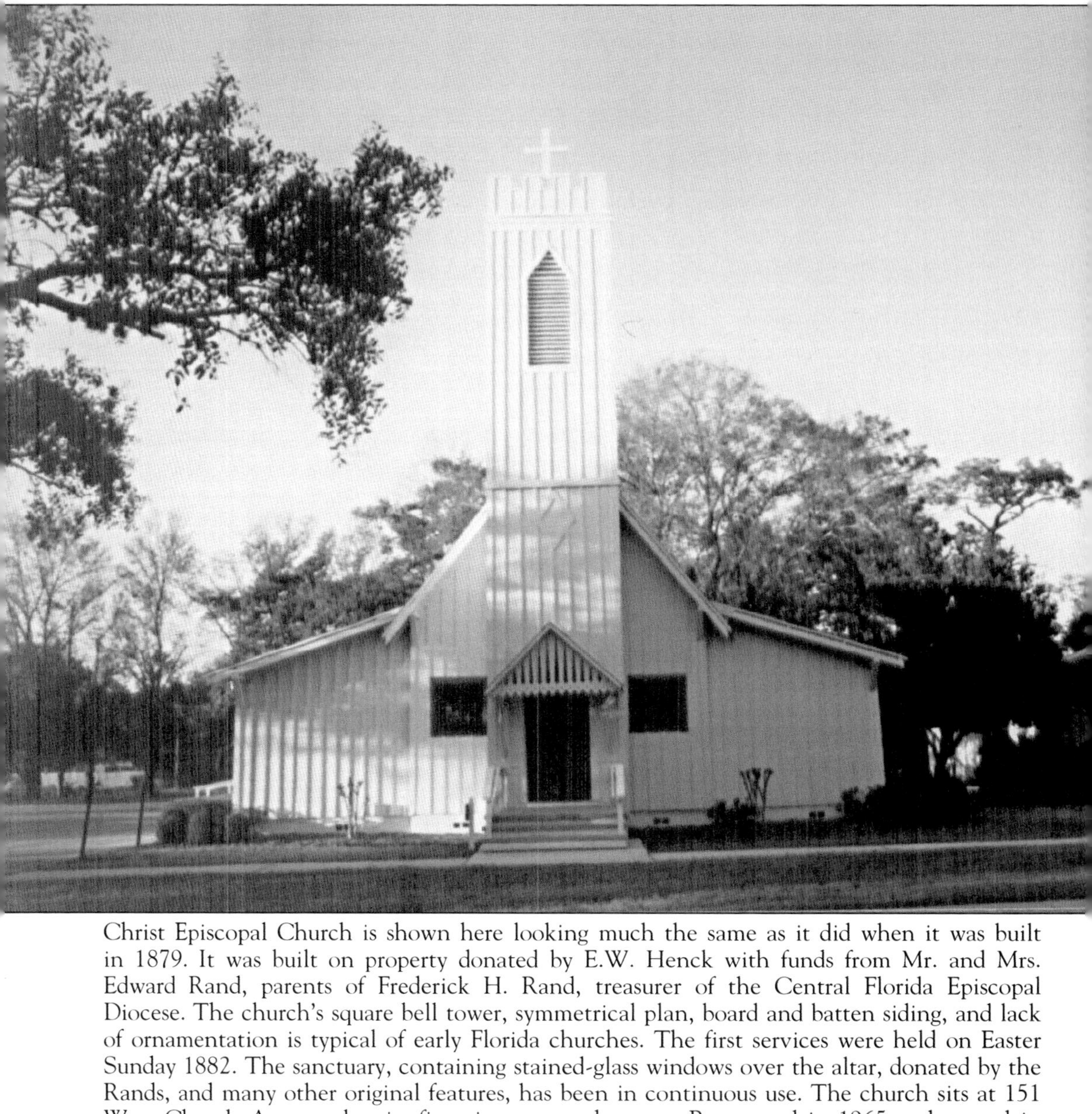

Christ Episcopal Church is shown here looking much the same as it did when it was built in 1879. It was built on property donated by E.W. Henck with funds from Mr. and Mrs. Edward Rand, parents of Frederick H. Rand, treasurer of the Central Florida Episcopal Diocese. The church's square bell tower, symmetrical plan, board and batten siding, and lack of ornamentation is typical of early Florida churches. The first services were held on Easter Sunday 1882. The sanctuary, containing stained-glass windows over the altar, donated by the Rands, and many other original features, has been in continuous use. The church sits at 151 West Church Avenue, but its first site was to the west. Renovated in 1965 and moved in 1988 to make room for additional buildings, it remains the oldest church in continuous use in Seminole County.

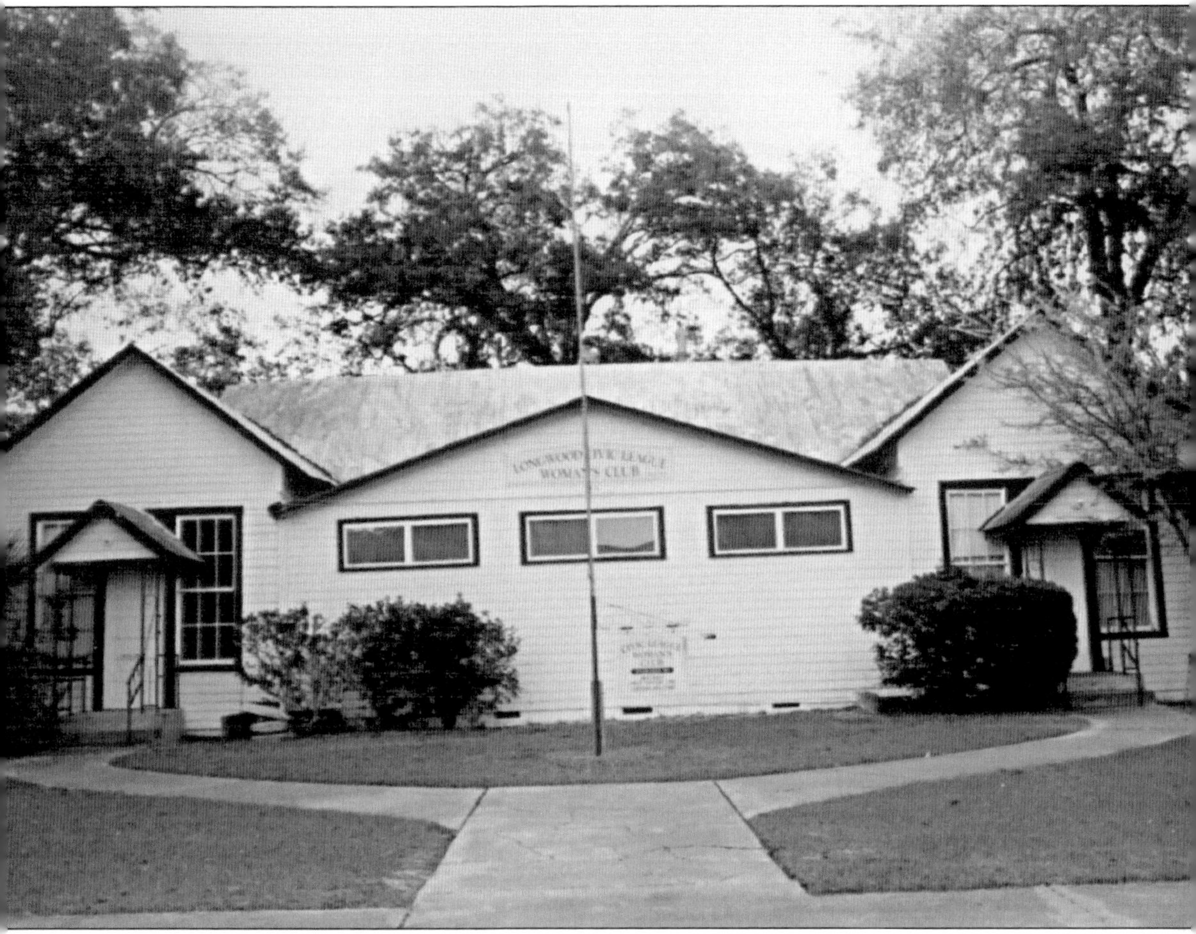

The Civic League Building, shown here at 135 West Church Avenue, is one of Longwood's first buildings and served as the village's first schoolhouse. It was built in 1875 as a one-room community building at the site of Christ Episcopal Church. It was later moved to the community of West Longwood and called the West Longwood Chapel. It also has been home to The West Longwood Pioneers and The Self Union. The Longwood Woman's Club established a library in the building in 1912. In 1914, the Civic League purchased the building, moving it to the present site east of the Inside-Outside House. The original building is behind additions on both sides and the center porch. Now owned by the Central Florida Society for Historical Preservation, the structure will be restored for use as a museum of Longwood history.

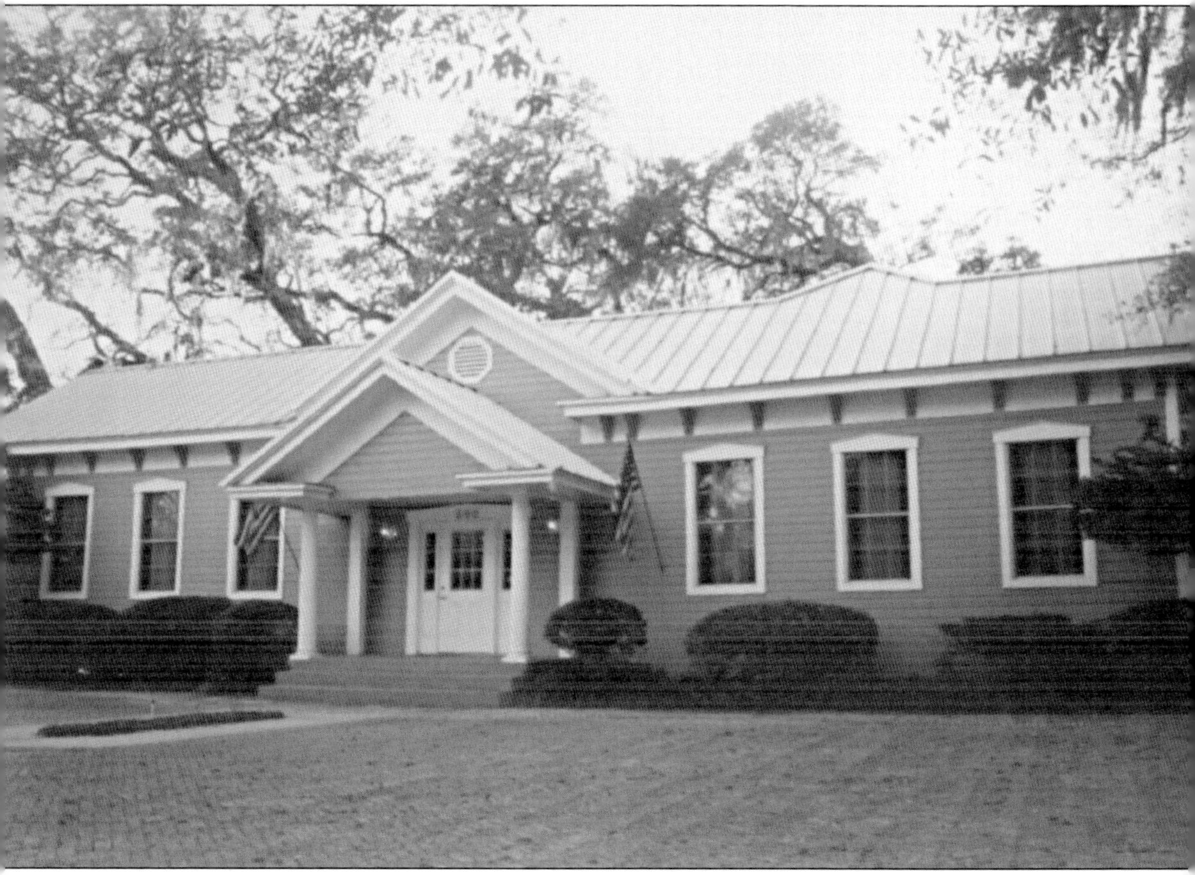

The schoolhouse, shown here, was built as a two-room school in the 1880s and used until 1924, when it became the City Hall and fire station until the 1960s. Renovated in the 1970s as a restaurant, it was damaged by fire in 1979. Since renovations in 1984, the building has been used for offices. It shares its architectural character with the nearby Longwood Hotel.

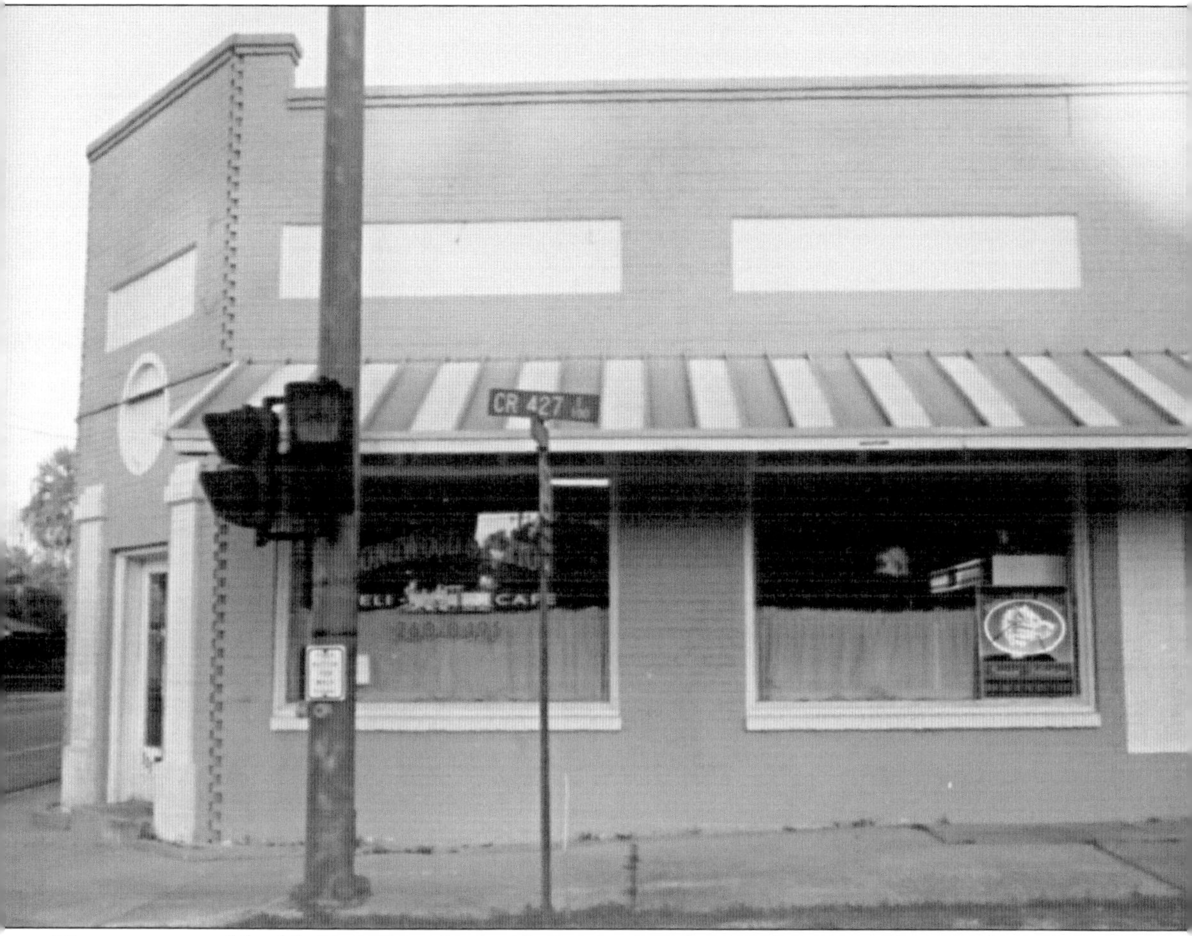

This commercial building at 101–159 South County Road 427 is known as the Henck-Tinker Building. Around 1925, E.W. Henck and baseball hall-of-famer Joe Tinker constructed this building for the Longwood State Bank, which occupied the north end of the building. The bank closed during the Great Depression. On the south end of the brick building was MacReynolds Drug Store, Jackson's Grocery, and a barbershop, drawing the town's business center from the railroad and Warren Avenue.

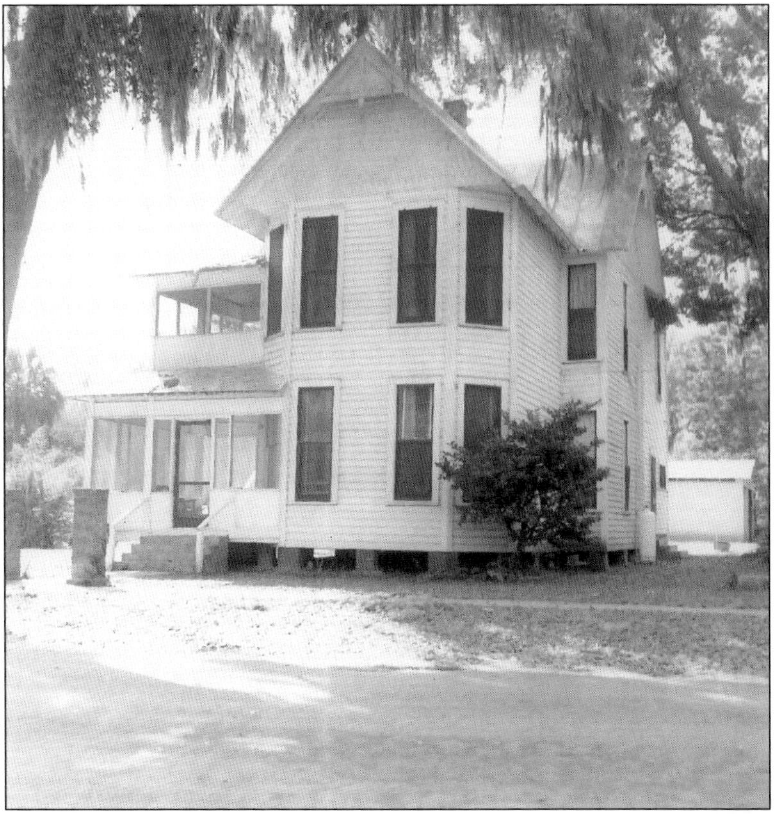

The Niemeyer House at 192 West Warren Avenue was built in 1889 by Josiah B. Clouser and Frederick Niemeyer. Originally constructed as a one-story home, the building got a second-story addition in 1905. As the home of one of the area's more prominent citizens, this house is appropriately one of the tallest structures in the Longwood Historic District.

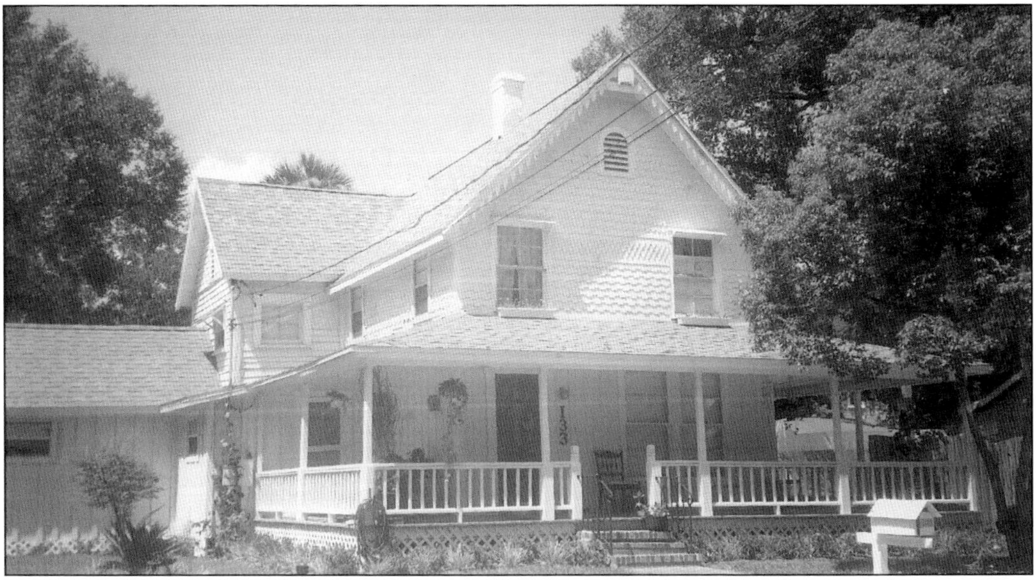

The LeRue House at 133 West Bay Avenue was built in 1885 by staircase builder and blacksmith J.S. LeRue. The decorative barge-board on the gable roof edge, elaborate porch handrail, and the multi-patterned shingles on the second floor clearly display a craftsman's handiwork. Grace and Robert Bradford restored the home in the 1970s, adding porch columns and a wing on the back.

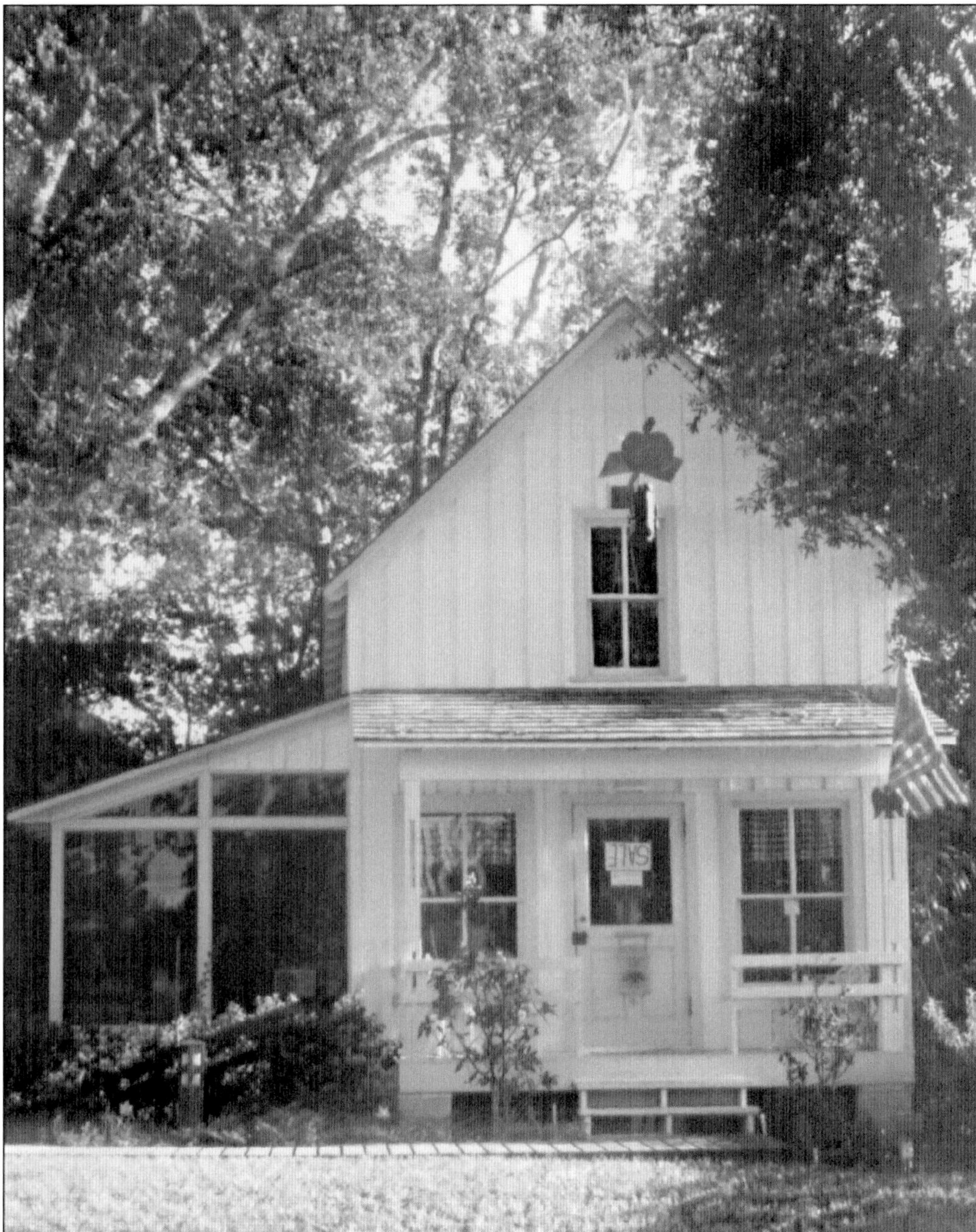

The Clouser Cottage, built by Josiah B. Clouser, shares its architectural style with the Pennsylvania farmhouses familiar to Clouser before he moved his family to Florida. The cottage at 218 West Church Avenue was the first house he built for his family. Hoping Florida's climate would improve his wife's health, Clouser responded to newspaper advertisements E.W. Henck placed in Northern newspapers seeking a master carpenter to build a hotel. The Clousers left Pennsylvania in 1881. The family briefly lived in a flea-infested house, prompting Clouser to build the cottage from salvaged lumber, nailing vertical board and batten siding to the interior paneling without stud framing.

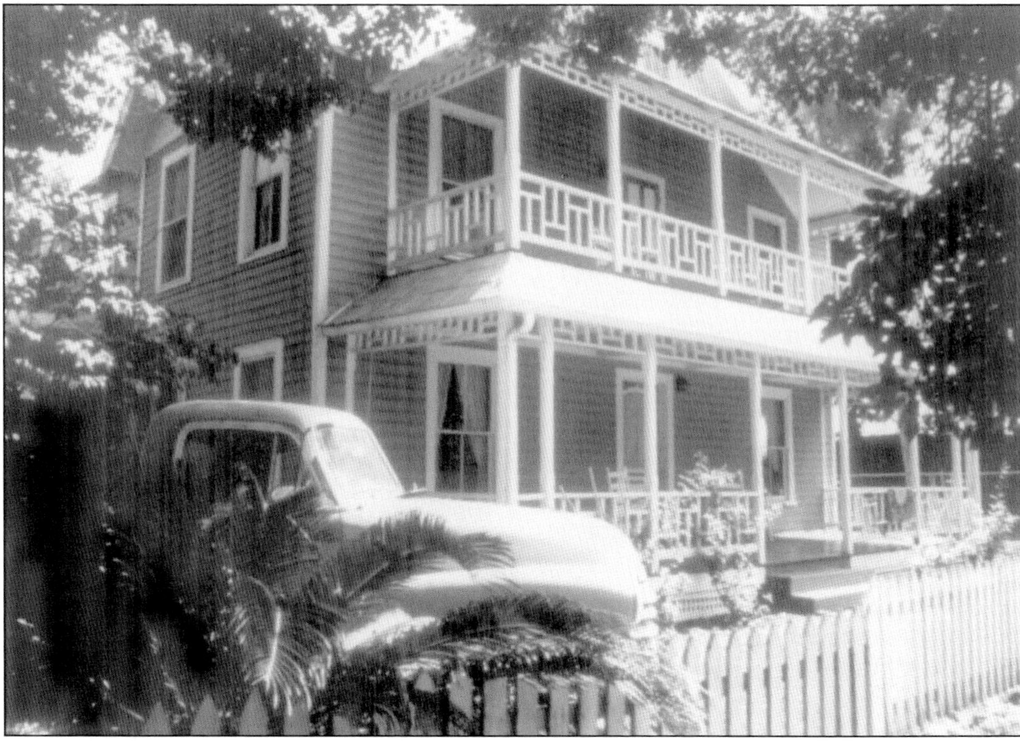

Josiah B. Clouser began building the Clouser House two years after he finished the cottage. The cottage was then used for an animal shed, storage, and was rented as a residence. Clouser's great grandsons Fred and John Bistline renovated it as a gift shop. The larger, more suitable Clouser House was built between 1885 and 1890. Later used as a birthing center, it is now a consignment gift shop.

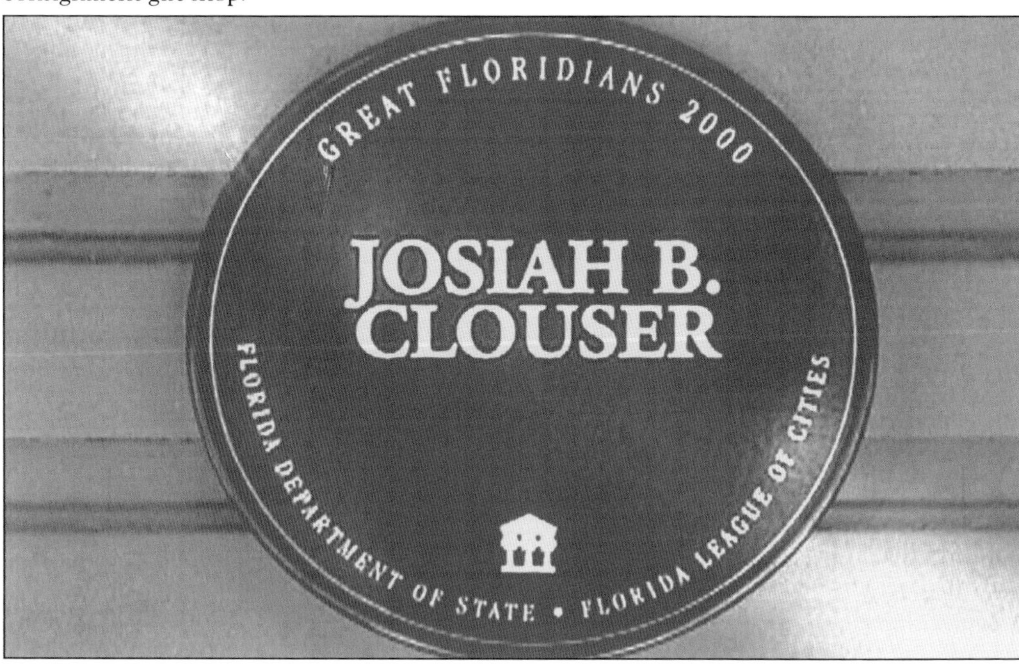

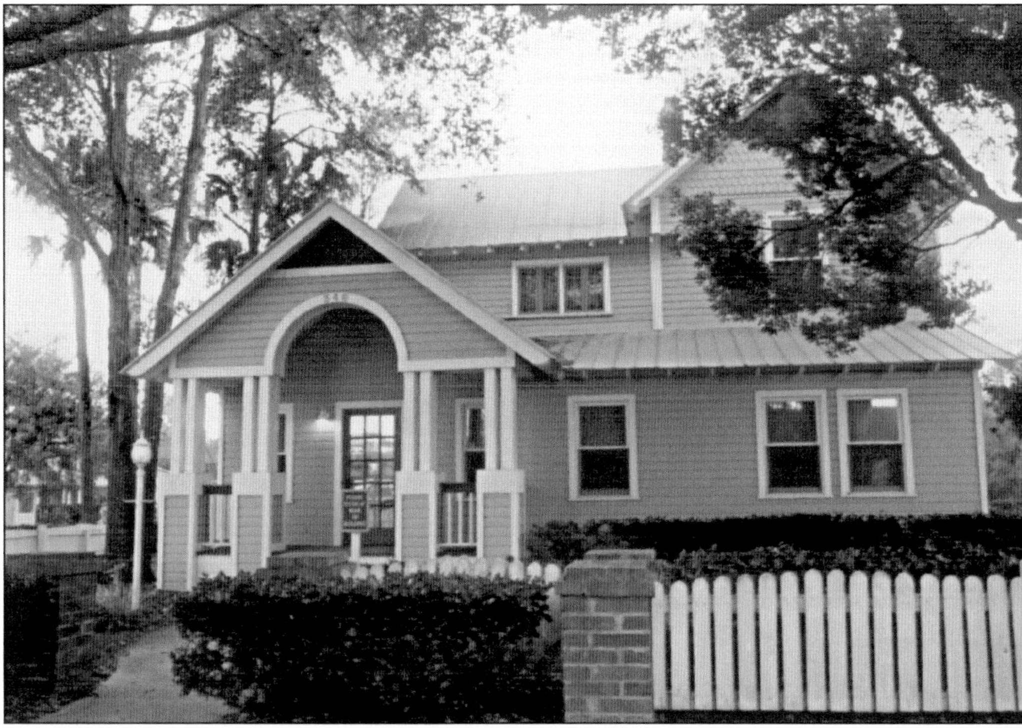

This house at 346 Freeman St. was constructed in 1888 for J.C. Fitch, an early settler who became an alderman in the mid-1880s. G.W. Hardaway, the minister of the Longwood Congregational Church, owned the house in the early 1890s. In 1920 Charles Entzminger bought the house and kept it for many years.

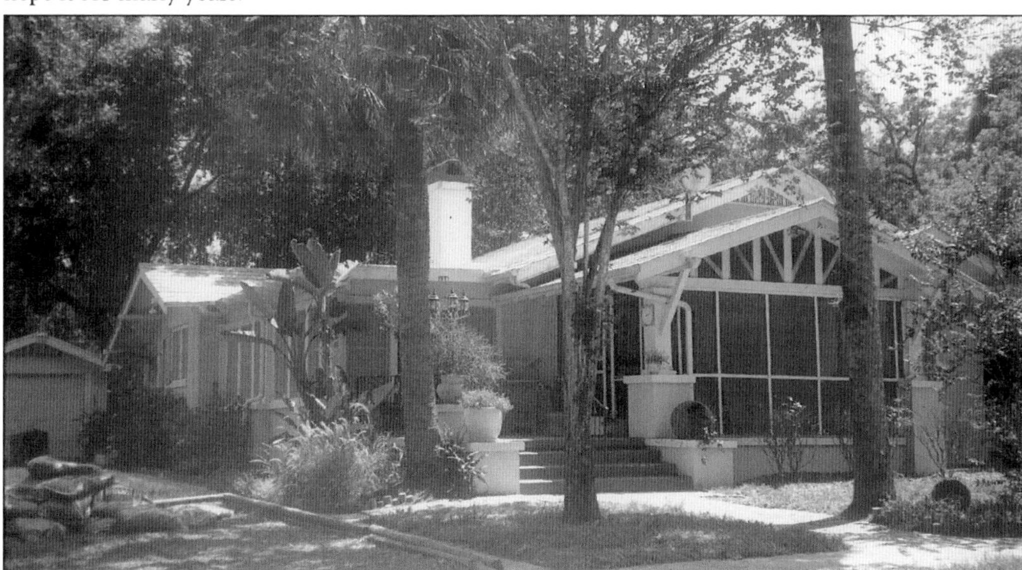

Constructed for L.R. Tucker, *c.* 1920, this house at 138 West Jessup Avenue is the most elaborate and detailed example of the Bungalow style in Longwood. Few, if any, changes have been made to the house since it was built. Even the original garage remains at the rear of the house.

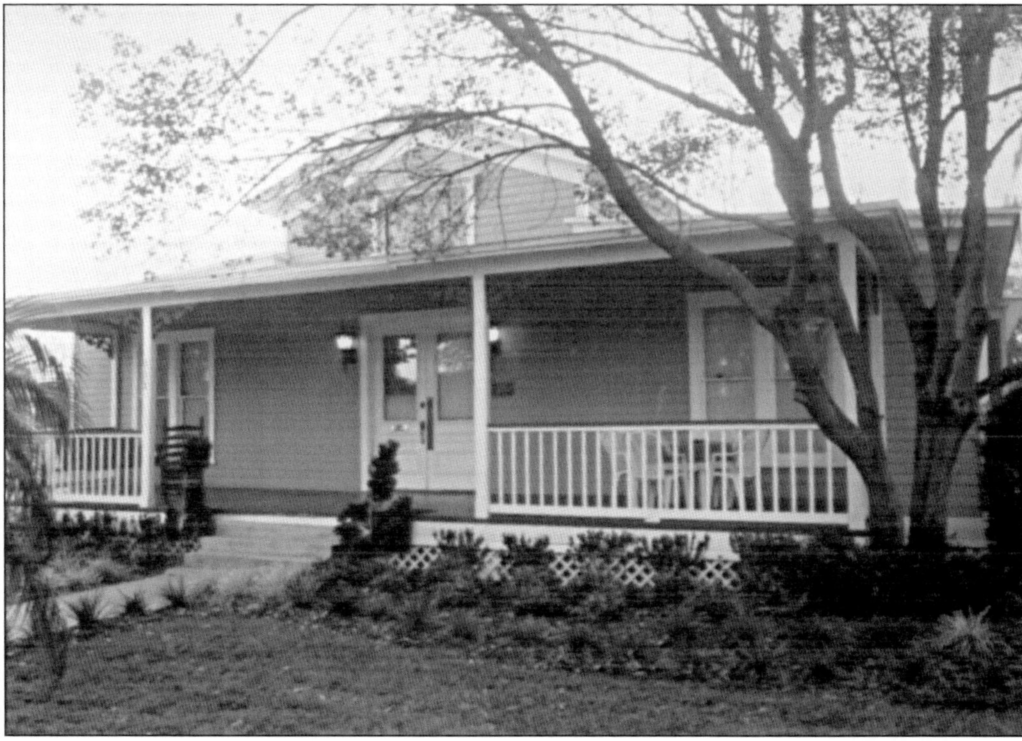

The E.W. Henck House, shown here, was built in 1875 for the Boston attorney and civil engineer who came to the area in 1873 and needed a winter residence.

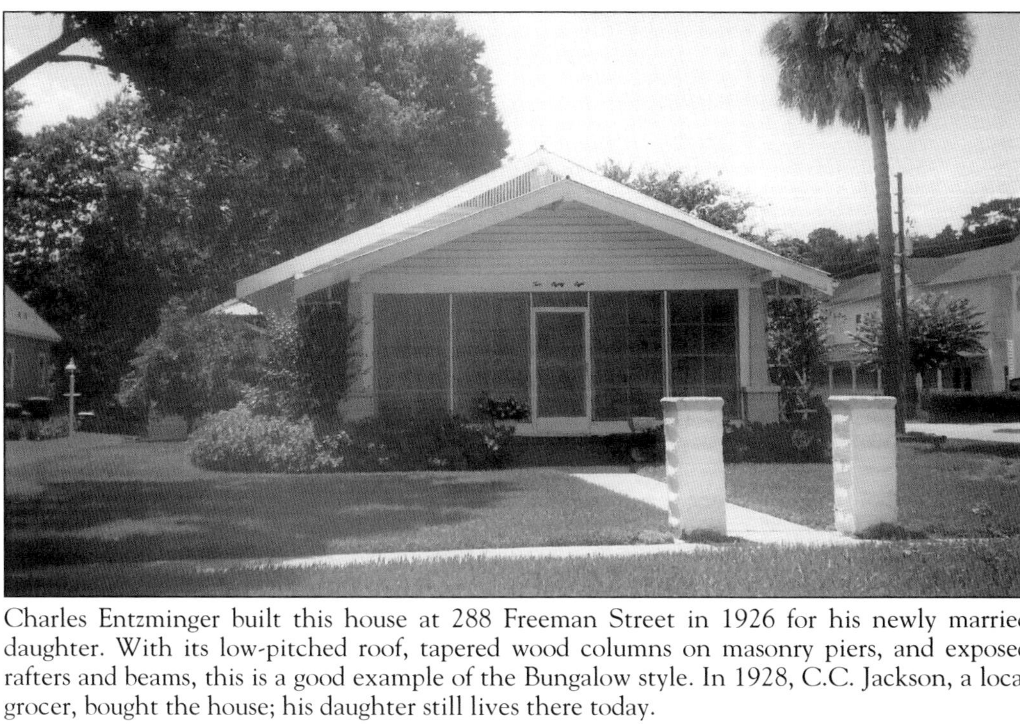

Charles Entzminger built this house at 288 Freeman Street in 1926 for his newly married daughter. With its low-pitched roof, tapered wood columns on masonry piers, and exposed rafters and beams, this is a good example of the Bungalow style. In 1928, C.C. Jackson, a local grocer, bought the house; his daughter still lives there today.

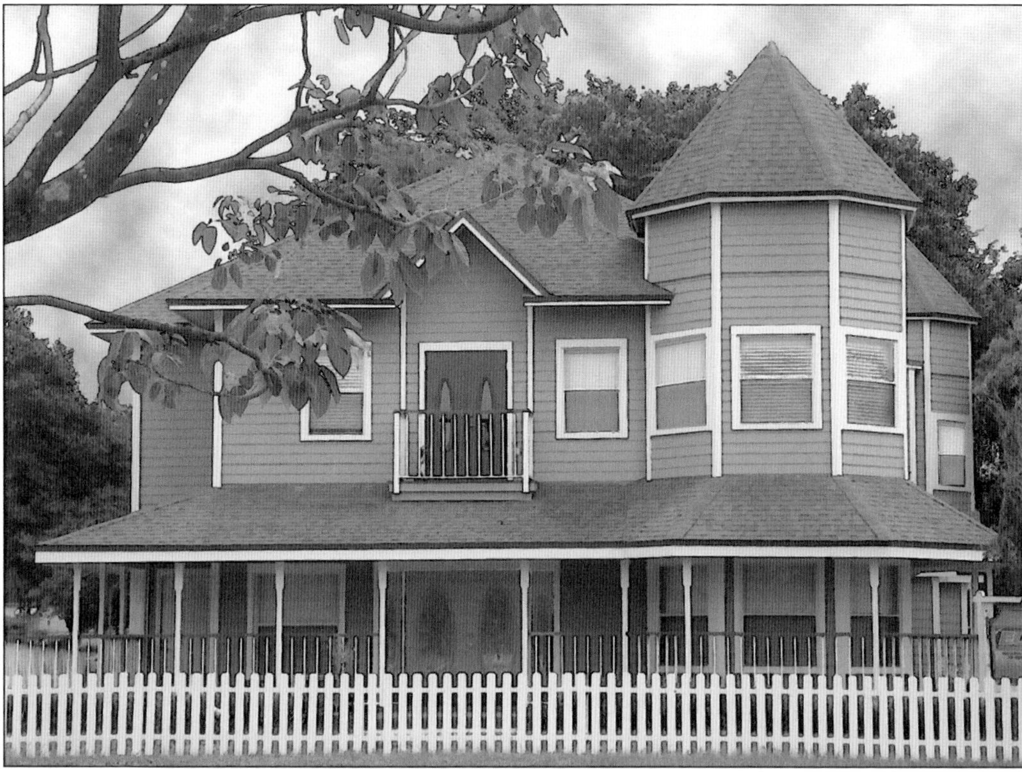

Several new buildings within the Longwood Historic District have been designed to fit in with the architecture of the district. This structure was built in the Victorian Queen Anne style in the 1990s and currently serves as a professional office.

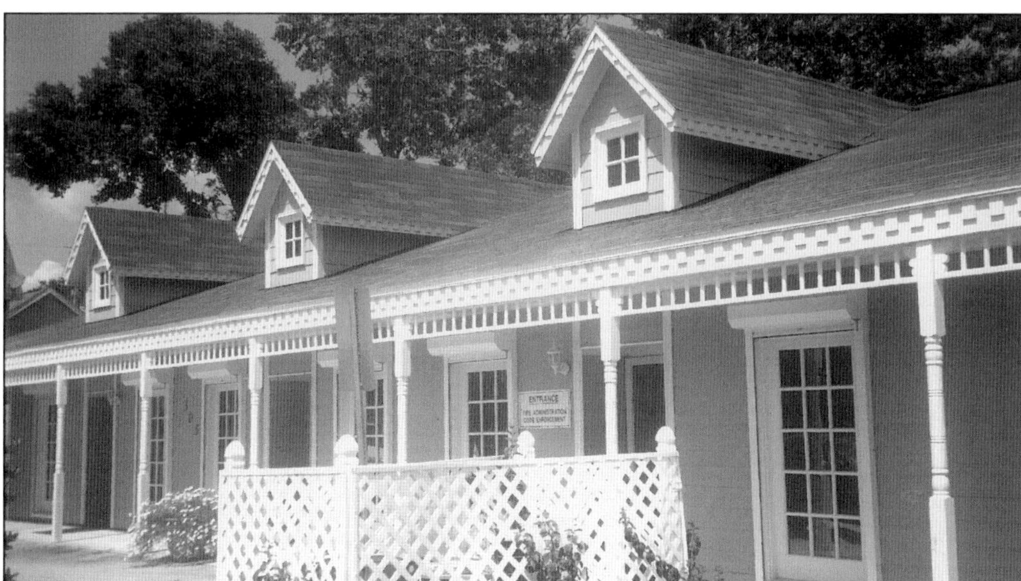

This City of Longwood office building is a prime example of a newly built structure that conforms to the Victorian architecture of some of the century-old buildings in the area.

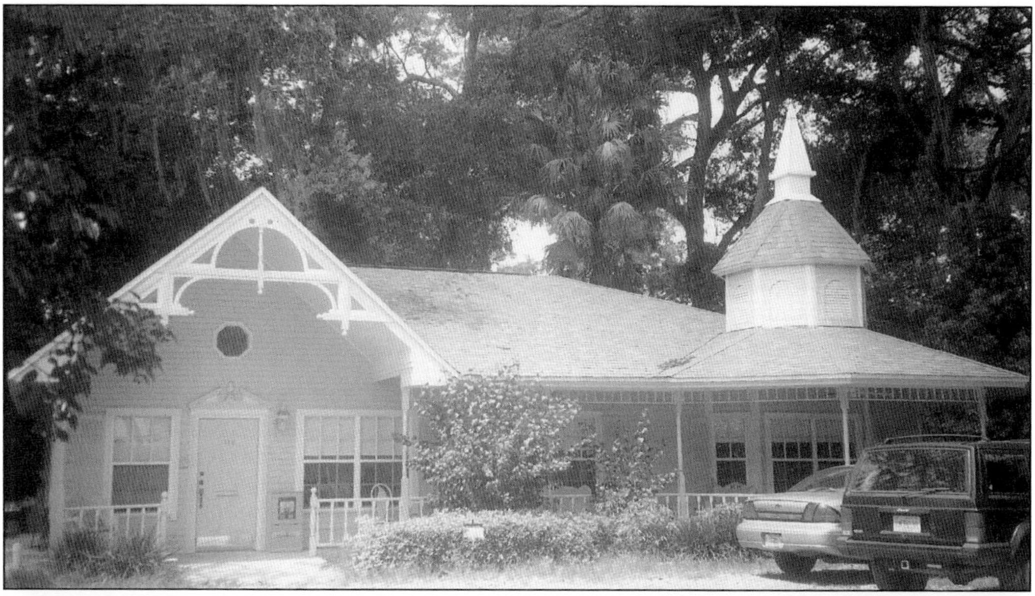

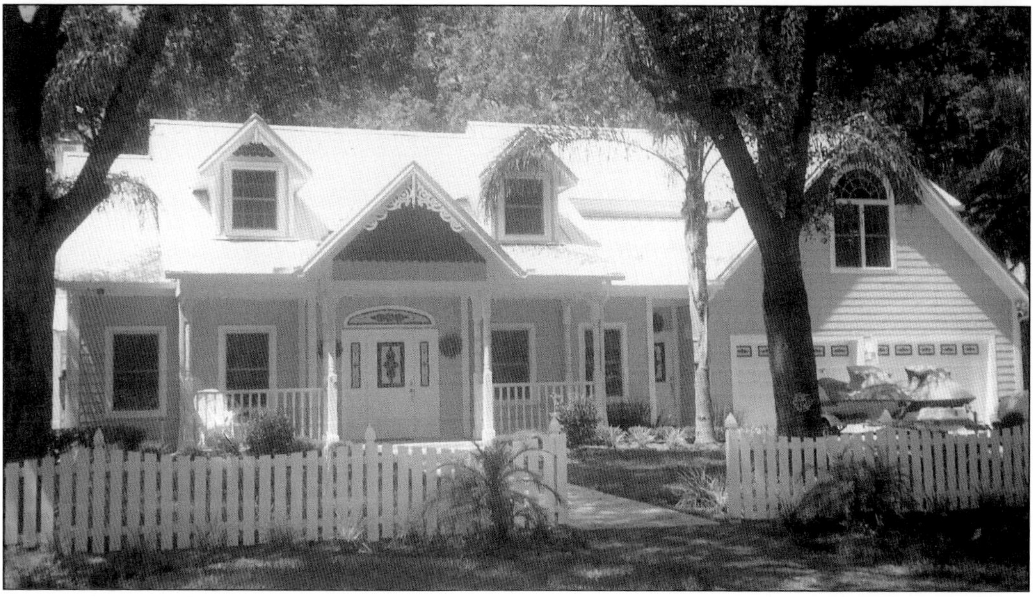

These office buildings at 125 and 135 Pine Avenue are excellent examples of business structures with a Victorian flair; they are in keeping with the character of the Longwood Historic District.

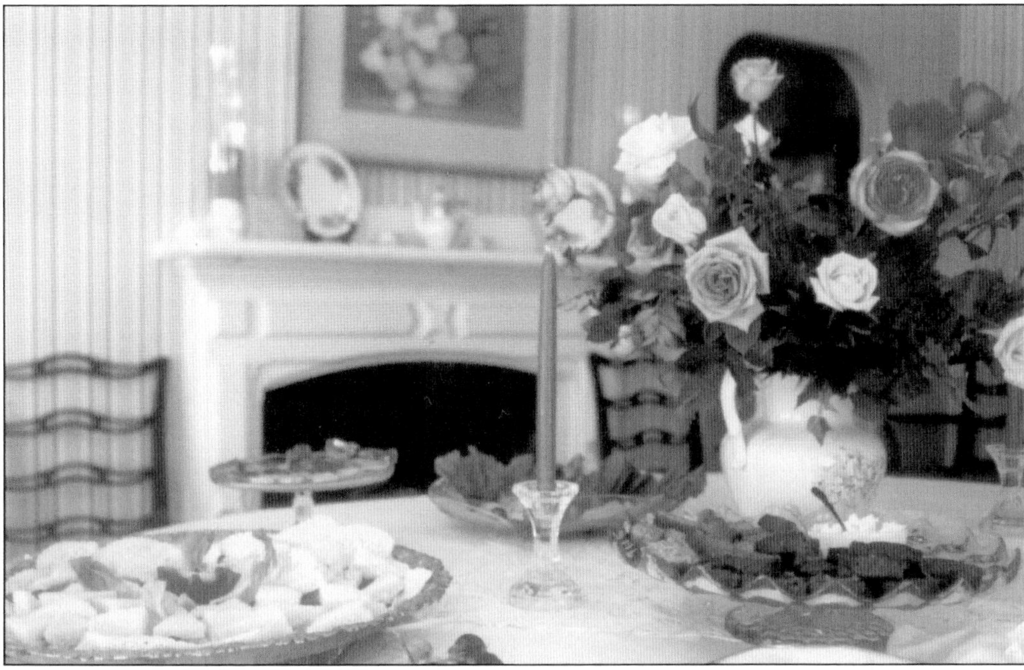

This is a holiday table setting at the Bradlee-McIntyre House, restored as a "truly Victorian" family house. On the first Monday, Tuesday, and Wednesday in December, the CFSHP hosts Christmas in Olde Longwood, which begins with carols at the Christ Episcopal Church followed by a holiday dinner at the Bradlee-McIntyre House.

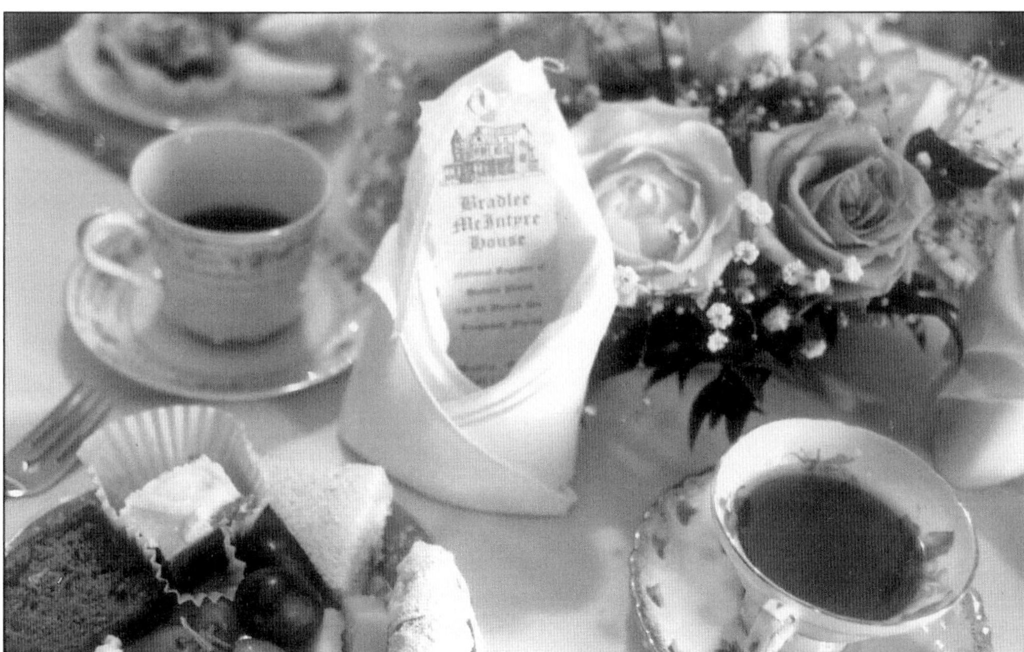

At the 2000 Victorian Tea held at the Bradlee-McIntyre House, the place settings reflected the refinement of the time.

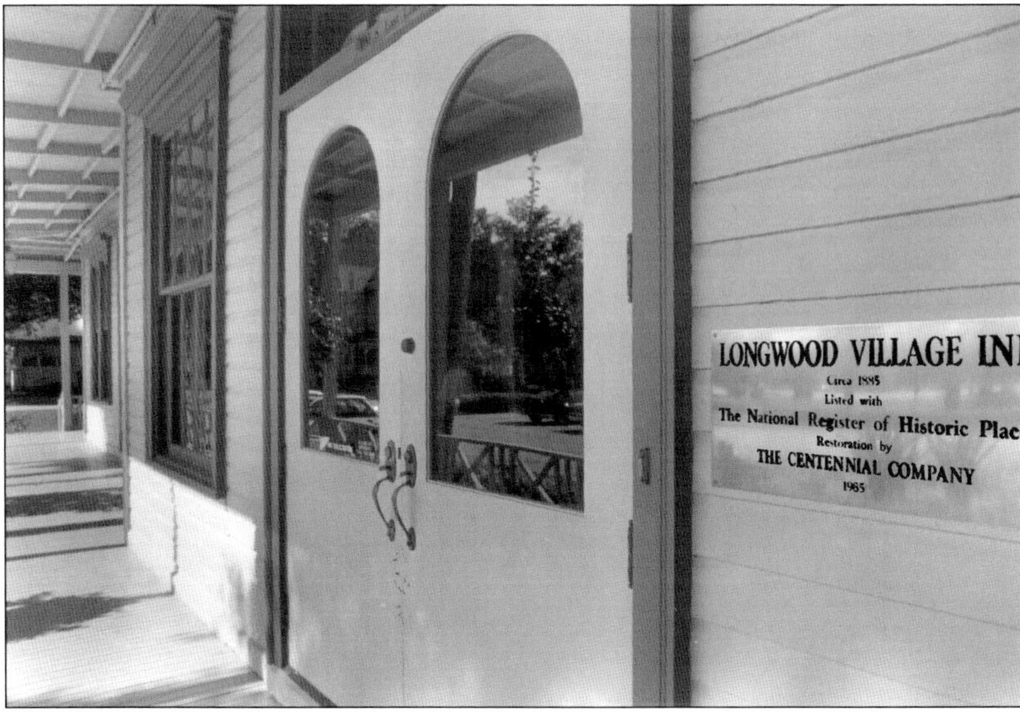

Shown here is the front porch of the Longwood Village Inn, now used for professional offices. The plaque notes that the hotel is listed on the National Register of Historic Places.

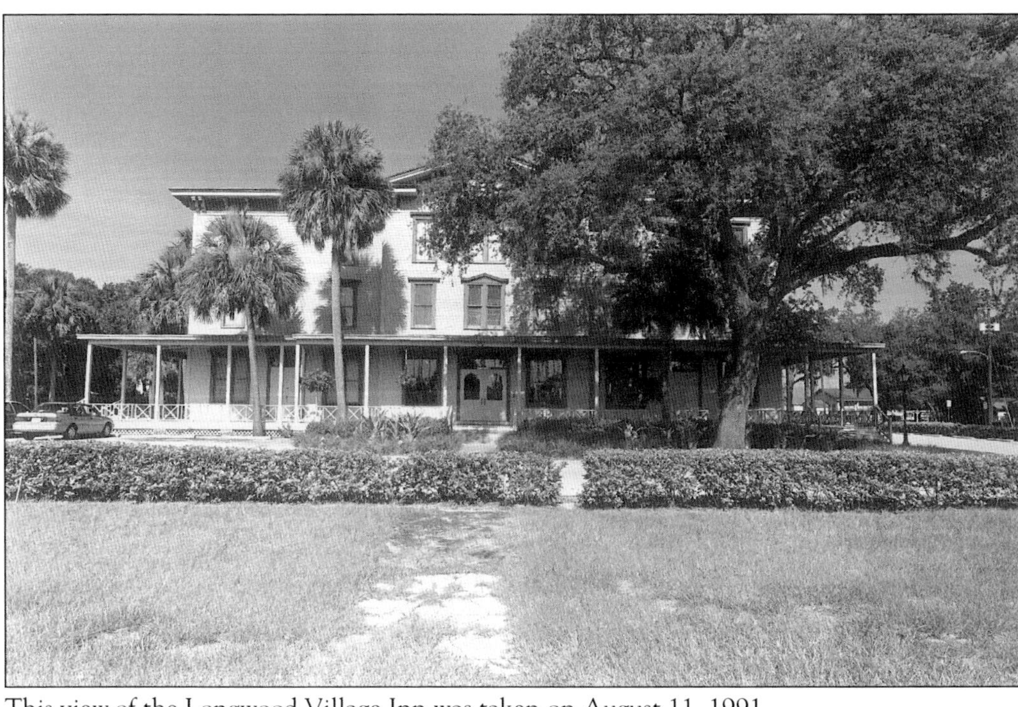

This view of the Longwood Village Inn was taken on August 11, 1991.

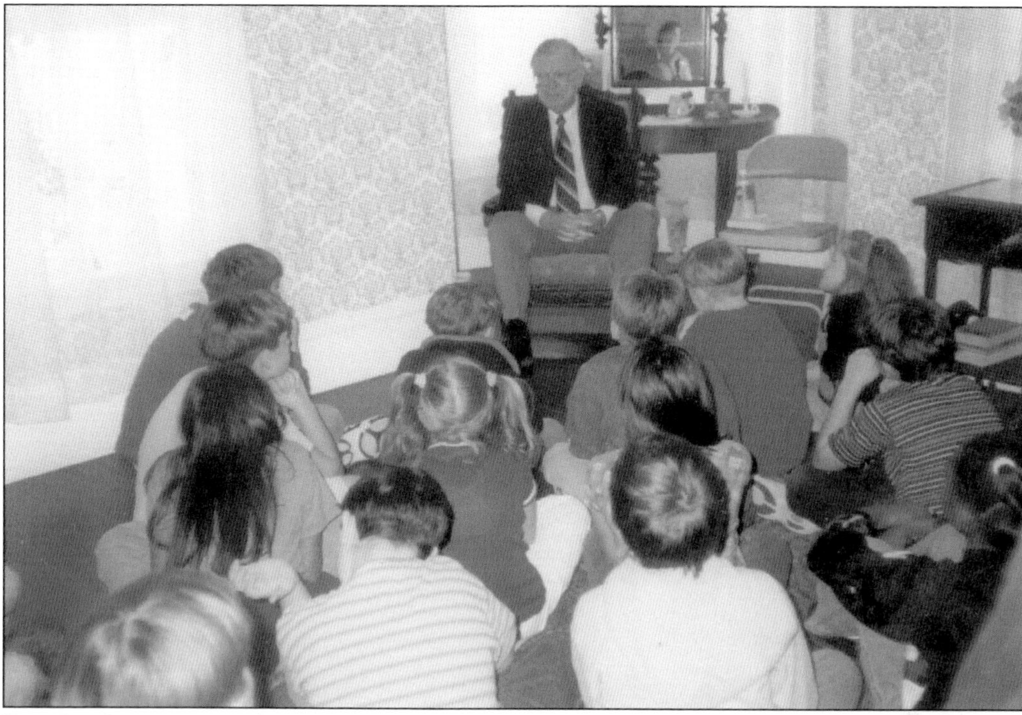

Douglas Stenstrom, a former state senator and Sanford lawyer, is shown here talking with schoolchildren during their visit to the Bradlee-McIntyre House. Stenstrom is one of many community volunteers who donate their time as speakers for the society's historical awareness program for students.

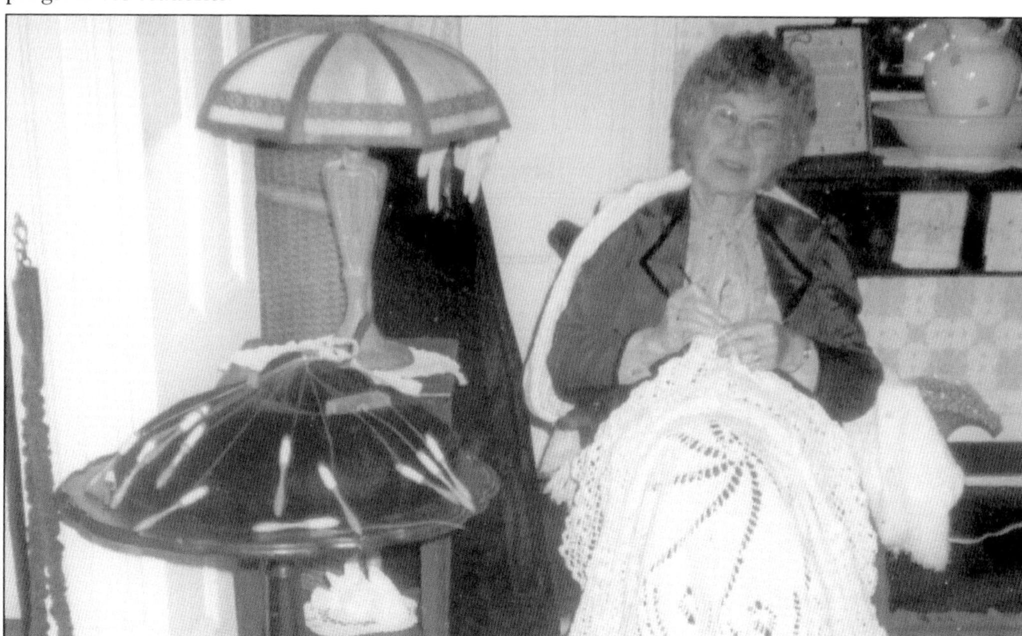

Lillian Miller, another of the society's volunteers, demonstrates some of the crafts people would have shared during the late 1800s and early 1900s at the Bradlee-McIntyre House.

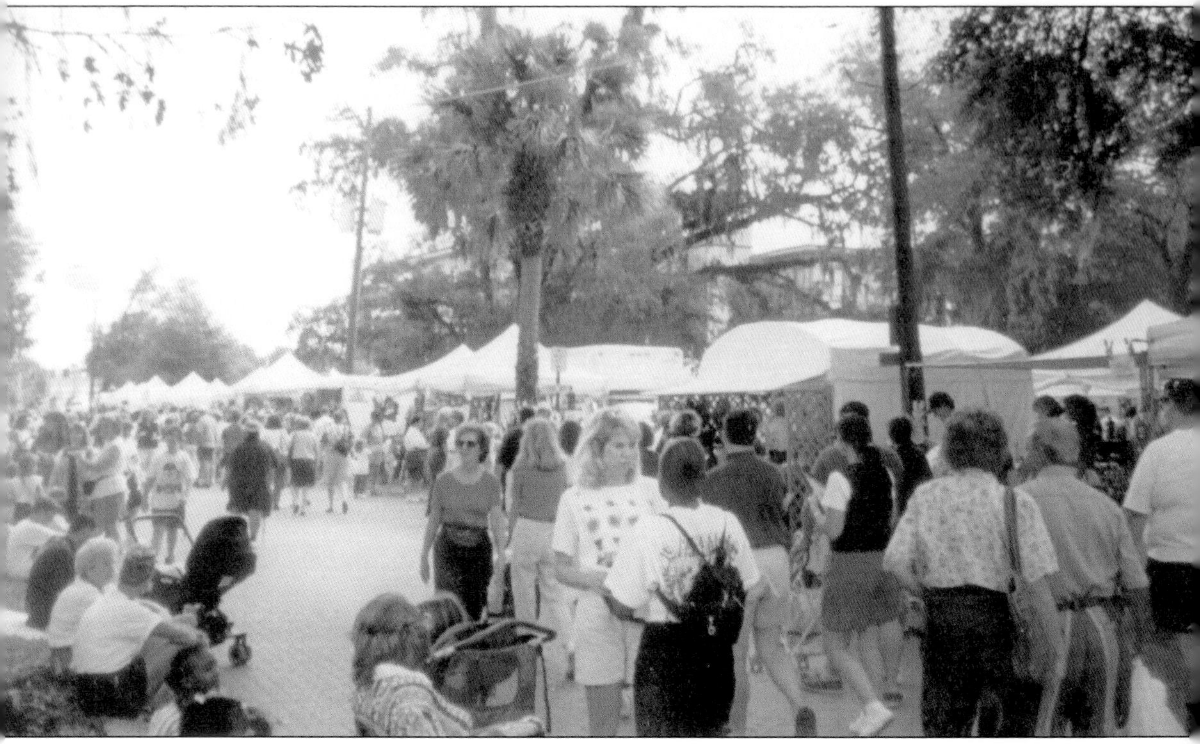

This is a scene from Church Avenue during the 2000 Fall Arts & Crafts Festival. The festival, which celebrates its 25th anniversary in 2001, is held every year on the weekend before Thanksgiving as the year's major fund-raising event for the maintenance of the Bradlee-McIntyre House, Inside-Outside House, and the society's other preservation efforts.

EPILOGUE

Longwood, one of Seminole County's first communities, enters the new millennium having preserved the best of its heritage for future generations to enjoy and treasure. Longwood's year-round population is about 14,000 people; however, about half of Seminole County's 345,000 residents live within five miles of Longwood. City founders Peter Demens and E.W. Henck and hundreds of settlers from the mid- to late-1800s were drawn to the high ground that rested along the clear lakes. Preservation of Longwood's historic district was probably ensured when the city leaders in the 1960s decided not to take advantage of the federal government's offer to provide 90 percent of the cost of putting in central sewer systems in the city's center that would draw redevelopment. City planner Chris Nagle, an ardent proponent of preservation, fought hard for the Longwood Historic District as suburban and industrial development in the 1960s threatened to destroy the character of this unique area. Longwood has become Central Florida's centerpiece of historic preservation. Efforts are still underway to preserve Longwood's prized collection of some of Florida's most historically significant, best-maintained older churches, businesses, and homes.